GENTLEMEN
OF THE
BLADE

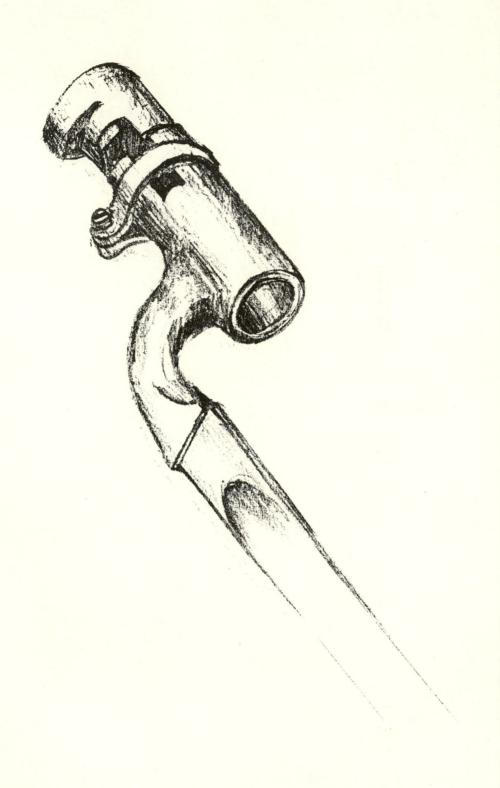

GENTLEMEN
OF THE
BLADE

A Social and Literary History
of the British Army Since 1660

G.W. STEPHEN BRODSKY

Contributions in Military Studies, Number 70

GREENWOOD PRESS
New York • Westport, Connecticut • London

Library of Congress Cataloging-in-Publication Data

Brodsky, G. W. Stephen, 1933-
    Gentlemen of the blade.

    (Contributions in military studies, ISSN 0883-6884 ;
no. 70)
    Bibliography: p.
    Includes index.
    1. Great Britain. Army—History.   2. Sociology,
Military—Great Britain.   I. Title.   II. Series.
UA649.B87   1988   355'.00941   87-23692
ISBN 0-313-26067-2 (lib. bdg. : alk. paper)

British Library Cataloguing in Publication Data is available.

Library of Congress Catalog Card Number: 87-23692
ISBN: 0-313-26067-2
ISSN: 0883-6884

First published in 1988

Greenwood Press, Inc.
88 Post Road West, Westport, Connecticut 06881

Printed in the United States of America

The paper used in this book complies with the
Permanent Paper Standard issued by the National
Information Standards Organization (Z39.48-1984).

10 9 8 7 6 5 4 3 2 1

Copyright Acknowledgments

The author and publisher gratefully wish to acknowledge the following sources for permission to
reprint copyrighted material:

A. D. Peters and Co. Ltd. for six lines from "War Cemetery" © 1940 by Edmund Blunden.

Victor Gollancz, Ltd. for excerpts from letters by the following list of soldiers in the work *War
Letters of Fallen Englishmen*, © 1930 edited by Laurence Housman: Cpl. James Parr, Lt. Harry
Sackville Lawson, Pte. Roger Marshall Livingstone, Capt. W. J. Mason, and Lt. Henry
Ratcliffe.

The estate and Chatto & Windus for excerpts from *Poems* by Issac Rozenberg.

The estate of Wilfrid Owen and Chatto & Windus for "Dulce et Decorum Est" © 1955 by
Wilfrid Owen.

To my student comrades in arms

Although you may honor—and rightly so—the great traditions of the past, the traditions of the future belong to you.

Field Marshal the Earl Alexander of Tunis

Contents

ILLUSTRATIONS

TITLE PAGE

Several patterns of this triple-edged socket bayonet were common in the nineteenth century. The British 1853 Enfield musket and the American 1848 Sharp's breech loader were only two of the many small arms so equipped. The idea of a "blade," reflecting the book's title, is expressed better as a bayonet than as an officer's sword. After all, the "gentlemen" this book is about are the rank and file, too. Cavalry troopers wore the curved sabre, of course, and the men of Rifle Regiments had a sword bayonet for close-quarter skirmishing.

CHAPTER ONE

The "G III R" on this guardsman's haversack dates him as late eighteenth century. In keeping with the theme of corrupt recruiting practices for colonial wars, and brutal and extortionate conditions of service, he wears an expression of trepidation and suffering. He kneels, perhaps in the front rank, waiting anxiously for the order to "present" and "fire", as his enemy—maybe General Washington's Continental Irregulars—advance on his firing line.

CHAPTER TWO

Pugnacity is evident in the features of this rapacious bully of the Embodied Militia. He is one of those who terrorized and plundered the English countryside on the pretext of searching out Commonwealth men, concealed arms caches, and smuggled goods.

CHAPTER THREE

This figure evinces the tough pride of the hard bitten regular in Britain's late nineteenth century Army in India. He wears the Slade-Wallace pattern buff leather kit, and carries a Martini-Henri single loader, soon to be replaced by the Lee-Metford magazine rifle. His white Wolseley pattern helmet with its khaki-dyed campaign cover was known from Khartoum to Delhi as a symbol of the Imperial Army's authority.

CHAPTER FOUR

The temporary soldier of the Great War is recognizably an imitation of Bruce Bairnsfather's style and subject in his "Old Bill" cartoons. His balaclava, the name itself reminiscent of an earlier war, is scarcely more comfort than the Lee-Enfield rifle he cradles. He is one of those ordinary men who waited in mud and misery for an end, while doing what they had to do.

CHAPTER FIVE

A World War Two soldier wearing battledress and 1937 pattern webbing Battle Order marches from victory in Europe into an uncertain future at the dawn of the nuclear age. Turned from us as he departs, he does not show us whether he advances confidently or if another sentiment dominates his countenance. As *Gentlemen of the Blade* concludes, his successors continue his march.

PREFACE

Having served the profession of arms from my youth and having pursued literary scholarship for much of that time, I have become aware that my convictions about the military vocation and my knowledge of our culture's literary past have been mutually enhancing. The more extensive my military experience, the more I saw in the literature; as my literary understanding increased, the more significance I saw in the events of my military life. I was long in arriving at a realization that these were not separate compartments of experience, but complementary parts of a whole. If I could integrate the two experiences by expressing in a book the meaning each gave to the other, I might in turn give greater meaning to my years of military service and literary study. This book is the first fruit of thirty-three years of soldiering and some twenty-four years of devotion to books.

The meaning of military service has not always been clear to me, and I have often thought about who I am. My own progress toward understanding has been gradual, and it remains incomplete. For most of my early life war was my state of mind. Visceral feelings of war-as-state-of-mind will always be with me, because of the world that shaped my youth. In World War I my father, who had already seen service in Imperial Russia's army, was an officer in a British Hussar regiment, and an uncle had died of wounds after Loos. As a schoolboy during World War Two I traded war souvenirs with other boys in the schoolyard—a Wehrmacht helmet, a .50 calibre casing, cap badges, and uniform buttons. In class on a warm spring day my daydreams were of brave deeds against impossible odds, and visions of blood spilled gloriously. Grainy black and white newsreels of the fighting shown at the movie house Saturday matinee; vegetables for the war effort from a Victory Garden patch in our back yard; campaigns for Victory Bonds and War Savings Stamps; door-to-door newspaper and coathanger drives for the "war effort;" posters in cafes cautioning that "the walls have ears": these were the facts of my early years.

My oldest brother who had been "Overseas" had assumed mythically heroic proportions for me, and his aspect when he returned in battledress with campaign ribbons and a decoration for gallantry did not disappoint me. He drank too much, his hand trembling as he held the glass; he would toss and groan in his sleep; and sometimes he suddenly would sit bolt upright in bed. As I watched from my own bed, pretending to be asleep, I would see his eyes glinting with terror in the moonlight from the window. He never talked of war, and my mother told me sotto voce never to ask him about it. I was deeply moved by the secret glamor of his heroic affliction.

Then there were cousins: one a Royal Airforce squadron leader who had been killed over the English Channel, and another who had served as a naval surgeon and survived to return to civilian practice. We had been a family at war, and we had spoken of "The War" as if it had always been. Because of some evanescent thread of thought and feeling I somehow assumed that I would be a soldier; at fifteen years of age I lied about my age to join a medium machine gun regiment as a reservist. Two years later I enlisted in the Regular Army.

The anomaly was that I had chosen a life as a professional soldier because of the example of amateurs. Those relatives of mine had hardly "soldiered"; they had only fought, and when hostilities were over, the ones who survived put aside their uniforms and returned to other lives. Through my years of professional service, it always bothered me that they could claim to have been "soldiers" in a way I could not, no matter how competent I was or how dedicated to the profession of arms. The experience of two world wars gave these amateurs membership in a warrior brotherhood I could never join. In no other calling do professionals emulate and admire amateurs, and keep the traditions made by them. Yet, there was consolation in knowing that they rose to their moment because they had been initiated into the brotherhood of arms by professionals like me, who had kept the flame. Whatever doubts I have had about the nature of military professionalism, they are small ones now.

In recent years there has been a great deal of discussion in staff colleges about the nature of the profession of arms, whether the military calling is a profession, and if so, by what measure. It generally is assumed that military amateurism is undesirable, and that the name "profession" ennobles a calling's practitioners. However, the British military tradition is different from that of other vocations. Amateurism historically had been central to the British profession of arms and vital to its special spirit. The professionals with whom I served were neither bellicose nor hungry for martial honors; they were content to sustain traditions of service created by amateurs. In turn, they were usually sustained adequately by those traditions, and by their belief in themselves and each other. They learned to accept and admire an ethos of service originating usually in regiments of wartime soldiers who imitated regulars for a time, but with the pride of being amateurs.

As an instructor at the Canadian Forces Staff School I put together some ideas in a lecture on the subject of my Army's tradition of professionalism. It seemed to work well, and it weathered most of the criticism leveled at it. Encouraged, I continued my research into the nebulous realm of "ethos," that institutional ambience which results indirectly in an army's consensus as to approved military conduct. Although at the time I had no idea of writing a book, that lecture formed the historical framework upon which this study is based. In the twilight of my career as a soldier, I became a military lecturer in English Literature at Royal Roads Military College. Seeking ways of imparting to my youthful comrades in arms an understanding of their cultural heritage, I devised a course of study devoted to literature about soldiers. A study of war and the warrior as represented in poetry and prose surely would help to broaden both appreciation of great literature and understanding of the dimensions of the military profession. Not only did the course appear to achieve its aim, it also forced me to develop themes and amass materials enough for a lifetime of authorship.

While I might have chosen to write about Canadian military history, I recognized that my army's tradition had been inherited from its British past, and its ethic and spirit had its origins in the British tradition tempered by the North American experience. So I decided to study first the British Army's evolution to understand my own army's tradition. The armies of all the one-time British dominions and territories have evolved naturally from British institutions, modified to suit local customs and increasingly independent national temperaments. Canadians, for instance, have had to adapt their British military heritage of inspired amateurism based on the British class structure to an ambience of professional urgency in the egalitarian North American culture they share with the United States. That delicate cultural balance will be apparent with a later work, "A Social and Literary History of the United States Army 1776–1975."

Armies have similarities and differences in ethos. "Ethos" is an elusive concept, its institutional attitudes and orientation observable in soldiers' daily conduct, their moral codes, and ultimately in their ethical choices. By and large, British and American military ethics, judgments about basic issues of moral conduct, differ hardly at all, because both armies have at their backs a single cultural history. But in other particulars the differences are vast.

Unlike the modern British army born of a revolutionary tyranny's failure in 1660, and 200 years of colonial competition, the American army was born of a revolutionary democracy's success and a continuing frontier experience which would clash with mass warfare's demands in the industrial age. The Civil War cast in sharp relief the difference between a small academy-trained cadre of intensely professional officers raised in a cavalier tradition, and large bodies of untrained and little-disciplined troops joining rapidly mobilized state militias. What had occurred two centuries earlier in pre-industrial Britian happened to the United States in conditions of modern war. The Civil War's officer corps perpetuated an ethos of rigorous yet politically shaded professionalism, distinct from their troops' spirit of enthusiastic amateurism which matured with the growth of competence. The legacy of those attitudes endured, as was apparent in the Vietnam conflict.

The opposite condition prevailed in the British Army. Insulated from modern war on a national scale until World War I, an officer corps drawn from Britain's leader class made a fetish of amateurism, while commanding a small army of superbly disciplined professional rankers. British and American soldiers have different views of the military profession. Their objects of loyalty also differ. For example, the Briton's mystical reverence for his "regiment" as a ceremonial institution is incomprehensible to most Americans, as are the subtleties of relationship between British officers and their senior noncommissioned ranks. The minute differences adding up to major differences of ethos are not the subjects of this book, however. Instead, we are interested here in the social and literary history behind the military traditions determining those differences.

From my vantage point as a soldier whose army and nation share both cultures, I have had a unique opportunity for insight into differences past and present. Although the late tradition of amateurism in the British Army has been quite different from American military amateurism, both peoples have a shared political and military experience from Charles II's Restoration, until George III's repetition of the Old World's follies in the New became intolerable. America's military culture may best be understood against a backdrop both of its British origins and its divergence from them; that is why this book tackled a history of the British Army, before a further work examining the American military experience. With both studies completed, I shall have laid the groundwork for a treatment of Canadian military culture in light of its British traditions and the American experience.

In the same way that my own Canadian military career was colored by both historical impulses, a gradual confluence of circumstances and interest, both military and academic, has made inevitable my writing of this book. It is a logical stage in a long march toward my understanding of the profession of arms and my life as a soldier. May it be worthy of the profession it has been written to serve.

ACKNOWLEDGMENTS

My debt of gratitude is to the soldiers, scholars, and friends who have contributed in so many ways to the success of this study. I cannot possibly name all my military mentors and comrades in arms to whom I owe more than they can ever know. These are the officers, noncommissioned officers, and men who have been my tutors, guides, and sources of inspiration throughout my life as a soldier. I also owe thanks to my professors at Queen's University, the University of British Columbia, and the University of Victoria for the knowledge and wisdom they have shared during my years of learning. More recently, my debt has been to my fellow instructors at the Canadian Forces Staff School, and my colleagues at Royal Roads Military College, Victoria, for their interest and encouragement.

As always, my greatest debt is to my wife Kathleen, the finest helpmate a soldier and scholar could have. Her preparation of typescript was the least of her trials. Her invaluable critical and editorial commentary, and her unflagging patience and moral support, were at the sacrifice of precious time and energy taken from her own scholarly labors.

Introduction

AMATEURS AND PROFESSIONALS

Of all the fair ladies that came to the show,
Sir Diddle's fair lady stood first in the row;
'O charming,' says she, 'how he looks, all in red;
How he turns up his toes! how he holds up his head!
. . . . : . . . .

The sweet-sounding notes of Sir Dilberry Diddle
More Ravished his ears than the sound of a fiddle,
And as it grew faint, that he heard it no more,
He softened the word of command to—encore.
                    Anon., "Sir Dilberry Diddle, Captain of Militia. . . ."[1]

The British Army has always been characterized by a spirit of endearing amateurism, a source both of its tragedy and its greatness. The historical causes have been threefold:

Political. British Constitutionalism from the Restoration was reflected in the presence of a large volunteer militia controlled by Parliament. This amateur soldiery was insurance against future absolutist tendencies on the part of the monarch, who had been given his own small Regular Army.

Commercial. As Britain acquired an empire in the eighteenth century, in competition with other European nations, temporary levees of militia augmented Regular troops for campaigns abroad. Militiamen became hardly distinguishable from Regulars as superbly drilled British troops won the Empire through discipline and sheer will. During most of the nineteenth century when militia was not needed, the Regular Army retained its amateur character through the deliberate ignorance of conservative officers who associated serious study with bourgeois values. Dilettantism, an air of negligent grace, and supreme self-confidence saw them through colonial skirmishes. Spared the mass wars experienced in continental Europe and in America, they had little need of military science.

Technological. When Britain experienced mass war on a national scale for the first time with World War I, a citizen army fought it. The skill of the Regulars with service in the colonies and South Africa was rendered valueless by the development of trench warfare. The wartime units gave to the British profession of arms the ethos of a citizen army.

The British Army suffered setbacks usually because of its officers' failures of knowledge, imagination, and competence. However, it always won through, because of its officers' character as a leader class, the discipline of its troops, and the indomitable courage of all. The officers who commanded meticulously drilled rank and file in the colonial wars were adventurous amateurs. When a massive citizen army fought World War I, temporary junior officers and troops persevered for senior commanders who had discovered professionalism too late. The paradox is that amateur verve usually produced success. If the British Army had been more professional after the fashion of Europe's nations-in-arms, a spirit of amateurism would not have existed to sustain British soldiers when they needed it.

By the measure of Samuel Huntington's widely accepted idea of classic professionalism in *The Soldier and the State* ("Expertise," "Responsibility," and "Corporateness"), there has never been a true "profession" of British arms.[2] The spirit of professionalism marking the officer corps of nineteenth-century continental Europe's armies simply foundered in the English Channel. Outrageous as it may seem, the British Army has never had "professionals" in the classic sense. By and large, the "officer corps' " corporate identity as merely a branch of an elite British leader class has been stronger than its identity as a military elite. The officer's virtue often has been his eccentric individuality rather than his corporate conformity, and his greatest virtue has been his character as leader rather than his intellect as strategist.

While for a time loyalties were split between King and Parliament, the British gentry never forgot the lesson of the Protectorate, when an illusory promise of equality brought a tyranny of generals. For these reasons, there never has been an idea of the army as autonomous purveyor of services to a client state. Rather, the overriding value has been one of dedicated service to the ideals of a Constitutional monarchy. Doubtless, it was Britain's fear of military professionalism that retarded the growth of a general staff and military education on continental lines. The army was to fight well and keep its nose out of national policy.

Because of the absence of grand strategy and mass armies, the army long remained a kaleidoscope of glittering fragments. Individual regiments, each with its own eccentricities of custom and uniform, commanded the loyalty of troops from the lower classes, who found in their regiments a home and a family. Indeed, for much of the British Army's history senior noncommissioned officers (NCOs) demonstrated greater corporate spirit as the regimental "backbone" than did their officers. In the British Army the term "sergeants' mess" means more than a facility; it connotes the equivalent of "officer corps," and implies its own body of codes and customs. By the standard of "expertise," the sergeants' mess has often shown more skill in the drills of minor tactics than have regimental officers.

The historical tendency reducing class distinctions in Britain has had an impact on the British Army. The officer corps' professional competence has improved vastly, while access is much greater into ranks that were once the preserve of gentry.[3] Yet, the officer corps, the sergeants' mess, and the regiment have retained the best of the British Army's unique spirit of inspired amateurism.

Britain has had no sustained tradition of conscripted service whereby a small professional cadre of officers and NCOs have trained and commanded a vast citizen rank and file. Nor has Britain ever felt the need of a standing army of any size. Indeed, the British are an unmilitary people. The result has been that professionalism and amateurism have been so interrelated, and even interdependent, that distinctions between military professionalism and amateurism have been difficult, if not impossible. The Regular officer has cultivated his amateurism as a mark of his professional status, and the temporary soldier has been at pains to pass as a regular. Regulars have "soldiered," but far more reservists and conscripts have fought.

With these complexities in mind, yet without losing sight of the classic features of professionalism, we may also say that the paradigm of military professionalism usually is a figure whose principal life's occupation is as a soldier. He is dedicated primarily to duty well done as an end in itself, rather than as merely a means to some other end. The professional is devoted to military institutions, traditions, and routines, which is not to say that he is militarism's extreme, quite in the mold of Alfred Vagts's classic concept of militarism.[4] Not necessarily bellicose, he finds aesthetic gratification in the sound execution of the military art in any of its forms, and he subscribes to an unforgiving code of conduct. For the professional a sense of vocation attaches to military service. He makes a fetish of the idea of duty, and he values highly the external rewards of military honors. Giving his primary loyalty to military institutions, he is apt to screen out from his considerations the larger purposes of his profession: the political, social, and religious ideologies served by the state, the complexities and contradictions of which might dilute his purely military resolve. Impatient with war's chaos, the professional traditionally has seen war as an unwelcome interruption to his true raison d'etre, "soldiering."

The Amateur Defined

By "amateur" we mean someone for whom soldiering and war hold the excitement and attraction of a fascinating avocation. The profession of arms is not the amateur's primary life's work, even though he may be a regular. For example, a midnineteenth-century officer of a fashionable Regular Army cavalry regiment typically spent more time on leave than on duty, never studied strategy, and thought that to do so was in bad taste. His officership was an adjunct to his class status. A regular "amateur," he was less "professional" than, say, an eighteenth-century volunteer soldier in the ranks of an embodied militia regiment on colonial service. As in other contexts, military amateurism connotes pursuit of the avocation for the love of it. Whereas in other callings, there is a pejorative connotation of limited competence, the military amateur often has been the source of new expertise. While the amateur has done things differently from the professional, he often has done them as well and even better. Less culturally conditioned by military life, he frequently has been more innovative than the professional.

Another category of soldiers must be excluded from the ranks of either professional or amateur. These are the temporary citizen-soldiers who have been conscripts or volunteers of conscience, and reluctantly on active service. Not imbued with military loyalties and ideals of military duty as virtues in themselves, the temporary soldier often has soldiered and fought only as an unfortunately necessary means to a larger ethical end pursued by the state. Sometimes he has become an amateur despite himself and has experienced self-revulsion in discovering that he has begun to like soldiering and fighting.

At their extremes of attitude, professionals and amateurs have differed because of the professional soldier's love of his craft as his raison d'etre, and the amateur's love of it as his favorite game. The temporary soldier who never becomes an amateur soldiers and fights either from love of his cause or by coercion. The professional soldier values loyalty and competence above all regardless of outcome, the amateur seeks the exhilaration of military romance, and the temporary soldier who served from conscience places justice and success first.

Probably no purely military type has ever existed except as a paradigmatic concept. Every soldier has complex feelings toward his calling. Love of duty, love of the game, and love of the cause may summarize the respective motivations of the three paradigms of soldier: professional, amateur, and reluctant temporary warrior. Those motivations and paradigms cross the boundaries of "regular," "mercenary," "militiaman," "reservist," and "conscript." While the regular has been thought of as a "professional soldier," the reservist as an "amateur," and the ideologically motivated temporary soldier as neither, they have shared each other's characteristics.

The Professional Soldier

The professional soldier traditionally has measured his enemy's virtue in terms of his fighting qualities, rather than in terms of the justice of his cause. Daniel Defoe's seventeenth-century Captain Carleton, for instance, is more upset by the lack of decorum he observes in a set-piece battle than by the waste of life. Both the professional and amateur view the enemy as an adversary whose honor depends on his fighting well, rather than as a foe without honor. Dilettante eighteenth-century British officers observed the punctilio of war partly from military expediency, and partly because their honor as gentlemen depended on their right conduct. Paradoxically, it is in that gaming spirit of inspired amateurism that Kipling's thoroughly professional Tommy respects the Sudanese "fuzzy-wuzzy" as "first-class fightin' man" who "broke the British square." The British Regular traditionally has admired an enemy who has played the game well.

By contrast, the Great War's typical subaltern, the "Temporary Gentleman," although often making the best of things by becoming an amateur and imitating the regulars, did not altogether regard war as a game. He averred that the Boche could not be treated fairly because he was no sportsman; and he was no sportsman because his cause was wrong. The "Temporary Gentleman" took comfort in the conviction that he could not lose, because he was convinced of the morality of his cause. That is not to say that he lacked the sporting spirit. He brought it from his public school background to his new avocation, and he applied his gaming rules to his own conduct. Unless he developed the true amateur's love of soldiering, however, military endeavor never developed for him its fascination as *his* game. Rather than adopting the profession's traditional rules of chivalric conduct, he brought *to* war the rules he had learned on the playing fields of the British public school. The differences were slight. Fair play was fair play, and the sporting metaphor of speech was as common among enthusiasts temporarily in uniform as the military metaphor had been common in civilian life.

World War I's temporary soldier usually missed out on one mark of professionalism which in battle had separated him from the nineteenth-century regular. For the regular, battle itself had been *the* game; for the temporary soldier battle was something else, but he believed he should play it according to rules of other *real* games. That made a difference in how he looked on his enemy. While the professional respected or scorned his adversary for his soldierly qualities, the temporary soldier commonly hated his foe for representing a principle of evil. Alternatively, he felt pity and compassion for him because he was a fellow sufferer sharing evil circumstances created by vicious governments.

In any selection of paradigm characters, distinctions between professional, amateur, and mere temporary soldier are imperfect at best. Although stoic professionals like the Great War's Frank Richards (*Old Soldiers Never Die*) have suppressed extremes of emotion in practicing their craft, temporary soldiers like Frederic Manning (*The Middle Parts of Fortune*) have seen drama in sacrifice. They have experienced the heights of battle ecstasy and the depth of anomie, or like Donald Hankey (*A Student in Arms*), the exaltation of inspired conviction. The contrasts between such examples of amateur and professional attitudes, discussed in later chapters, are not as apparent as their parallels in other nations.

The distinction between professional and amateur has been less pronounced in Britain than in nations that traditionally have had large conscripted armies. In European armies a hard core of professionals has been seen as clearly separate from the much larger component of reserves and conscripts it has commanded and trained. That has not been the British experience. Daniel Defoe's "professional" Captain Carleton eventually commands irregulars at home because of his belief in his monarch's cause, and the real life ex-regular Frank Richards returned to the colors from the reserves to serve among the World War One's Territorials. Each attitude, professional, amateur, and simple devotion to a cause, has interpenetrated, and has pervaded, the military society of regulars and reservists alike to produce a special regimental loyalty and military ethos. Neither amateurism nor professionalism has existed in isolation. The professional soldier had been influenced by the traditions and attitudes of amateurs who went before, and vice versa. This interpenetration of attitudes toward military service has been complemented by the exchange of learning between those who have soldiered and those who have fought. The result has been a spirit of service unique among nations, which has permeated the regimental messes of the British Army and armies sharing its tradition.

THE HISTORY

> Curse on the star, dear Harry, that betrayed
> My choice from law, divinity or trade,
> To turn a rambling brother o' the blade!
> Of all professions sure the worst is war.
> How whimsical our fortune! how bizarre!
> This week we shine in scarlet and in gold:
> The next, the cloak is pawned—the watch is sold.
> Richard Pack "An Epistle from a Half-Pay Officer..."[5]

Our chronology of amateurism begins in 1660, when Britons ended a dozen years of military dictatorship and returned a sovereign to the throne. Charles II and his Parliament were soon disagreeing over the distribution of power, but at least the principle had been firmly established that neither should have an edge, as long as the other had a voice. Chapter One of this book, "That Devouring Profession," addresses the impact of the Constitutional issue on the British Army's character. Parliament allowed the King his own small army, but kept its own citizen militia as insurance. Through the Restoration, militiamen policed a disaffected citizenry, and through the following century, militia volunteers augmented the Regular Army as Britain's imperial interests grew.

Chapter Two, "A Sort of Public Nuisance," shows the character of a volunteer militia vastly expanded under the impetus of Britain's commercial interests abroad. Beginning with opposed roles, the Army and the Militia gradually adopted complementary functions. As Britain competed with other nations for territory, requirements for large levies of troops on short notice were met by Volunteer Militiamen. The mercenary character of the Regular had yielded to an ethic of loyalty to the sovereign, and the Militiaman's former character as citizen-soldier defending the hearth changed to resemble the Regular's ethos. So, first for political reasons, and later for Britain's commercial interests, the roles and characteristics of army and Militia began to merge.

As the *Pax Britannica*'s frontiers stabilized in the nineteenth century, the Militia was rarely embodied and it withered away. Chapter Three, "The Devil's Code," enters the nineteenth-century world of the British Regular. The colonies were garrisoned by a tough little army of long-service soldiers; at home a predominantly conservative Parliament which had common cause with Queen Victoria against the forces of liberalism and reform had no cause to fear the Regular Army. The Army's officers, after all, were themselves from the governing class. Meanwhile, the tradition of loyalty to regiments, nurtured both by regular battalions and an embodied militia during the previous century, grew to the proportions of a secular religion in the isolated units of the Regular Army both at home and abroad. But the insularity which bred regimental loyalty and devotion also nurtured ignorance and ineffi-ciency. Reform was slow, even after the revelations following the Crimean War. The concessions made in the century's closing decades let in some light. Length of service was shortened, and literacy and educational require-ments were imposed as conditions for promotion among the rank and file. However, the Regular Army's conservative officer corps, conditioned to a view of war only as frontier skirmishing, remained stubbornly ignorant of military science in the industrial age. To be a gentleman demanded that one remain a dilettante. The Regular officer therefore idealized his own gentlemanly amateurism, which afforded him the character, but not the knowledge, he would soon need.

The technology of mass war brought the British regular's day to a close. Chapter Four, "The Shrieking Pyre," traces the fortunes of a new kind of temporary soldier. At the start of World War I, civilian volunteers quickly learned what little they could about soldiering from the old sweats, then went into the trenches to learn an entirely different reality of war. By 1916 few of the old regulars were left, and what they knew of warfare was of little value to citizen-soldiers blooded in the trenches. Many temporary soldiers who enthusiastically enlisted and displayed the swagger and dash of the inspired amateur lost their early infatuation with military service when they exchanged the camaraderie of the barrack room for the desperate comrade-ship of battle. The ceremonies of war contracted then to an elementary struggle to endure and survive. Nevertheless, it was the regular's sense of tradition and discipline imparted to the new breed that saw the British Army through. Again, the characteristics of professional and amateur had merged.

Chapter Five, "A Just Cause," tells the story of the legacy of amateurism from World War I, through the twilight of the Empire, to the present. The tradition of amateurism which had been forged in World War I dramatically reduced later distinctions between professional and amateur soldier. The Second World War's conditions were ideal for the amateur soldier's flare for novelty, and the influence of professional orthodoxy did not seriously impede amateur invention. In the postwar era, and most recently in the 1982 Falklands War, the British Army's soldiers have displayed a unique integration of the essential elements of professionalism, amateurism, and simple dedication to a moral purpose. These elements have been the objects of the modern soldier's devotion: duty, the game, and the cause.

The amateur's exhilaration, inventiveness, and love of the game of soldiering and fighting served the Regular soldier well in the years after the Second World War, while Britain was dismantling its empire. The same spirit of adventure and gamemanship which the British soldier needed to take and hold territories in the eighteenth and nineteenth centuries were needed for the army to dispose of them in an orderly fashion. But it was the professional tradition of discipline, competence, and attention to duty which countered the disillusioning aspect of tasks that otherwise could have damaged British military pride.

By turns, the politics of state, national commercial interest, and the technology of mass war have determined the British Army's role and character. Regulars have provided the backbone of steadiness and competence at the start of every period of crisis, tempering the citizen-soldier's spirit of adventure. However, the amateur's ethos, seasoned by full-time service, has lived on in regular regiments after each crisis has passed.

The regimental ethos which has remained strong at unit level has become increasingly anachronistic in the new "systems-oriented" bureaucracy of mass violence. The old amateur values of the regular have had progressively less application for the modern war of nuclear deterrence, because they do not square with the new reality. The conclusion gives a glimpse of the future and an end of amateurism in the British Army. Amateurism has always thrived in the context of conventional war, the "totality" of which has been relative, and an essential feature of the amateur spirit has been the idea of arms as a game with limits and rules. The Nuclear Age has removed the gaming element and has rendered the military gamesman obsolescent. With the Nuclear Age, deterrence, rather than fighting well, has become the warrior's fulfillment. The possibility of conventional war as an alternative to Armageddon may temporarily prolong the need for professional soldiers with the amateur's gaming spirit, but the risk of escalation may soon be too great even for minor skirmishing wars by major powers or their surrogates. The nuclear warrior, the new professional who began appearing in large numbers during the 1960s is an "endgamesman." Rational, unromantic, competent, and obedient, he is forbade using the judgment demanded of soldiers on the conventional battlefield. The Nuclear Age is ending the age of amateurism in the British Army.

THE LITERATURE

I've tinkered at my bits of rhymes
In weary, woeful, waiting times;
In doleful hours of battle-din,
Ere yet they brought the wounded in...

My job is done; my rhymes are ranked and ready,
My word-battalions marching verse by verse;
Here stanza-companies are none too steady;
There print-platoons are weak, but might be worse....
>   Robert W. Service, "Rhymes of a Red Cross Man"[6]

The Problem of Critical Choice: Typicality and Merit

The chapters which follow draw liberally on the verse and prose of each period discussed, to evoke the texture of each age and a sense of how being a soldier must have felt. However, as a literary history *Gentlemen of the Blade* is not an exhaustive compendium of literature relating to the British soldier, and constraints of space have dictated rigorous selection.

In any review of the past, the scholar is faced with the task of selecting the most appropriate material to support and illustrate a particular vision of historical truth. Finding the right poetry and prose fiction is like deciding on the right ordinances, Orders-in-Council, or minor occurrences, to evoke a sense of the temper of a time. The choice that sometimes has to be made between the typicality of sentiment in a work of literature and its artistic merit is a problem not usually facing military historians who rely on more conventional sources. Injudicious use of atypical but compelling literature may result in special pleading to produce a perverse view of history, regardless of its intrinsic worth.

As an example, Evelyn Waugh's genius in his *Sword of Honour* trilogy could result in a distorted view of the World War II citizen-soldier, to show an army of cynics and hypocrites thriving on the misfortunes of a few quixotic heroes they victimize for selfish purposes. Obviously, there has been baseness in any great enterprise, but that must be seen in the context of the author's state of mind. A Roman Catholic in an Anglican state, and an indifferent soldier not well liked by his peers and subordinates, Waugh has presented the alienated vision of a martyr to corrupt motives and impersonal military systems. He does so with such brilliance that his novel fiction demands inclusion in Chapter Five. Nonetheless, Waugh's thesis of moral decay should not be seen as typical of prevailing attitudes, which commonly were more optimistic. To balance the scale of historical judgment, World War II poetry of lesser stature than Waugh's fiction is shown cumulatively to have equal and perhaps greater importance in illustrating the anger, grim determination, and hope that characterized the time.

The way the British soldier regarded himself and how he was regarded by the civilian world also were often at odds with each other, and the reader may be tempted to regard emotionally congenial art as the typical or definitive view. For example, the British public's common vision in World War I of young Galahads experiencing the joy of martyrdom bore little resemblance to how most temporary soldiers viewed their own situation. There are occasional echoes of the approved body of attitude in novels by men who lived through World War I and seem not to have experienced the general disillusionment.

These examples are worth mentioning at the outset, simply as a way of accounting for their existence. Beyond that, however, they are not sufficiently typical, nor of such quality, to merit later inclusion. Ernest Raymond's 1922 novel *Tell England* maintains its excruciating jingoism and chivalric mysticism from start to finish.[7] The author's heroic persona Rupert Ray is a model of dedication, humility, and British sportsmanship. He tells with absolute conviction how, as a subaltern on a troopship headed for Gallipoli, he hears a padre liken the voyage to a knight's vigil before combat. He is to "pursue beauty . . . like the Holy Grail."[8] Raymond had served in World War I, but for whatever reasons of temperament and experience, his exaltation apparently was never tainted by doubt, and *Tell England* has no hint of irony.

By contrast, Richard Aldington's *Death of a Hero*, shows the author's indignation and bitterness at the glorious delusion.[9] His novel is indifferent art, and the subjectivity of his anger pushes his prose toward a querulous extreme, verging on hysteria in places. He probably had good cause, and while the work's merit is limited, it nevertheless is a cogent expression of feelings typical of many upper-middle-class young men crushed first by Edwardian conformity, then by war.

On the one hand, Aldington's private Winterbourne is a reluctant victim, and on the other, Raymond's Rupert Ray is a willing martyr, full of the military amateur's love of adventure, expressed continually through a sporting metaphor. Both novels are of the second rank but *Death of a Hero* clearly is more representative of the sentiments of its time in light of letters, biographies, histories, verse, other fiction, and even living memory. While *Tell England* "reflects the climate of opinion of those years with their ardent, if uncritical patriotism" as a reviewer has claimed,[10] the weight of evidence shows Aldington's inner experience to be more typical, and its expression more genuine. So, although some account is made of beliefs professed publicly by many but felt inwardly by few, the weight of attention in Chapter Four is given to the poetry and novel fiction which probably represents the feelings of most soldiers.

For most of the literature, little choice has been needed between the best and most typical of prevailing attitudes. For example, eighteenth-century literary sentiments showing the military man as stupid and brutish presumably reinforced those attitudes among the literate publics and in turn enhanced the military community's defiance. The soldier's swaggering contempt for civilians probably was partly his reaction to their contempt for him. His marginality is underscored by Samuel Johnson's apothegms, by satirical verse, and by novel fiction. Literature was both arbiter and echo of the opinions of the social elite and those who wished they were, in an age when social mores were held to be more important than private ideas of virtue. The best literature, acknowledged as such by a discriminating salon society, was also the most representative of public opinion. Chapter Two therefore adverts only to the best of picaresque novels, such as *Tom Jones*, and others in which soldiers appear.

A hoard of incidental minor verse supports a compassionate mood expressed by the important authors and poets late in the eighteenth century. Together, verses of this sort amount virtually to a genre, which may be termed "poetry of pity." Individually, the pieces have little literary value, and those dating from early in the century are not as typical of the general sentiment as those written later. Therefore, in Chapter 2 the account of the poetry of pity acknowledges the minor poetry only briefly and focuses on the period's more influential and noteworthy poets: Wordsworth, Goldsmith, and Cowper.

Decisions as to which literary works would be included from each age were unavoidably subjective in some instances, and were always based on the major and sometimes conflicting criteria of representativeness and artistic merit. By and large, however, the choices match scholarship's general consensus made by Alexander Pope's measure, "that which oft was thought, but ne'er so well expressed."

Military Literature of Historical Value

What *Gentlemen of the Blade* attempts through literary commentary is approximately parallel to what John Keegan's *The Face of Battle* achieves for military history through analysis of the soldier's circumstances and environment.[11] Keegan's approach redresses the inadequacy of traditional historiography by showing the human side of war. In his introductory remarks about the shortcomings of various approaches, Keegan touches on literary fiction and the "literary challenge" battle has presented. Giving honorable mention to some of the great names of novel fiction for taking up the gauntlet, he issues a word of caution, however: "imagination and sentiment, which quite properly delimit the dimensions of the novelist's realm, are a dangerous medium, however, through which to approach the subject of battle." Admittedly, mounds of horrid stuff, what Keegan calls the "Zap-Blatt-Banzai-Gott in Himmel-Bayonet in the Guts"[12] sort of military fiction, has been written, and literary discrimination has to come into play. Genuine artistic imagination has a truth greater than mere fidelity to fact. Good literature about the soldier is an *event in itself* in revealing men's universal psychology, shaped and conditioned by circumstance.

Although the literature shows the attitudes of "professional" and "amateur," "regular" and "reservist," it also shows the common humanity underlying the differences. For example, Frederic Manning's persona Private Bourne in *The Middle Parts of Fortune* experiences the basest and most exalted emotions in battle when during the attack fear and restraint become unbridled anger. It is only Bourne's cultural overlay of revulsion to his essential self which, even before its being revealed to him in battle, has prompted him to refuse a commission. But under social pressure as compelling in its own way as battle stress, by the novel's close he has agreed to become an officer. Death intervenes. Through this sort of art as event-in-itself, one sees the soldier's inner landscape. Josiah Bunting has commented on the worth of subjective experience imaginatively conceived:

[T]he best war novelists frequently come closer to the reality of war in their work than military historians. . . . Ideally the military historian and military novelist have complementary missions. The historian describes how wars were fought and for what reason; the novelist is concerned with what the fighting meant to those who suffered, failed, or succeeded in it.[13]

Keegan comments, "historians, traditionally and rightly, are expected to ride their feelings on a tighter rein than the man of letters can allow himself." It is the "military historian, with his specialized ability to check for veracity and probability," who should tackle the fiction, to "relate battles more closely to the social context of their own times."[14] Few literary historians have addressed the literature of war and warriors, and Keegan rightly observes, "the treatment of battle fiction is a subject almost untouched by literary critics."

Gentlemen of the Blade attempts to redress this oversight. Because literature both expresses and helps to create a culture, it participates in the ambience of its age, to show customs, attitudes, hopes, and fears. The *Spectator*'s satirical "letters," for instance, reflect the eighteenth century's deeply ingrained fear of standing armies expressed through the disparaging wit of a superficially secure and complacent literate class. By contrast, "The Volunteer," which tells of a returned soldier "to the halberts tied" for "stealing two chick-eggs" for his starving family, shows an altered awareness about military service in the century's closing years, as compassion replaces derogatory wit.[15]

The literary historian needs also the military historian's knowledge of custom and culture. For example, a detailed grasp of practices relating to regular and militia commissions and conditions of service enhances an understanding of Jane Austen's villainous captain of militia, Wickham (*Pride and Prejudice*), discussed in Chapter Three as a stock social type. Similarly, a grasp of Paul Scott's *Staying On* demands an understanding of British military society and regimental life in India before Independence. The tale requires knowledge of, and sensitivity to, the feelings of the British Army's *Barra Sahibs*, and *Memsahibs* who had invested their entire lives in what they believed themselves to be in British-Indian society and culture. Chapter Five describes the place of the British soldier at the end of the Empire, so that the mention of *Staying On* in the Conclusion is against a historical backdrop of fact and feeling. For the factual background, *Gentlemen of the Blade* relies on traditional kinds of historical sources to show how the literature typifies views. The world of art is illuminated by the world of fact, and vice versa, to complete a portrait of the soldier in his time.

Distinctions in literature between the regular and the temporary soldier can mislead unless they are carefully drawn. A false distinction may seem to imply some fundamental difference in emotional makeup. But the hypocrite, the martinet, the stoic hero, the military romantic, the zealot, the coward, and the bureaucratic pedant know no boundaries of circumstance or occupation. Frank Richards's wry memoir of World War I, *Old Soldiers Never Die*, has all those types, and Evelyn Waugh's somewhat biographical *Sword of Honour* trilogy has them even as facets of individual characters. In that respect, the military setting, although central, is incidental to what the literature reveals about the human condition.

Cultural differences between the regular and the temporary soldier have nonetheless been real. Because the regular soldier rarely is in a majority during war itself, fiction and verse about men in war are usually about civilians who have donned uniform for a time, and who have responded to military life and the shock of combat either with exhilaration and enthusiasm or with revulsion. Much of the Great War literature discussed in Chapter 5 shows how these feelings often are mixed. Ford Madox Ford's Christopher Tietjens (*Parade's End*) is a Temporary Gentleman who despises war and the hypocrisy causing it; yet, he finds himself longing for command of his battalion. Although World War I breaks him in body and spirit, it also leads him to the revelation that he shares a common humanity with other men of all classes and kinds.

By contrast, some military fiction set in peacetime is about men who are self-consciously separate. Kipling's romantic *Soldiers Three*, for instance, shows the dash and brutality, the humor and banality, of the special military world of the Raj. The fiction is not about war, as much as it is about a way of life. While officers sweated at polo on the *maidan* in the cantonments, the likes of Private Ortheris toiled over their kit for guard inspection, their feelings a complexity of exasperation and pride, alienation and comradeship.

Verse and fiction that impart the flavor of a discrete military society, as Kipling's does, are rare in English letters, probably because the private world of marginal men on the frontiers of Empire held little interest for Britons.

The home army was not a closed society in the same way, so that satirical verse, picaresque fiction, and novels of manners have shown the military officer's place in the larger society. (Until the Great War the rank and file hardly existed for the literate classes.) Many authors have indulged usefully in historical discursiveness in the interests of realism. William Makepeace Thackeray's *Vanity Fair*, for instance, affords valuable historical insights into the officer's social context during the Napoleonic wars, so is discussed briefly in Chapter Three. Similarly, Ford Madox Ford's portrait of Edward Ashburnham (*The Good Soldier*) and H. G. Wells's observations as his persona William Clissold (*The World of William Clissold*) provide a sense of enervated Edwardian society, reflected in characters who are incidentally and ineffectually military.

Military Literature and Inner Experience

War as *concept* has often been called "inhuman"; yet war and the military life as *experience* are intensely "human." A perspective on the British military figure in civilian society, regimental life, and war cannot always be created adequately through memoirs, letters, or even eyewitness accounts. These are all necessary grist for the historian, of course. But it is literature's imaginative force which has power to evoke and recreate the *inner* experience of Siegfried Sassoon's autobiographical Great War character Sherston (*The Sherston Memoirs*), David Jones's John Ball (*In Parenthesis*), and even John Collier's eighteenth-century "Old Soldier," "maimed and in the beggars' list."[16] Fearful exhilaration and desolate despair in battle, pride and pathos in peace, are at the artist's command.

Through war fiction, material facts of existence take on a life of their own: " 'And—and when it thaws we—we've got to slap 'em back with a spa-ade! Remember those Frenchmen's little boots under the duckboards? . . . What'll I do? What'll I do about it?' "[17] "Debutantes flutter less than we do, as we put on our best battledress, with its cut-throat creases; and our best boots, glistening with quarts of spit and tins of polish; and our gaiters blancoed to a perfect pallor, and our brasses blindingly burnished."[18] The banal horror of bits of corpse poking accusingly out of the trench muck; the antiseptic smell of heel ball, webbing blanco, and brass polish conjuring up the terrors of Commanding Officer's parade for the recruit; and the tingling in the groin at the imagined steel splinter that will not just plop like heavy rain into the mud with the rest—these are images of war and military life, fictive expressions of the soldier's truth.

Soldiers' Letters

Letters by and about soldiers are used sparingly in this book. A letter's artlessness may afford a view of its author's psychology, unobstructed by the mask of anonymity and objectivity an author of fiction imposes between himself and his characters. But a letter as often obscures the view, because the author may be at pains to appear as he would have his reader see him. This self-idealizing tendency was particularly prevalent in letters written by military men before the mid to late nineteenth century. With literacy confined almost exclusively to the upper classes, letters were for the most part by senior officers and the occasional man of letters for whom military adventure was a passing avocation.

Such belles lettres portray war as a romantic escapade and the writers as men of great affairs (which many were). The prose is sometimes extravagant, and there is hardly a word of the squalor, hunger, and hardship which were the lot of the common fighting man. They are a grand source of historical knowledge, but they hold few revelations about either soldiers or war. Letters by earnest Cromwell, haughty Marlborough, contemptuous Wellington, witty Napier, and romantic Byron give us war as seen from the lofty heights of privilege and power.[19] So these are omitted from this history. Instead, some letters by the few literate eighteenth-century rankers are included in Chapter Three, to show conditions of service.

Occasionally, a letter by a civilian reveals attitudes toward the soldiery. William Blake, for example, recounted in 1804 an unseemly encounter with a trooper of Dragoons. Required by military authorities to stand trial for alleged seditious utterances during the altercation, Blake wrote, "Every man is now afraid of speaking to, or looking at, a Soldier."[20] Regrettably, letters about soldiers by the citizenry are rare.

By the late nineteenth century, the increase in literacy in the British Army was so marked that by one reliable estimate "at least half of the NCOs and private soldiers were capable of writing letters from active service."[21] The letters of the period have for the first time the virtue of "tak[ing] us with the individual soldiers directly to the sharp end of battle, behind the official dispatches to the realities of dangerous encounter," and the Victorian rank and file cease to be a "mute and anonymous body of men marching past in scarlet or khaki columns."[22] Some of the letters express the misery and fear to which men are subject in every war, but commonly they were written for the popular press. Jingoistic sentiments excited an armchair readership and bought approbation for the writer; hardships often were exaggerated, and, predictably, letters widely circulated in print never reflected "un-British" disenchantment. While these letters are useful to the military historian, they afford only limited insight into genuine attitudes.

By contrast, many letters by World War I soldiers were more frank, and even their prose excesses of patriotism probably expressed real conviction. Some letters reproduced in Chapter Four show stock attitudes fostered by propagandist literature, and others suggest disillusionment setting in as early optimism dissipated. Besides literature, letters form the largest body of evidence for the ethos of each period discussed.

A Chronology of Military Literature in Brief

After initial reticence bred by revulsion to war soon after the Restoration, a literature of satire ridiculed the eighteenth-century soldier as villain at worst and buffoon at best. By century's end, however, the victimizing of Britain's poor who as "Volunteers" served the nation's interests abroad and returned thankless and broken in health evoked poets' sympathy. At the same time, the fiction novel was reaching maturity as a genre. For the unmilitaristic British, war literature had less appeal than commentary on social mores. So while picaresque novels continued to show the roguish soldier of fortune, novels of manners mirrored the military officer in his social context, usually as fool or villain.

The nineteenth century's heady spirit of nationalism soon drowned both contempt and pity, and at midcentury the remembered heroism of Waterloo had more appeal. Ironically, the near-disaster of the Crimean War only whetted the public's appetite for military romance. In the century's closing decades the usually sordid life of the British Tommy on the frontiers of Empire was exalted in verse and prose, all in the spirit of the popular *Boy's Own Paper*. Love of the Tommy, synonymous with love of Empire, happily coincided with a resurgence of interest in folk balladry, a form ideally suited to Kipling's epic exuberance.

With a tide of skepticism against late Victorian complacency from the turn of the century, Edwardian novels began to measure the passing of England's second Renaissance. "Psychological" novels such as *Clissold* and *The Good Soldier* became a jaded society's mirror on its own time, showing the tawdriness of military glory.

World War I found a generation of well-educated young men in uniform as temporary officers. Trained in the classics, they gave vivid expression to what it was like to be a citizen-soldier for the "duration." Later literature perpetuated the tradition of complaint, but in the Second World War the enterprise itself was not held up to question. The poetry and fiction assumed a just war.

The literature did more than reflect the historical process which has given the British Army its unique combination of professional and amateur ethos; it helped mold the army's spirit. Kipling's Tommy and Robert Graves's Temporary Gentleman, the tough and loyal regular and the patriotic citizen, remained as ideals for later generations of soldiers. Taken as a whole, the literature mirrors the historical process of institutionalized amateurism, from its beginnings in 1660 with the merging influences of Regular Army and militia, to its completion at the end of Empire.

In the Nuclear Age, a language of science militarized is replacing the language of military science as the possibility of limits on war recedes. The language of the militarized state echoes a loss of distinctions between peace and war, soldier and civilian. *Gentlemen of the Blade* concludes with a note

about language, war, and the warrior in the Nuclear Age. The age of amateurism is drawing to a close, and what that will mean for military literature
is as yet unclear.

NOTES

1. Anon., "Sir Dilberry Diddle, Captain of Militia . . . " (1766), *The New Oxford Book of Eighteenth Century Verse*, ed. Roger Lonsdale (Oxford: Oxford University Press, 1984), p. 544.

2. Samuel P. Huntington, *The Soldier and the State* (Cambridge, Mass.: Harvard University Press), 1957.

3. For a summary of recruiting practices and commissioning opportunities since Britain's first Labour government in 1945, see Dominick Graham, "England," in *Fighting Armies of the World*, ed. Richard A. Gabriel (Westport, Conn.: Greenwood Press, 1983), pp. 63–79.

4. Alfred Vagts, *A History of Militarism: Romance and Realities of a Profession* (New York: W. W. Norton, 1937).

5. Richard Pack, "An Epistle from a Half-Pay Officer. . . . " (written 1714; published 1719), in Lonsdale, ed., *The New Oxford Both of Eighteenth Century Verse*, p. 111.

6. From Foreword and *Envoi* of Robert Service's collected war poetry, "Rhymes of a Red Cross Man" (Toronto: Ryerson Press, 1931).

7. Ernest Raymond, *Tell England* (1922), (London: Corgi, 1973), p. 215.

8. Ibid., p. 312.

9. Richard Aldington, *Death of a Hero* (London: Chatto & Windus, 1929).

10. The comment, attributed to a *Times Literary Supplement* review, is printed with the 1873 edition of *Tell England*.

11. John Keegan, *The Face of Battle* (New York: Viking Press, 1976).

12. Ibid., pp. 30, 31.

13. Josiah Bunting III, "The Military Novel," *Naval War College Review*, 26 No. 3, Sequence No. 246 (November-December 1973), pp. 30–37.

14. Keegan, *The Face of Battle*, p. 53.

15. Anon., "The Volunteer" (1971), in Lonsdale, ed., *The New Oxford Book of Eighteenth Century Verse*, p. 786.

16. John Collier, "The Pluralist and the Old Soldier" (1763), in Lonsdale, ed., *The New Oxford Book of Eighteenth Century Verse*, p. 510.

17. Rudyard Kipling, "A Madonna of the Trenches," *Debits and Credits* (New York: Doubleday, Page & Co., 1926), p. 205.

18. Gerald Kersh, *They Die with Their Boots Clean* (London: William Heinemann, Ltd., 1941), p. 100.

19. E.g., see H. Wragg, ed., *Letters Written in Wartime (XV-XIX Centuries)* (London: Oxford University Press, 1915).

20. James Aitken, ed., *English Letters of the XVIII Century* (Harmondsworth: Pelican Books, Ltd., 1946), pp. 152–54.

21. Bunting, "The Military Novel," p. 31.

22. Ibid.

1

That Devouring Profession: The Restoration and Eighteenth-Century Regular Army

THE BIRTH AND LIFE OF A NEW BRITISH ARMY

Some for Hard Masters, broken under arms,
In battle lopt away, with half their limbs,
Beg bitter bread thro' realms their valour saved.
                                    Edward Young, "Night Thoughts"[1]

Cromwell's New Model army and the rule of the generals during the Commonwealth period had less lasting impact on the future of British arms than the appearance of ideologically motivated citizen-soldiers. Of more importance still was the political climate after the Protectorate which determined the character of Charles II's Restoration army. What had started as high idealism ended as petty political wrangling. When Richard Cromwell arbitrarily dissolved Parliament and a docile Rump Parliament assembled, he split the already politicized army into factions that stood either for the democratic principles for which they had fought or for a continued dictatorship of generals. It was adherence to the principle of Parliamentary rule which brought General George Monck to London from Scotland and led to the restoration of the monarchy in the person of Charles II, who now appeared infinitely preferable to the dictator under whose boot the much-vaunted "Commonwealth" had suffered. Monck, who had served Oliver Cromwell faithfully and now was instrumental in ending Britain's experiment with revolution, has been seen variously as patriot and time-server. Indeed, Milton may well have allegorized him as Beelzebub in *Paradise Lost*.[2] Whatever the case, as architect of the Restoration army, Monck may be called the father of the English-speaking world's modern armies.

It was with a sigh of relief that most Englishmen welcomed a return to monarchy and some degree of reconciliation between King and Parliament. That the monarchy would be Constitutional was a principle accepted by all but the most militant royalists. For the time being there was no serious questioning of the precept that the sovereign ruled with consent of Parliament, and that Parliament in turn represented the people's will. In practice, the monarchy could neither forget old ways nor learn new ones, so that the

Constitutional balance would remain in question until the Glorious Revolution of 1688 provided final resolution.

Whatever political struggles remained after the Protectorate, one principle relating to the military ethic at last was clear: the British soldier could boast a unity of loyalty denied him in the past. His oath to the sovereign had in earlier times been a royal ploy to afford the king military strength at the expense of subject lords or other factions who otherwise might have claims on the army's loyalty. Now for the first time an oath to the sovereign was an oath also to state and people, because the sovereign stood as the symbolic embodiment of the state and the people's will. At least, that was the theory. In actuality, King and Parliament eyed each other warily. Parliament begrudgingly acknowledged the need for protection against external threat, and the monarchy's traditional right to maintain a retinue for his own and his realm's defense; on the other hand, Parliament also feared the internal threat to constitutional liberties posed by a standing army. The answer seemed to lie in a strong militia under Parliament's control. So whereas in theory the military ethic entailed unity of loyalty, the army's sentiments were supportive of the central power, and those of the militia were jealously parliamentary and regional. On the whole, these differences cannot be thought of as political orientations as in the days of the Civil War. Rather, they were more in the way of attachments motivated by self-interest. So in looking at the Regular Army we should regard it as one of two military organizations which, distinct at first, influenced each other increasingly.

Small though the Restoration army was, the character it assumed formed the basis for the characters of modern armies in the English-speaking world. In contrast to the ideologically motivated Commonwealth army, the new standing army was apolitical, and accepted its subordination to civil government in executing its functions of national defense and internal security. Symbolic of the new order and the military's place in it were the desecration of Cromwell's corpse by disinterment and public hanging at Tyburn, and the execution of his principal army commander, Major General Thomas Harrison (signer of Charles I's death warrant, who was hanged, drawn, and quartered at Charing Cross). The message for the army was clear: neither King nor Parliament would stand for military meddling in affairs of state, a tradition of political neutrality which has been a cornerstone of the British military ethic.

The army which Charles II inherited when he returned from exile was a threat to the Crown, because although General Monck had already given all regimental commands to royalist officers, the very fact of a standing army had become associated with antimonarchist doctrine. Not surprisingly, Charles II set about disbanding the army. At the end of 1660 only two regiments and some ineffectual garrison companies remained in England, and England's Dunkirk Brigade (which remained there for two more years) was officered entirely by royalists. Human nature being what it is, a large armed body is a volatile mass, and in light of the decade just past, the army's loyalty was not a certainty. On the other hand, if a standing army were controlled by the monarch, it could also be a threat to Parliament.

By the spring of 1661 Charles II had founded the core of a new army which necessarily would remain small because of Parliament's fears. Throughout his reign, a suspicious Parliament dreaded the prospect of a standing army which might further monarchist and even popish ambitions. Rumors of plots and conspiracies, some real but most imaginary, were rife. Before the disbandment of the Commonwealth army was complete, an insurrection by some anabaptist fanatics in London made it apparent to all that the King would need troops to protect his person, if nothing else.

Much of the formal justification for a standing force loyal to the monarch was derived from the ancient precedent that entitled him to a personal retinue. Theoretically, then, the regiments were not a standing army but a "guard." The term was less frightening for opponents of standing armies and was the euphemism which graced new unit titles. The regiment raised by Colonel John Russell became the First Guards (later the Grenadier Guards), and the Earl of Oxford's cavalry was the First Life Guards. The Duke of York's cavalry troop recalled from Holland became the Second Life Guards, and Lord Gerard raised his troop of Royal Horse Guards. Lord Monck's regiment of foot which had been in the parliamentary service ceremonially laid down arms, took an oath to the Crown, and took up arms again as the Coldstream Guards.[3] This miniscule army of about 6,000 could hardly pose a threat to Constitutional government. It was intended largely for ceremonial duties, for protection of the King's person, and as a training cadre if the army had to expand in view of France's standing army of 16,000.

Because of its size, the army had no difficulty in filling its ranks with volunteers. The infantry certainly were not of the class of dismounted minor gentry who had manned the fifteenth- and sixteenth-century "free companies,"[4] nor were they the ideologically motivated citizen troops of the recent troubles. Like the men of the old levies, they were recruited mainly from the dregs of society—the unemployed and unemployable, the poverty-stricken and debt-ridden, vagrants and criminals. Nonetheless, they *were* volunteers. The ministers of the Crown had to resort to levies and press gangs later only during three brief periods of expansion for the Dutch wars, and then largely because most Englishmen loathed foreign service. In the Regular regiments anyway, home service was usually reserved for Englishmen, and except for those who served aboard ship, foreign duty was generally assigned to Scots and Irish soldiers. (A separate corps of Marines did not appear until Queen Anne's reign.)

By modern standards the quality of troops was abominable, but for the times it was good. The long tradition of equestrian superiority was reflected in the cavalry, which resembled the volunteer troops mentioned by Daniel Defoe in his persona as the Cavalier. With the sole exception of Lord Oxford's First Life Guards, the cavalry was an elite made up entirely of troopers from the lower gentry. All were from royalist backgrounds, and some even had held commissions during the civil war. Indeed, the cavalry was a training ground for young men who would later become officers. The officers both of horse and foot regiments were drawn from the peerage and gentry, and the army was seen as an honorable profession for sons who did not inherit land, and had no inclination for the navy, the legal profession, or the church.

As for the rank and file, education was surprisingly high, to the extent that out of 150 noncommissioned officers serving in Tangier, sixty-two "could write their own names."[5] This was no mean feat in an age of almost universal illiteracy among the laboring classes. Commissioning from the ranks was still unthinkable, however. Literate rankers more commonly were gunners or engineers, because they had to read the manuals of their craft, which they "deliberately surrounded . . . with a mystique."[6] They can hardly be counted as rankers, however; they still came under the direction of an Ordnance Office that was not subject to the Army's command. As in the previous century, gunners thought of themselves as practitioners of a science that set them above and apart from the soldiery.

Generally speaking, there were three kinds of officer, and while occasionally an officer might exchange roles, his family circumstances usually dictated which kind he would be: (1) The most professional usually was a member of the poorer gentry, without family and connections adequate to provide sufficient independent means to supplement his pay, and to make service in England affordable. If he did not offer his services to a continental power, an officer of this sort would find service with a British regiment on foreign service. (2) Then there were the officers of the garrison companies manning the king's forts and castles. They usually were old and incompetent, and knew little else of military matters but the routine duties of watches and guards. (3) The officers who most influenced the Regular Army's character were those of the Regular regiments on home service. Owing their commissions and ranks to their status as peers and upper gentry, they were "more politicians then [sic] soldiers."[7] Of independent means, they essentially were amateurs who took on military service as a credential qualifying them for later political leadership.

The singularly unmilitary aspect of English society, and its revulsion for standing armies and fear of military influence in state affairs, had a profound impact on the development of the Regular Army's ethos. The nobility and gentry brought status and prestige to their commissions and regiments, rather than the commission and the regiment according status to its officers. Ironically, then, the supposedly professional practitioners of the military art as applied science were least thought of as soldiers. However, the numbers of untitled gentry with commissions increased, especially after the expansion of 1674. Senior rank remained the preserve of peers and knights, and helped to perpetuate the association of the idea of "gentleman" with "officer," with some vague connotation of aristocracy attaching to commissioned rank. Thus, in the later seventeenth century a gentleman could enhance his social status by the regiment to which he could afford to belong. No qualifications of physique or intelligence were required, and military training was thought unnecessary. Natural nobility from generations of breeding would take care of any requirement for courage, and courage would compensate for any shortfall in competence. Formal qualifications of birth and money required for entry into the officer corps had only to be supplemented by knowledge and experience gained through foreign service. Aside from other obvious holes in that theory, the socially "best" regiments were least competent because they saw the least service outside England.

In time, keen competition among the gentry for the few officer vacancies resulted in fiscal abuses which were so common and traditional that they seemed more like time-honored custom than corruption. Gentlemen sought commissions and promotions for social status and political advantage, and even for the financial rewards that would come from false accounts of levy bounties, sales of licenses to sutlers, and all sorts of devices to part the Crown and the soldier from their purses. Although an officer might not be able to live off his pay, he had cause enough to buy a commission and subsequent promotions. As Crown appointments, commissions technically were paid by the officer to the Court. In practice and with the Crown's tacit complicity, however, a purchased rank was regarded as the holder's property, and he could sell it to the successor of his choice. As initial vendor, the Crown would benefit financially, as would the outgoing officer, who in his turn might have purchased a higher rank.

A young gentleman seeking a commission needed court favor, which required his having the patronage of someone influential in government who was sympathetic to the Crown. Oliver Goldsmith's *The Vicar of Wakefield* (1766) relates with frank acceptance an episode revealing the squirearchy's intricate system of influence and patronage. Not altogether cynical, the practice accommodated the patriotic fervor and tragically heroic sentiment which have always been weaknesses of the military romantic:

Mr. Thornhill came to me with looks of real pleasure, to inform me of a piece of service he had done for his friend George. This was nothing less than his having procured him an ensign's commission in one of the regiments that was going to the West Indies, for which he had promised but one hundred pounds, his interest having been sufficient to get an abatement of the other two. . . . George was to depart for town the next day, to secure his commission, in pursuance of his generous patron's directions, who judged it highly expedient to use dispatch, lest in the meantime another should step in with more advantageous proposals. . . .
After (our young soldier) had taken leave of the rest of the company, I gave him all I had, my blessing. "And, now, my boy," cried I, "thou art going to fight for thy country: remember how thy brave grandfather fought for his sacred king, when loyalty among Britons was a virtue. . . . Go, my boy, and if you fall, though distant exposed,

and unwept by those that love you, the most precious tears are those with which
Heaven bedews the unburied head of a soldier."[8]

In return for the rewards of that patronage, an officer who held a peerage
or a seat in the Commons was expected to vote with the King's faction. This
practice of royalist patronage did not make the army political. Quite the
contrary: the officer owed his authority and loyalty ultimately to the civil
authority which had secured his commission, and the army thus remained
subordinate to government. On the other hand, the purchase system ensured
a linking of aristocratic interests with the military status quo, and the military
officer in turn identified his interests and the interests of the army with the
political status quo. This conservatism and perceived social legitimacy accorded to military rank was to characterize the officer class for the next two
centuries.

In the three brief periods of expansion during the Restoration period,
patronage worked for mass levies in a looser but equally compelling way,
reminiscent in a way of England's feudal past. Royal commissions as colonel
were extended to members of the county gentry who had special political
and economic influence, and it was left to them to raise regiments, appoint
officers, and recruit troops. The trained bands, ineffective in themselves,
nevertheless were a source of semi-trained troops around which conscripted
county regiments could be built. The regional character of "county regiments" grew out of this recruitment practice, and was enhanced by the new
importance of the militia during the Restoration period.

Some practices to encourage recruiting involved a good deal of misrepre-
sentation:

On the three enlargements of the army recruiting parties scoured the length and
breadth of the country. Each group consisted of a captain, a sergeant, a corporal, a
drummer, and two privates. They would halt in a suitable village, plant the captain's
flag, and then summon the inhabitants by beating the drum. With the villagers assembled the captain mounted an improvised rostrum and delivered a speech, couched
in properly heroic and glamourous language, enticing the able-bodied men to come
to the drum-head and enlist for a bounty of five shillings.[9]

Other recruiting practices were more deceitful and brutal, such as false
promises and blackmail. George Farquar's love comedy *The Recruiting Officer*
(1706) about the adventures of Captain Plume and Sergeant Kite gives a
revealing glimpse of the corrupt recruiting methods of its age. Farquar, an
army officer-turned-actor, knew well whereof he wrote.

While this method of raising levies lent itself to influence peddling, it was
fundamentally sound. A recruiting system which relied on social and political
relationships was essentially benign, paternal, and grounded in existing social
structures. Consequently, there was a basis for mutual affection and loyalty
between officers and men. While these relationships did not always enhance

the efficiency and discipline of the militia when it was not embodied, they certainly increased the cohesiveness of units raised to augment the regular army in time of crisis. Certainly, the "regimental families" of British county units achieved miracles of endurance and courage in battle. But it would be easy to overemphasize regional bonds in the *regular* army. They were not a permanent feature, and a county regimental system had yet to evolve. Vicious discipline, shared misery, and a perverse pride in both put the starch into the regular regiments. It was not the ranker's love for his officers that made him toe the mark.

With pay, discipline, and training methods far more regularized and standardized, conditions of service were on the whole far better than they ever had been. Military discipline was still vicious, however, and care of troops was slipshod and incomplete by modern standards. Whether volunteer or pressed man, a soldier's initial engagement was for life; only disbandment of units, injury, illness, or death terminated his service. Although the soldier suffered brutal punishment, the administration of discipline in the early years after the Restoration was at least regulated in keeping with the example of the Earl of Essex's *Laws and Ordinances of Warre*, which in the Parliamentary army had established the principle that military justice was not the arbitrary will of the local commander.[10] That is not to say that discipline was humane. Flogging was the customary punishment, and rides on the "wooden horse" were common. "[T]he object of military law was not—and is not—to make men virtuous by punishing moral default, but to produce instant and complete obedience."[11]

As the quality of officer declined with time, punishment became more brutal and ingenious, and more in the nature of torture than correction. In the following century executions, branding, the cutting off of ears, "picketing," stocks, and running the gauntlet were common.[12] Many were permanently crippled as a result of torture, which abated only in the latter years of the eighteenth century. (By 1812 most of the more refined tortures had been proscribed, and only flogging remained. It was not abolished entirely until 1881.).

Some of the old fiscal abuses soon reappeared in the new army, because the common soldier was at the mercy of the recruiting sergeant for his bounty entitlement and the graces of his captain for his pay. As military command extended increasingly to officers who depended on military service for their livelihood, captains of companies lined their pockets through all the old dodges—false musters (nonexistent men were called "faggots")[13], and illicit charges against the soldiers' pay. Despite a gradual devaluation of currency, there was no increase in the soldier's daily eight pence pay for over a century, when in 1797 it went up to a shilling. He saw little enough of it anyway. "Subsistence," "off-reckonings," innkeeper's payment, laundry, replacement of worn or damaged kit and equipment, and even "waste of ammunition" were pretexts for company officers and their NCOs to part the soldier from his pay.

Civilians hired off the street were put into uniform to fill out the ranks at musters, and one soldier might answer for two or more others who did not exist. Another form of exploitation was the payment of debentures in lieu of cash. When the treasury was low, the soldier was forced to accept a promissory note payable at a later date. With the many charges made on him, both legitimate and illegitimate, for billets, equipment, and rations, he had little choice but to sell his debenture to a civilian speculator at much less than its real value.

Regular Army life in England was as idle as it was brutal. Unlike the dedicated and rigorously disciplined New Model's officers, the gentlemen officers of the Restoration Army were dilettantes who even abused a leave policy so liberal that it might allow absence from duty for six months. Thus emerged an image of the languid and charmingly useless officer aristocrat who rarely was to be found with his soldiers until it was time to die. The day-to-day conduct of a company's affairs in garrison was left pretty much up to the noncommissioned officers, and so grew a tradition of affectionate contempt by NCOs for their officers, whom they came to regard as only nominal commanders except in war. This subtle relationship between officers and senior NCOs has dictated the traditional sanctity of the NCO's responsibility for enforcement of discipline and garrison routine.

Training was tedious and unimaginative; the soldier's day was a round of drills, guards, inspections, and abuse by sergeants. Tactical drills and formations, differing little from methods employed before the civil war, were limited by the technology of the period. There was still little reliance on aimed fire, and no change from dependence on the hollow square and the charge in line. Although flintlock muskets and bayonets made their appearance during the Restoration period, they did not supplant the matchlock and pike as basic infantry weapons until the end of the seventeenth century, so that there was little call for tactical innovation. Not until speed of loading, together with reduced weight of small arms, increased the requirement for mobility would military commanders have to complement their bravery with intelligence.

The flintlock musket remained the basic infantry weapon throughout the eighteenth century. Although some French cavalry regiments had been equipped with rifled carbines as early as 1680, the time required for ramming home the bullet made rifled bores impractical for battle. Not until the War of Independence, and the prodigious feats of American marksmen, would the rifle receive serious attention. In the meantime troops had to maneuver into very close range, then depend on volume of fire and a final charge to break their enemy's formation. Commanders therefore usually occupied high ground where, surrounded by their staff aides and liaison officers, they could survey the battleground and direct operations. Not surprisingly, these spectator commanders were apt to view their troops as chess pieces whose ability to retain formation was essential. Hence, the incessant drilling and vicious punishment. For the British this rigidity and precision was all the more necessary, because British armies abroad had problems of logistics and transportation which kept their numbers small. They could not afford numbers in depth as a substitute for training and discipline.

Reverence for stasis and order, reflected also in the thought and art of the period, resulted in conservatism and reluctance to change, which enhanced military traditionalism and inflexibility. Particularly when engaged in irregular warfare abroad, commanders preferred irrational and rigid practices of "honorable" warfare to imaginative tactics, at terrible cost.[14] Similarly, the styles for uniforms reflected archconservative methods of discipline. Symbolically inflexible, the skintight gaiters, trousers, and tunic, the high leather stock, the greased, powdered, and minutely measured cue, the cinched-up buff leather belt, and the brasses, were all means of ceremonial torment for the soldier, long after their functional value had ceased.[15]

Now that the army had no ideological basis and had the uninviting task of garrisoning Britain's new possessions at Tangier and Bombay, it soon became a body of marginal men. Enduring virtual banishment on foreign service for years on end, they could look forward to a military career which in many cases amounted to a life sentence.[16] With the advent of foreign service, the government made virtually no provision for special clothing, equipment, supply or medical attention. Consequently, many who did not die of infected wounds died anyway, of disease. (By the late nineteenth century, an aura of romance enveloped death from disease in foreign climes.)

Soldiers who remained on home service suffered another disease: the hatred and contempt of the citizenry. As always, hatred of war had its reflection as hatred of the warrior. Weary of civil strife and military repression, many thinking men did not share the assumption that war was an inevitable dimension of international competition, and those who took up arms as a profession were "unnatural," they believed. Edward Hyde, Earl of Clarendon, restored as Charles II's major Constitutional architect until his banishment in 1667, wrote in exile of his loathing of military professionals:

[A]ll war hath much of the beast in it. . . . [P]rinces must be obeyed, and because they may have just cause of war, their subjects must obey and serve them in it, without taking upon them to examine whether it be just or no . . . : they have no liberty to doubt when their duty is clear to obey; but where there is none of that obligation, it is wonderful, and an unnatural appetite that disposes men to be soldiers, that they may know how to live, as if the understanding the advantage how to kill most men together were a commendable science to raise their fortune; . . . [T]he guilt contracted by shedding the blood of one single innocent man, is too dear a price to pay for all the skills that is to be learned in that devouring profession.[17]

Clarendon's subsequent comment that the perpetrator of a "skilful, and injurious aggression" incurs guilt which "often makes his understanding too weak to go through an unjust attempt, against a resolute though less experienced defender," is a sophistic argument against a standing army. If the cause is just and the soldier is motivated by it, so went the argument, his sheer righteousness and enthusiasm will prevail over military competence which presumably is without sustaining spirit. Arguments of this sort accorded legitimacy and respectability to the militia, while denying it to the Regular Army. Other arguments attacked the army on Constitutional grounds, so that Daniel Defoe, for one, saw need to refute assertions that "a standing army is inconsistent with free government."[18]

In the backlash of Commonwealth excesses, the soldier was widely despised, and in turn he had little pride in himself or his calling. The sight of the soldier's red coat—ironically, the New Model army's color which Charles II's troops retained—prompted fear, loathing, and insult. Soon only men with neither pride nor cause for it would join the army willingly; debtors could be drafted as punishment, convicts were offered pardons for enlisting, and unemployed vagrants could be ordered into the army.[19]

Although indiscriminate looting by victorious troops was forbidden, the rule was often violated, and attempts to control the practice by regulating division of spoils and paying prize money according to rank had little effect.[20] Therefore, by the early eighteenth century the British Army was attracting volunteer adventurers whose purpose was to grow rich with booty. In any case, soldiers often needed booty to trade with camp-following suppliers for subsistence. The overall result was an army of drunkards, rapists, and looters, who understood only the lash. Military service became so unattractive to ordinary folk that from 1779 even cripples were welcome in the ranks. During the campaign in Ireland against the deposed James II, the troops were so ignorant and lazy that they would not even build shelter huts for themselves when ordered.[21] One may only marvel at the truth of John Laffin's observation, "[F]aced with real fighting, somehow the men redeemed themselves."[22]

Deceitful and draconian recruiting practices, corruption which deprived soldiers of their pay, the brutalizing effects of military life, and the public's fear of armies all resulted in a vicious circle of civilian contempt for the military, and the military's contempt for rules of decency. There were no barracks until 1792, and although free quartering of troops on civilians was proscribed, the regulation was commonly violated. Otherwise, troops were quartered in public houses kept by publicans for the purpose. Thus, the civilian population was subject to continuous contact with whole companies of soldiers in garrison towns, where their drunkenness and violence made them odious. Billeted with civilians in towns, soldiers bullied, abused, and plundered their hosts, or simply failed to settle their accounts. Town and countryside were infested with beggars either wounded in foreign wars or crippled through punishment. Added to their numbers were fake military beggars who made it hard for real veterans to beg a living, and probably drove many to theft. Certainly, military beggars and thieves were a social blight of epidemic proportions in the late seventeenth century and throughout the eighteenth. The Royal Hospital at Chelsea for disabled veterans, established in 1681, could not begin to cope with the numbers needing its services; nor could the pittance awarded in the eighteenth century as pensions for old soldiers or bounty for amputees.

From the Restoration and through most of the eighteenth century, the relationship between civilian society and the army was worse than ever. This mutual hostility had Constitutional causes, which in turn had a direct bearing on the civilians' sense of impotence in the face of abuses by the soldiery. As we have seen, King and Parliament coexisted uneasily during the Restoration period, and the very existence of a royal army was a focus of contention. The army's legal status was never quite clear, because the monarch's traditional right to his own "guards" did not square with the equally well-established tradition that only Parliament could authorize a standing army. Thus, the Militia Act of 1662 was remarkably conciliatory in allowing the King autonomy in military affairs.

This military independence from parliamentary control was reflected in the dangerously elitist view the army had of itself. Officers held that military law took precedence over common law in its application to soldiers because they were the King's property, not Parliament's. Generally, politicians were content to let the army run itself, so that internal breaches of military law such as insubordination and desertion, which were not civil offenses anyway, were handled by the army's officers. On the other hand, the civil authorities insisted that crimes against common law such as murder, felony, and treason should be handled by civil magistrates.

Expansion by levy created further complications, because desertion and other offenses related to recruitment fell under the purview of civil commissioners. Convention held, too, that even for civil offenses local authorities first would obtain the permission of a soldier's commanding officer for his arrest and trial by a civil magistrate. This remained the practice even after Parliament gained control of the army by the Mutiny Act of 1689 (which not coincidentally was the year of Britain's Bill of Rights).

The attitude of officer and common soldier alike thus might be likened to that of medieval church, which insisted on the primacy of ecclesiastical law for clerics. The military came to think of itself as a separate class beyond the reach of common law, and held civilian officialdom in contempt. With officers rarely in evidence, crimes against civilians often went unpunished, moreover, the litigation procedures for recovery of debts were so unwieldy and long-drawn-out that publicans and shopkeepers had little recourse but to accept their losses with ill grace. Nominally guardian of the realm, the British Army of the Restoration and eighteenth century was a plague on decent folk, and probably did more damage at home than it ever prevented. It was despised for every reason:

Politically and socially the standing army in England represented a force which worked for the good of the king, but to the supposed detriment of both the lower and upper classes. To the gentlemen of Parliament the army was one of the central questions of the age and formed the core of the struggle between king and Parliament for executive supremacy. Non-Parliamentary gentry in the counties saw the standing troops as an attempt to undermine the position of their cherished militia, indirectly threatening their roles in county politics. The ordinary people in the towns and the country loathed the army. In their eyes it stood for everything that was bad and hateful.[23]

The civilian population had to tolerate not only a quarrelsome and rapacious soldiery, but also arrogant and contemptuous officers. Infatuated with French military fashion, officers paraded themselves in uniforms bedecked with Frenchified frills; nor was their posturing wholly innocuous. Unconcerned and unsympathetic with the complaints of merchants and burghers who suffered at the hands of the soldiers, the officers were also pugnaciously jealous of their own honor. Although military duelling in Britain did not reach quite the epidemic proportions it did in the French army, it was sufficiently prevalent to make ominous any dispute with a military officer. Regular officers were hardly accorded higher esteem in polite society than were the other ranks by the lower classes. Yet as always, class attitudes were curiously ambivalent. Many of the gentry were eager to obtain commissions because of the dash and romance associated with military service. The prospect of a life of glamorous idleness was seductive.

Militant elitism, together with the Regular Army's marginality, found expression in the common soldier's professed ethic of unthinking loyalty to the sovereign. The pre-civil war mercenary had professed loyalty to the military calling as an honorable trade for profit, and the civil war Royalist and parliamentary soldier had embraced political and religious doctrines. Later, events both during and subsequent to the Restoration period directed the soldier's loyalty to the Crown, so that service to the sovereign took precedence over every other consideration, and became part of the soldier's ethic. Unlike the "constitutional" soldiery of the militia, the "mercenary" soldier of the Regular Army was a fanatical royalist because he thought of himself as the King's property, and no longer knew nor cared about the Constitutional wrangles that had had so much impact on the profession. Nor had the soldier to worry himself about the morality of his trade. His allegiance to his monarch justified all, so that the King even shouldered blood guilt:

"But Jack," says I, "are you not thankful to God, for your preservation?" "How do you mean," he answered. "Fine talking of God with a soldier, whose trade and occupation is cutting throats. Divinity and slaughter sound very well together, they jangle like a crack'd bell in the hand of a noisy crier. Our king is answerable to God for us. I fight for him. My religion consists in a firelock, open touch-hole, good flint, well rammed charge, and seventy rounds of powder and ball, this is my military creed."[24]

Although the military code as its own cult justification was a barrier to new ideas, the eighteenth-century army nevertheless progressed toward modern military organization. To be sure, structural unity was still lacking. There was no general staff, and the king ran his army through his lord general (later commander-in-chief), who in turn directed regimental commanders. There were no divisional or brigade command structures or tactical formations; regiments were nearly autonomous in matters of dress and custom; and even the companies of a single regiment were billeted in different towns. On the other hand, the offices of adjutant, quartermaster, provost marshal, and chaplain became regimental appointments, and surgeons became regimental officers. After 1751 regiments no longer bore the names of their colonels, but were numbered; they thus took on a permanent identity and a recognizable place in the army's ceremonial "order of battle."

Medical, commissariat, and pay and pension services were still rudimentary, but regularization and centralization of administrative systems were making slow headway. The Earl of Marlborough's enlightened command did much to regularize campaign logistics. Ironically, the sixteen-year-old John Churchill was commissioned as ensign in the Guards in the same year as Clarendon's exile. A regular soldier, Marlborough was a living contradiction of the argument against a standing army. Marlborough's intuitive strategic genius, and his belief in rigid discipline, thorough training, and sound administration led to such resounding British victories as Blenheim (1702), Ramillies (1706), Oudenarde (1708), and Malplaquet (1709).

The establishment of field hospitals of sorts in defended garrison towns, and the provision of ambulance carts and barges for evacuation of dead and wounded, introduced some rationality and order to the aftermath of battle. If the hospitals were not much more than casualty dumps, they were at least a beginning of care for the soldier. Marlborough's insistence on sanitation helped to cope with problems of morale and disease; he paid the troops in advance so that they could buy their rations; and on the march he sent advance parties ahead to establish staging areas for care of troops on their arrival.[25] Harsh, paternalistic, and contemptuous toward his troops, Marlborough was nevertheless scrupulously fair. While the low standard of officers was more than one commander could improve fundamentally and permanently, he demanded and largely got honesty and efficiency.

After Marlborough's campaigns, the army continued to suffer from political neglect and social contempt. Numbers fell off, until by 1720 there were only 18,000 regular troops under arms (aside from garrison troops in Ireland and the troops of the Honourable East India Company). British troops continued to compare well with continental armies, as was evident at Minden, but only with the imperatives of the Seven-Years' War would the quality of officers and efficiency of formations begin to improve, when war eliminated the "more useless."[26]

Above all, what made the Restoration and eighteenth-century army recognizably modern was the principle established immediately after the Protectorate:

Charles' army was modern in that it was the servant of the civil power and not its dictator. Throughout the reign the military was subordinate to the civilian government, establishing a precedent for the following centuries for the British Army.[27]

THE POST-RESTORATION SOLDIER
ADVENTURER: "MEMOIRS" BY DEFOE

> This Peace leaving those youthful Spirits, that had by the late Naval War been rais'd into a generous Ferment, under a perfect Inactivity at Home, they found themselves, to avoid a Sort of Life that was their Aversion, oblig'd to look out for one more active, and more suitable to their vigorous Tempers Abroad. I must acknowledge my self one of that Number.
>
> Daniel Defoe, *Memoirs of an English Officer*[28]

The paucity of contemporary fiction and drama dealing with military figures from the civil war through the Restoration and the eighteenth century lends special importance to the work of Daniel Defoe (c. 1660–1731). Although Defoe grew up during the Restoration, the fictional accounts in the first person which are commonly attributed to him are so accurate in flavor and technical detail that they provide invaluable representations of men at arms from the Thirty Years' War and early Scottish campaigns to the early eighteenth century.

Defoe's own military experience spanned a turbulent period. A dissenter of low birth, he was about twenty-five years old when he took part in Monmouth's rebellion (1685), and somehow came away unscathed. Subsequently, he joined William III's triumphant march into London when the "Glorious Revolution" unseated James II in 1688. From 1697 to 1701 he was an agent for William III in England and Scotland. Best known for his *Robinson Crusoe* (1719), his racy *Moll Flanders* (1722), and such picaresque tales as *Captain Singleton* (1720) and *Colonel Jack* (1722), the pseudonymous "memoirs" which he is credited with writing are of more significance for present purposes: *Memoirs of an English Officer*.... (1728) and *Memoirs of... a Highland Officer* (1718). Always forward to a fault in his protest against intolerance and injustice, Defoe wrote about military matters usually to some current purpose. Yet whatever his satirical and political purposes may have been, his personae present unadorned narrative and personal comment, unencumbered by any sense of more profound authorial purpose beyond a knowledgeable description of seventeenth-century military manners, mores, and practices.

Defoe's apocryphal "The Military memoirs of Captain George Carleton" and "The Memoirs of Major Ramkins, A Highland Officer" (1719) are particularly valuable as examples of the late seventeenth and early eighteenth centuries' military conventions and attitudes. In terms of the military professional ethic, this was a time of transition. The courtesies of siege warfare were giving way to skirmishing, French military fashion was being aped in debased form in Britain, and national politics were adulterating the military adventurer's mercenary motives.

Carleton recounts his volunteer service with the Dutch William of Orange, and his later service for him as William III of England. The tale continues with his campaigning in Scotland and Spain until he is wounded and taken prisoner. In beginning his military career in 1672 by volunteering to fight against the Dutch, Carleton exemplifies the growth of nationalist sentiment among the upper classes: "[I]t was looked upon among the Nobility and Gentry as a Blemish, not to attend the Duke of York aboard the Fleet." Carleton's enlistment as "voluntier" does not guarantee him a commission or a command, although he is a British envoy's son and an ambassador's nephew. (Defoe's bourgeois background, rather than Carleton's aristocratic origins, might account for such grotesque excesses of description as that of a wounded soldier being eaten alive by hogs!) So Carleton is a gentleman ranker like those of the civil war and the King's Restoration cavalry; unlike them, he evidently is not a regular.

Hostilities with Holland were short-lived because of the French threat, and Carleton relates that this "generous Ferment" of temperament prompts him to serve the Dutch in Flanders as a member of William's Company of Guards, made up of English gentlemen. He does not think of himself as a mercenary in any pejorative sense, because soldiering by contract for a foreign state was still quite respectable, unless one's employer were pursuing a strategy counter to England's interests. Similarly, Carleton finds no fault with his precipitate escape from the French by vaulting a hedge more nimbly than his comrades. For the English mercenary of the period, utility seems to have been the best measure of action. As Carleton points out, his retreat not only saves his life, but also gives him a chance to find a spectator's vantage-point for the "glorious conflict!"

Ironically, the age that was becoming infatuated with classical ideals of order witnessed warfare which was becoming less ordered and rational. The relative simplicity—and even decorum—of siege tactics had suffered from use of diversionary attacks, ambushes of supply columns, pursuits of stragglers, employment of spies, and subversion by disinformation. In the tradition of Shakespeare's Fluellen, Carleton complains of the battle he watches (Seneff):

[T]hough the common Vogue has given it the Name of a Battle, in my weak Opinion, it might rather deserve that of a confus'd Skirmish; all things having been forcibly carried on without Regularity, or even Design enough to allow it any higher Denomination: For . . . , I found it very often impossible to distinguish one Party from another.

However, conventions of siege warfare were still being observed. Carleton reports that at the siege of Ghent the French military governor's refusal to capitulate brings on cannon and mortar fire which change his mind,

[U]pon which Hostages were exchanged, and articles agreed on next Morning. Pursuant to which, the Garrison march'd out with Drums Beating and Colours flying, two Days after, and were conducted to *Charleroy*.

Carleton's account is credible and accurate, in its resemblance to verifiably genuine accounts of conditional surrenders. This is a report of a formal siege in the Low Countries (seventeenth century):

[B]y ten a Clock the batteries were mounted, and ready for fireing, w. .[ch] the Governor perceiving, and very well knowing the dreadfull callamity ensued upon the Obstinacy of the Govern.[r] of the Cittadel, a few days ago was resolved that he would not putt himself in such a hazard, whereupon he ordered a Chamade and a flagg to be hung out to signify his inclination to come to a Treaty, the which being observed, Hostages were exchanged and the Articles were in a very short time agreed upon, and the Garrison marched out the next day upon Hon . . .[ble] Terms.[29]

There is paradox in this nice observance of martial etiquette at a juncture when warfare was becoming more vicious and diverse of method. The need for stability of relationships between nation states, together with the growth of an international military culture, proved to be civilizing influences on warfare. Earlier, convention held that the commander of the attacking army would threaten to loose his soldiery to rape and pillage at will after victory, if the defending commander refused to capitulate and negotiate conditions of surrender. By contrast, Parley as Carleton appears to understand it merely establishes the attacker's right to use arms as necessary to force surrender, and the besieged force may "cry quarter" at any time. Parley no longer afforded the attacker an opportunity to disclaim responsibility for humane treatment of the vanquished.

At the siege of Maestricht (1676), Carleton receives a commission when an "Ensign of Sir John Fenwick's Regiment" is killed. The practice was that a fixed number of commissions by rank were allotted to a regiment. The commission and its attendant rank became transferable property, although a candidate for a higher commissioned rank usually had held the rank below it. Carleton's "natural Desire to serve [his] native Country" prompts him to obtain a lieutenancy from James II. When James abdicates, Carleton has his commission renewed in William III's name. As with the argument advanced by militia officers by which they thought to choose allegiances,

Carleton does not think his commission is necessarily valid under the monarch's heirs and successors.

Fighting against the Scots, Carleton has further experience of irregular warfare. Called upon to surrender "with an Offer of Mercy," the Scottish gentleman "refus'd the proffer'd Quarter, and fir'd upon our Men, killing two of our Grenadiers, and wounding another." Carleton's commander angrily promises to "cut them all to Pieces." But some of the Scots are Carleton's old comrades-in-arms from Flanders, and they are given quarter when they surrender. Membership in the brotherhood of arms has saved them; otherwise, they would be regarded simply as murderous rebels. Such distinctions by military men are evidence of the growth of a military culture with internal ties more binding than loyalty to king or country.

Carleton's conduct during the Highlands campaign results in another commission in a regiment fighting the French. The French, having very nearly suffered a serious defeat, "fail'd not, in their customary Way, to express the Sense of their Vexation, at this Disappointment, with Fire and Sword in the Neighbourhood round." However, while French armies had not come far in the development of a military ethic, an aristocratic code bound the officers. Carleton relates this vignette of exquisite military manners:

But before they fir'd..., Villeroy, in complement to the Duke of Bavaria, sent a Messenger to know in what Part of the Town his Dutchess chose to reside, that they might, as much as possible, avoid incommoding her, by directing their Fire to other Parts. Answer was return'd that she was at her usual Place of Residence, the Palace; and accordingly their fireing [*sic*] from Battery or Mortars little incommoded her that Way.

If this incident has historical truth, it suggests that French romantic sentiment, so strong in the seventeenth century, was being translated into fact by a nobility consciously trying to fulfill its self-ideal. This Quixotic remnant of *amour courtoise* is treated as bathos by Defoe, yet paradoxically the British officer was infatuated with French military fashion. The rules of war may not have been humane, but they showed acute concern for gentlemanly honor.

After a period of inactivity "too long lamented," Carleton soldiers in the War of the Spanish Succession (1705) for the Earl of Peterborough. Peterborough commanded an international force for the second Grand Alliance forged by William III, and Carleton hints at the difficulties of command in a polyglot force. Peterborough is described as subject to "Instructions from England, the repeated Desires of the Archduke [of Austria], and the Importunities of the Prince of Hesse." Attempts at unity arrived at through Councils of War prove hopeless, and Peterborough is "reduc'd to the utmost Perplexity." His planning for the siege of Barcelona reflects these difficulties:

[Peterborough was] directed . . . by those at a Distance, upon well grounded and confident Reports . . . , and compell'd . . . , though General, to follow the Sentiments of Strangers, who either had private Views of Ambition, or had no immediate Care or Concern for the Troops employ'd in this Expedition.

Cooperation and competition by nation states in both peace and war had added new complexities to the profession of arms, and Peterborough's problems would soon be typical of those faced by military officers who would have to be diplomatists and strategists as well as field commanders. Resuming his reminiscences of the Spanish campaign with instances of deception and atrocity by soldier and civilian alike, Carleton hints at the growing moral complexity of early eighteenth-century warfare, and so his tale concludes.

For a view from the other side, Defoe relates "The Memoirs of Major Ramkins . . . " Ramkins, a Jacobite, soldiers for James II in Ireland, escapes to France after capture at the Boyne, and is wounded in French service, which included Malplaquet (1709). Ramkins begins his narrative with his departure from the University of Aberdeen "to observe the Martial Call" after the Battle of Killiecrankie (1689). Equipping himself from the sale of his books and furniture, he joins the remnant of a force that had fought for James II against rebel highlanders.

Raising money against his land as collateral, Ramkins fits himself out to campaign in Germany, where he joins a French army besieging Mainz. Told by a Scottish officer that he must gain experience either by serving as rank and file in a "Common Foot Regiment" or by undergoing two months' training as a cadet at Strasbourg, Ramkins decides to be a cadet, a not unusual choice. Later, Wellington also would be the product of a French military education. The description of the academy's curriculum is revealing of the state of continental military education at the time:

'Tis [in] the Nature of a College, where young Gentlemen are instructed in the Rudiments of War. . . . During my Stay . . . I omitted no Opportunity of improving Myself as to the French and High Dutch Fortifications, and other Parts of the Mathematicks which were useful in War. I was also present at some Lectures of Politicks which were given to those more advanc'd in Years, in which they handled the interest of Nations, and brought down their Reflections to the present Times. This I look'd upon as an excellent Method of educating young Officers; for it qualified them to be serviceable to their Country under a double Capacity; that is, as well to Argue as to Fight for it, and defend it equally with their Tongue and Sword.

Having finished his training, Ramkins buys his way into a body of "grand Musketeers," elite mounted English troops. An acquisitive lot, they angle for his purse with a threatening sort of camaraderie, which to refuse could mean a duel. Ramkins extricates himself by leaving the French army to join James II, out of loyalty. However, his inner promptings do not generate much haste, and he sojourns in Paris. He recounts his brother's imbroglio there. Typical of the image of soldier, the elder Ramkins is "somewhat addicted to Gallantry and Intriguing with the Fair Sex"; and through a series of mixups a French lieutenant challenges him to a duel. The young Frenchman's obsession with the *pointe d'honneur* costs him his life. Hopelessly outmatched by Ramkins who at first merely parries his thrusts, he persists in pressing his attack, and Ramkins has to run him through. A French officer dead and an English officer fleeing for his life from the law, and all over a supposed *affaire* which was entirely innocent! The maiden virtue of the Frenchman's cousin has never been in danger, but the bellicose young man has had to prove himself. Goaded by brother officers to seek an opportunity, he has not been inclined to listen to sense. Having sought manhood through a blood ritual, the French officer achieves a rite of passage he has not anticipated. There is bathos in this tragedy of honor perverted. The woman who has been the object of the whole episode has been oblivious. Horrified by the news of her cousin's death, she indulges her "Curiosity to peep" at his killer.

The younger Ramkins, being mistaken for his elder brother, is imprisoned until he proves his identity. Freed and still in Paris, he obtains a commission for service in Ireland, "which was no difficult Matter at the Time, especially to one who was provided with a little Money to facilitate the Grant." Satisfied to be "Registered as a lieutenant," Ramkins "according to usual custom, upon receival dexterously improv[es]" his rank to captain.

Despite Ramkins's protestations of loyalty as motive, he also admits that he has had "very lofty Expectations, and the Affairs of King James went so well at that time in Ireland, that there was not a Footman who follow'd that Prince, but look'd upon his Fortune as made." In Ireland Ramkins commands a company of "Fingalian Grenadiers"; at least, he "make[s] bold to stile" them as such, although they are "arm'd rather like Pioneers than Grenadiers." (Ramkins probably means axes and shovels. James's army became ragtag because French promises of arms and troops never materialized.) Ramkins pays for his pretension; an inexperienced captain who has wrought his own promotion, he is himself surrounded when he attempts an ambush. He accepts quarter and becomes a prisoner of William's army in Dublin. Because Ramkins has ample means and his family is known to many of William's English officers, he can enjoy his captivity. However, disillusioned with French duplicity and unable to accept William as his new monarch, he chooses to remain in Ireland. He breaks his parole and rejoins James's army.

Ramkins's apparently dishonorable violation of the code of arms points up a change in the nature of the military profession. When in the recent past the soldier's motives had been wholly mercenary, his parole would have been ahead of any other consideration; but with Ramkins factional loyalty takes precedence over military propriety. Although the trend in the late sixteenth century was toward the regulating and civilizing of war, another trend was also at work. This trend had been set in motion by the appearance of citizen-soldiers on the battlefield during England's civil war and the rise of irregular modes of warfare in Scotland, Ireland, and the New World. Those who took up arms for political or other reasons were not as likely to observe the profession's civilizing niceties, until eventually demands for unconditional surrender and attempted escape by prisoners would be deemed honorable.

Ramkins is wounded in the Irish campaign which ends in James's defeat. He leaves the army, returns to Paris to "solace [him]self," and falls prey to the soldier's traditional weakness. Hitherto so "bent upon War" that he could never waste time with a "Trolloping Girl," a "Breach of Idleness" makes him vulnerable; "The Roving Deity seiz'd the Advantage and enter'd Sword in Hand." Following the tradition of earlier literary warriors who are as incompetent in love as they are great in war, he is ensnared by a Spanish gentlewoman's charms. Having been made a fool by jealousy, he recovers his senses "by spending [his] Time in a Treatise of Algebra and Fortifications."

Restored to himself by his military studies, Ramkins continues in James II's service, knowing that the situation is hopeless. Unlike earlier professionals, he soldiers from conviction and remains loyal to a lost cause. Regarding himself as a "banish'd man," he observes that "there are a great many Charms in some Sort of Delusions, especially if they flatter Inclination." Next, Ramkins is ordered into Flanders with his French company. He is wounded at the Battle of Landen, and is briefly held prisoner by the English. His account concludes with his delirium, convalescence, and subsequent service in the Jacobite cause. Frank in pointing out his own follies as well as the military follies of his time, he expresses his consciousness of the moral complexity of the profession in words that would make a fitting epitaph for any soldier who knows himself:

> A Soldiers Life has many Occurrances which are not
> reconcileable to strict Morality
> I was neither a Saint nor a Devil

NOTES

1. Edward Young, "Night Thoughts" (1742–45), Book I, 11. 250–52.

2. For contemporary views of General Monck's motivations and role, see Albert C. Baugh, ed., *A Literary History of England* (New York: Appleton-Century-Crofts, 1967), p. 692; and Charles E. Ward, *The Life of John Dryden* (Chapel Hill: University of North Carolina Press, 1961), pp. 20, 21.

3. Hence the Coldstreams' motto, *"Nulli Secundus."* Founded as a Parliamentary regiment in 1650, they predate the Grenadiers.

4. J. W. Fortescue, *A History of the British Army*, vol. 1 (London: Macmillan & Co., 1918).

5. John Child, *The Army of Charles II* (London: Routledge & Kegan Paul, 1976), p. 24.

6. Ibid., p. 110.

7. Ibid., p. 30.

8. Oliver Goldsmith, *The Vicar of Wakefield* (Toronto: Macmillan, 1942), p. 192.

9. Child, *Army of Charles II*, p. 23.

10. John Laffin, *Tommy Atkins: The Story of the English Soldier* (London: Cassell, 1966), p. 100.

11. Ibid.

12. Ibid., pp. 102–4.

13. Ibid., p. 26.

14. Ibid., p. 43.

15. Ibid., pp. 30–32.

16. John Laffin (*Tommy Atkins*, p. 38) cites the 38th Regiment, which was sent to the West Indies in 1707, only to remain "abandoned" for sixty years!

17. From Edward Hyde, First Earl of Clarendon's (1609–74), "Of War," in *A Book of English Essays 1600–1900*, eds. Stanley V. Makower and Basil H. Blackwell (London: Oxford University Press, 1912), pp. 24–32.

18. "An Argument shewing that a standing Army, with Consent of Parliament, is not inconsistent with a free Government, & c. . . . " (London: Printed for E. Whitlock, 1698). (Reply to "An Argument shewing that a standing Army is inconsistent with a free Government" by John Trenchard and Walter Moyle.) See also Defoe's "A brief Reply to the History of standing Armies in England. With some Account of the Authors" (London, printed 1698).

19. Laffin, *Tommy Atkins*, p. 28.

20. Ibid., p. 27.

21. Ibid.

22. Ibid.

23. Child, *Army of Charles II*, p. 213.

24. From Samuel Ancell's *A Circumstantial Account of the Long and Tedious Blockade and Siege of Gibraltar* (Liverpool: 1785), and quoted at length in Laffin, *Tommy Atkins*, p. 56. Samuel Ancell apparently served in the 58th Regiment of Foot when Gibraltar was under siege by the Spanish (1779–83). Here Ancell recounts a purported conversation with "Jack Careless."

25. See John Laffin's detailed account of some of these innovations (*Tommy Atkins*, p. 35).

26. Laffin, *Tommy Atkins*, p. 48.

27. Child, *Army of Charles II*, p. 232.

28. Daniel Defoe, "The Military Memoirs of Capt. George Carleton from the Dutch War, 1672. . . . " (1728), in *Memoirs of an English Officer*, ed. Martin Seymour Smith (London: Victor Gollanz, 1970). The question of Defoe's authorship of *Memoirs* is dealt with in detail by Stieg Hargevik, who argues compellingly but not conclusively that a Captain Carleton was the true author. (See Stieg Hargevik, *The Disputed Assignment of Memoirs of an English Officer to Daniel Defoe* [Stockholm: Almquist & Wiksell, 1974), Part II, p. 1).

29. From "The Journal of Serjeant John Wilson (15th Regiment of Foot (1701–11)," in *Rank and File: The Common Soldier at Peace and War 1642–1914*, ed. T. H. McGuffie (London: Hutchinson, 1964), pp. 279–80.

2

A SORT OF PUBLIC NUISANCE: THE RESTORATION AND EIGHTEENTH-CENTURY CITIZEN MILITIA

CONSTITUTIONAL SAFEGUARDS AND THE CITIZEN MILITIA

> The county rings around with loud alarms,
> And raw in fields the rude militia swarms;
> Mouths without hands; maintain'd at vast expense,
> In peace a charge, in war a weak defense:
> Stout once a month they march, a blust'ring band,
> And ever, but in times of need, at hand.
> This was the morn when, issuing on the guard,
> Drawn up in rank and file they stood prepar'd
> Of seeming arms to make a short essay,
> Then hasten to be drunk, the business of the day.
> The cowards would have fled, but that they knew
> Themselves so many, and their foes so few. . . .
>
> John Dryden[1]

One of the consequences of the civil war and Protectorate was that the militia assumed a new importance which would significantly alter the nature of the military profession in Britain and the character of its soldiers. If the New Model army may be seen in any sense as Britain's first modern force, it is largely because of the emergence of a citizen-soldier whose belief in a cause made him amenable to iron discipline, and whose commitment was to an ideal not itself part of the code of arms. Perhaps more innovative than the New Model army was the increased competence and importance of the town militias, a factor influencing the character of England's future armies. Town militia, by and large comprised of, and loyal to, the bourgeoisie of the craft industries and commerce, were for the most part on the side of the Parliamentary army. In Daniel Defoe's apocryphal *Memoirs of a Cavalier*, the Cavalier says of the troops who resisted Prince Rupert at Ailsbury that although they were "two Regiments of the Country Militia, whom we made light of, . . . we found they stood to their tackle better than *well enough*"; and they "fired their Lines very regularly, considering them as Militia only. . . . [T]he City Train-Bands, of which there were two Regiments, and whom we used to despise, fought very well: They lost one of their Collonels, and several Officers in the Action; and I heard our Men say, they behaved themselves as well as any Forces Parliament had."[2] A citizen militia which formerly was without any real motivation except exemption from impressment had become a force to be reckoned with when they had a cause.

While the feudally derived tradition of privately raised regiments would wither away over the next two centuries, the earlier Anglosaxon tradition of the *fyrd* perpetuated in the Militia temporarily took on new life following the civil war. The war once more gave Englishmen a personal stake in military affairs. What more natural than that the regimental system, essentially feudal in character, should eventually be adopted by the Militia Trained Bands? The Militia soon lapsed into its traditional ineptitude. Yet it assumed social and political importance out of all proportion to its effectiveness. For that reason, we have to look back briefly at the Militia's traditional role before and during the Protectorate. Britain's irregular soldiery had always been an expression of the reciprocal right and obligation of the Crown and its free yeomanry. The right and duty to bear arms, having its origins in the twelfth-century Assize of Arms and the Statute of Winchester (1285) epitomized the dual nature of militia service: a pride in local autonomy and freedom on the one hand, and loyalty to central authority on the other. It had been this same tension in its political form, after all, which had led to disputes between Crown and Parliament, and to civil war. The tension had continued during the Protectorate, between Parliament and the Protector's standing army.

Self-righteous, religiously zealous, and egalitarian, Cromwell's victorious army had been ripe for exploitation by its leaders for political purposes.[3] A New Model Army Chaplain (who admittedly would not have been free of all bias) wrote in 1646:

One thing there is most singular in this your Army: that whereas soldiers usually spend and make forfeiture even of the civility they bring into other armies; here men grow religious, and more spiritual-thriving than in any place of the kingdom.[4]

Yet these most pious soldiers, like others, were soon seen by the citizenry as an unwelcome burden. Among other complaints another chaplain cited the "free-quartering of soldiers." He did not inveigh against the soldiery as such. Indeed, he advocated as the alternative, "provision for soldiers' pay, lest the cure seem more heavy than the disease."[5]

The vaguely threatening tone of the chaplain's words suggests the potential for confrontation between the nation's defenders and its lawmakers, especially when the army might make demands for the protection of the rank and file against a dilatory government. *Advertisements for the Managing of the Counsels of the Army* reflect a political, belligerent, and vocal army, determined to have its way, demanding mutinous protection by its own commanders.[6] Cromwell's army had ample cause for indignation, as the *Apology of the Soldiers to their Officers* (3 May 1647) attested.[7] After all, were not the rank and file also of the people, and therefore did their commanders dare oppose their just demands, democratically set forth?

Therefore, brave commanders, the Lord put a spirit of courage into your hearts that you may stand fast in your integrity that you have manifested to us your soldiers; and we do declare to you that if any of you shall not, he shall be marked with a brand of infamy for ever as a traitor to his country and an enemy to this Army. Read and consider. Was there ever such things done by a Parliament, to proclaim us enemies to the state, as they could have done about the late petition, [For disbandment of the Army].

Soon the confrontation had reached a point that clandestine "committees of correspondence" appeared, led by "agitators" ready for violence if necessary, to prevent Parliament's disbandment of the New Model army. Agreeing to "cheerfully and readily disband when thereunto required by Parliament," but only after "having first such satisfaction to the Army in relation to our grievances," the soldiery in a *Solemn Engagement* (5 June 1647) had advanced as its representatives "a council to consist of those general officers of the Army who have concurred with the Army in the premises, with two commission-officers and two soldiers to be chosen for each regiment."[8] In a *Representation* ... (14 June, 1647) the army's authors made a telling point which serves to show a fundamental difference between this and Britain's earlier armies, giving it a new and fundamentally different relationship with the state:[9]

Especially considering that we were not a mere mercenary army, hired to serve any arbitrary power of a state, but called forth and conjured by the several declarations of Parliament to the defence of our own and the people's just rights and liberties. And so we took up arms in judgment and conscience to those ends.

The army demanded "[t]hat the Houses may be speedily purged of such members as for their delinquency, or for corruption, or abuse to the state, or undue election, ought not to sit there," and that those who "have the will, the confidence, credit, and power to abuse the Parliament and the Army ... may be some way speedily disabled from doing the like or worse to us, when disbanded or dispersed, and in the condition of private men, or to other free-born people of England."[10]

The political and ideological intricacies which gave rise to the Army's march on London, Pride's Purge, Charles II's execution, and the Cromwellian Protectorate need not concern us here. Of more importance for present purposes is that (1) Britain's standing army had taken on the character of a citizen-soldiery which expected and demanded all the rights and obligations of free men; (2) the army expected to exert political influence as a body, for its own interests and for the good of the realm; (3) the standing army, which had been the victorious Parliamentary army, ironically became regarded by Parliament as a threat; (4) the Army saw a Militia enlisted and controlled by Parliament as a threat to its continued condition of privilege, prestige, and even existence. To be fair, we should note that what the junior officers and the rank and file wanted were payment of wages in arrears and indemnity on discharge for acts committed on military service. More senior officers with political ambitions might have hoped secretly that continued grievance would prevent the spread of sentiment for disbandment among the troops.

Central to this struggle between Parliament and the army had been the struggle for control of the Militia. The Army was successful in controlling a "Rump Parliament" for a time, and predictably the Militia came under the control of the generals; if the soldier of the standing army had taken on the character of citizen-soldier, it is also true that members of the Militia took on a professional role and character. Embodied to prevent and control disaffection among the citizenry, and itself selected and thoroughly controlled by a central military polity with a standing army at its back the Protectorate's Militia was for a time something quite other than a parochial and regional institution opposed to central authority. In attaining quasi-professional status the Protectorate Militia was briefly more efficient than it had been in its earlier incarnation as the Trained Bands.

The Restoration Militia declined in quality, but its new prominence made its ambivalent role politically and militarily critical. It was both the Crown's protection against any resurgence of popular unrest, and Parliament's guarantee of constitutional autonomy. Conflict over the Militia epitomized the Constitutional dispute which earlier had led to civil war, and which with the Restoration made it either a blessing or a threat depending on the point of view. During the Restoration the Militia's role in relation to Parliament and Crown remained contentious until the Glorious Revolution of 1688, when the principle of Constitutional monarchy was established in Britain once and for all.

The militiaman of whatever rank probably did not bother his head much about this matter of divided loyalties, unless he happened to be a member of the House of Commons. His loyalty remained as indeterminate and potentially volatile as the character of the institution itself. Not until the interests of the state became embodied in the Sovereign's will could the man at arms resolve the question of unity of loyalty. While the principle had equal application to the Regular soldiery, the emergence of the Militia was vital to the development of that military ethic. During the civil war the very idea of "Cavaliers" and "Roundheads" fighting as citizen-soldiers in fully constituted armies dedicated to causes had forever altered the nature of British arms. The Militia which emerged, nearly dormant and ineffective as it often was in times of peace, became the foundation for the armies that fought Britain's national wars.

Paradoxically it had been during the Protectorate, when irregular troops were becoming more "regular" and regular troops had taken on the attitudes of irregulars, that for the first time a clear distinction appeared between the Militia and the standing army. Similarly, it was during the Protectorate that a standing army had first appeared as distinct from earlier armies which really had been Royal retinues supplemented for specific campaigns with ad hoc levies. For the first time a force could be mobilized which could counterbalance the power of the state's standing army. Every political faction therefore sought control of its financing, equipping, recruiting, and command authority. Parliament's running battle with Cromwell and later with his son Richard had been marked by unremitting insistence on a series of Militia Ordinances designed to reform, codify and regularize laws and customs of finance, muster, levy and training of militia; other legislation attempted to reduce drastically the standing army's size. The civil war and the army's subsequent abuses of power had produced fear and revulsion in Parliament and among the public; so ironically both Parliament and ex-Cavalier Royalists found common ground in wanting a strong militia not subject to the head of state's authority.

By 1660 two distinct views of militia had emerged: the country view and the court view.[11] The "country" view was in the tradition of the Trained Bands, whereby the militia was for home defense, and all fit males had an obligation to keep arms or armed men according to their means and social rank. In practice, membership in the Trained Bands had become largely voluntary and was a refuge for the prosperous to avoid Crown levies. The result was that levied armies consisted of the penniless and predatory; if there was to be a standing army in peace these would be its members by default. There were ground here for militia soldiers to be thought respectable by comparison with the Regulars, an attitude held through the eighteenth century and into the nineteenth.

The "court" view was in keeping with the militia system instituted by Cromwell. The Commonwealth Militia had been composed of paid volunteers who were required to appear at quarterly musters, and who were available for service both at home and abroad. About one tenth the size of the Trained Bands, they were much better trained and organized. The prospect of pay and occasional full-time service attracted adventurers who might otherwise have gone into the Regulars. After the Restoration proposals for similar organizations were unpopular, because this kind of militia was too much like a standing army. Both Parliament and the public were as fearful of either an army or a militia controlled by Charles II as they had been of the New Model Army.

The Militia Acts of 1661–63 exemplified the English capacity for compromise, in accommodating both the "country" and "court" views. Charles was given control of the Regular Army and the right to appoint its officers, but control of its budget and powers of levy and muster remained with Parliament. Furthermore, Parliament carefully curtailed the Militia's powers as an internal police force, in the hope that militiamen could not indiscriminately hunt down and persecute suspected dissidents and subversives as Cromwell's men had done, having been given very nearly arbitrary powers. With the Restoration a balance was achieved, whereby the Militia was *responsible* to the Crown and *responsive* to Parliament.

As long as the honeymoon of King and Parliament lasted, the soldiers would not have to choose between sovereign and state. But the delicate balance of authority was short-lived. After its recent experience with tyranny, Parliament was a little too ready to accede more power to the restored Charles II than he was able to handle with restraint. Much of that power was in the King's authority over the Militia, so that soon the "court" view predominated and the Militia took on the character of royal troops. Lieutenancies for "finding" troops were issued solely by the Crown, which also controlled pay and accounting systems. As in the past, property owners had to provide troops and equipment as directed by the king's lieutenants, and every militiaman was required to maintain his equipment according to a set scale. As early as 1662 rumors of subversive activities by disaffected Commonwealth men resulted in Parliament's granting the king a substantial budget to enable part of the Militia to be "permanently embodied for the maintainance of order."[12]

Whatever its newly strengthened sovereign allegiance and police powers, the Militia was no more free from corruption and inefficiency than it ever had been. The landed gentry and yeomanry disliked the new liability to serve away from home, and found paid proxies when any real soldiering was called for. So the squirearchy enjoyed the prestige of uniforms and rank titles without exercising command, and the Militia's rank and file soon were much like the dissolute Regulars, whose habits they emulated, the more to feel like real soldiers. The annual training requirement of four days including traveling time was little enough. Even at that, musters in many regions were not held for years on end. Because musters were by regiment and at different times, the same men often served as proxies at several musters.

A militia subject to embodiment for service at home or abroad for limited periods gave rise to the institution of "volunteer", a man not ordinarily a Militiaman, but who would join a Militia regiment only when it was embodied in response to a particular emergency. Especially in the early Restoration period when civil unrest threatened and the ordinary Militia was in disarray, the "volunteer" bands which kept the peace were not much better than medieval *ecorcheurs*, persecuting the innocent and scouring the countryside for booty.

The emergence of the "volunteer" was an important development in the British soldier's attitude towards his calling, signifying the merging of central and regional systems of military service. The Militia thus became regarded, and came to regard itself ideally, as a permanent mobilization base ready to answer the sovereign's call to arms, not only with men, but also with complete regimental organizations ready to serve on an equal footing with the army. The very term "army" eventually ceased to distinguish between regulars, reserves, or reserves called to active service.

Until about 1670 the Militia was essentially a constabulary operating with the impetus of the government's fear of uprisings by Commonwealth men. Militiamen set about catching customs violators, seizing arms, searching homes, and breaking up conventicles and seditious meetings. Beginning in 1663 one-twentieth of the Militia was always on full-time duty for a fortnight at a stretch. By 1666 its constant harassment had pretty well broken the dissidents' morale. With the Second Dutch War (1666–67) the Militia rallied for national defense, and several companies assembled to deal with coastal raids by privateers. Organized essentially for internal security and untrained for war, it could not have taken the field as a proper army. After the war scare the Militia became increasingly unpopular. Much of its *raison d'etre* as an instrument of search and seizure had disappeared, largely because stringent game laws had deprived most citizens of arms.[13] The Militia's continued repression of suspects long after the wounds of the Commonwealth had begun to heal alienated a people who have always been acutely jealous of their freedom. Dissenters gained public sympathy and support, even from many of the county officials who were responsible for the Militia's administration, and many of the Militia themselves lost their taste for police duties. However, with the excuse of the Popish Plot in 1678 there were enough militiamen ready to abuse their power; and as late as 1689 militiamen were plundering papist livestock and property. The Militia became despised, its officers and men lost their self-respect, and efficiency declined.

From the 1670s to the 1750s the Militia continued on a downhill slide. It may have appeared equal to its tasks, but that was because it required few of the military virtues. Whenever Militiamen practiced tactical drills in town squares they provided a laughable spectacle for the townsfolk. To be the butt of one's neighbors' jokes is demoralizing, and understandably recruitment fell off. During the Monmouth Rebellion in 1685 the Militia's resistance was hopelessly inept, and troops of several regiments fled shamelessly before the advancing rebels.[14] Their only value was as a deterrent, merely by occupying ground and by disarming potential rebels.

Along with this general decay there was the Militia's natural tendency toward political partisanship and patronage. Because the king controlled commissions and lieutenancies, he sought a military administration favorable to his interests and less sympathetic to Parliament. So those responsible for recruiting were of Charles II's political color, and were apt to select officers and men of similar persuasion. The Militia thus had the effect of making the military ethic more political than in the past. However, the kind of politics had less to do with ideological and social aims than with the Militia's own interests to ensure its officers' continued well-being. The Militia's political tendency thus made it vulnerable to shifts in government, so that when James II survived Exclusionist forces in Parliament and succeeded Charles II, one of his early moves during 1687–88 was a purge of lieutenancies to fill positions with Catholics and dissenters.[15]

Not only did partisan appointments give the Militia a "party character,"[16] but class interests were served as well.[16] A property qualification dating from the 1648 Militia Ordinance required that only those with adequate estates to "find" at least one mounted soldier could be Crown deputies or officers.[17] The lieutenancy had to woo the gentry, therefore; and officership and rank, legally tied to property and social standing, became virtually a hereditary right among many families of county gentry.[18] Predictably, officers used their positions to influence elections through intimidation of voters, and by granting rank and privilege to militiamen of the right persuasion.

The Militia's decay and disrepute as a military institution was accompanied by its growth in strength as a social and political institution. Not only were junior officer appointments sought after, but lords lieutenant, deputies, and influential senior officers wielded political and economic power merely by being able to bestow commissions in return for political support. Because the lieutenancies were royalist and Tory virtually by definition, they were an important counterpoise to the growing power of the Parliament-leaning city and town corporations. Whig militiamen were scarce, and even they were reluctant to persecute their fellow gentry who might be dissenters, papists or Jacobites. The Militia's last notable achievement of this sort was its harassment of the Exclusionists, who from 1681 were conspiring to ensure that the Catholic-leaning James II did not stand heir to the throne.

In the late eighteenth and early nineteenth centuries demands for reform and for an end to persecution mounted; yet, even an inept militia was thought preferable to a standing army. So it survived even the ridicule so well typified by Dryden's verse.[19] A war of words raged between pamphleteers who wanted a standing army and those who feared one.[20] In the political intrigues by advocates of weak and strong monarchy and between the Parliamentary majority and its opposition, the militiaman had become a pawn in the emerging two-party system. As such, he became a political animal to protect his own interests.

It was this characteristic above all else that distinguished the army ethic from that of the Militia. Admittedly, regular officers held commissions by purchase, had landed interests, and in many instances had influence in Parliament; but their loyalty was more exclusively to the Crown, and was not influenced much by regional politics. However, a thoroughgoing doctrine of nonpartisanship would not become firmly established until the midnineteenth century, when the Prussian army set the tone for Europe's armies as institutions ideally aloof from politics.

During the 1740s and 1750s Britain, although mistress of the seas and a colonizing power without equal, felt her back to the wall. By 1745 France appeared about to become Spain's ally against Britain, and at home Jacobite agitation in support of "Bonnie Prince Charlie" brought the return of the British Army from the Continent. Again the need for home defense raised cries for militia reform and saved it from extinction, and there was a movement to make the Militia a trained citizen force-in-being, after the fashion of Continental nations.

Although no serious consideration was given to disbandment of the Militia, largely because of France and Spain's threatening postures, there was much debate over schemes for reform. Supporters of a strong militia working to minimize the importance of military education, ensured continued amateurism just when the idea of professionalism was emerging in other armies. Education in arms—that is to say, the study of strategy and principles of war as distinct from technical training or the learning of manuals—had only begun to appear, because broad national strategies had not emerged fully and wars were still limited. Of course, officers of artillery and engineers had to know their crafts, but those "trades" were usually the province of the bourgeois who otherwise would not have been thought fit for commissions. Gentlemen had character and courage bequeathed by breeding and background, so went the argument; and for officers of cavalry and infantry, nothing more was needed. By the same token a free militiaman's motivation and belief in the justness of his cause would make him more than a match for any professional—by definition a mercenary—whose profession of killing could not impart moral strength. Indeed, the Earl of Clarendon had asserted that the amateur's strength born of innocence would always prevail:

[A]ll the science that is necessary for just defence may be attained without contracting a guilt, which is like to make the defence the more difficult. And we have instances enough of the most brave and effectual defences made upon the advantage of innocence, against the boldest, skilful, and injurious aggressor, whose guilt often makes his understanding too weak to go through an unjust attempt, against a resolute though less experienced defender.[21]

The new fashion for light infantry, derived largely from the colonial experience in the West Indies and North America, meant that precision of formation drill diminished somewhat in importance. This sentiment, favorable to faith in an ill-trained but enthusiastic militia, anticipated by only a few years the theories of European military thinkers who advocated speed, flexibility, initiative, and maneuver as the highest battlefield virtues, in contrast to rigid discipline, unthinking obedience, and steadiness under fire.[22] The new military theory combined with urgency to support universal training and constant partial embodiment of the Militia.

Of course, there were objections: military training destroyed a man's will and ability for honest labor and encouraged drunkenness and loose living. The result would be the decline of the working class at the expense of

Britain's foreign trade. The argument reflected the age and nation; commercialism, utilitarianism, and cynical pragmatism underlay this concern for citizens' morals. The argument did not differ much from arguments against employment of the despised Hessian and Hanoverian mercenaries for the Jacobite uprising of 1745 and the beginning of the Seven Years' War in 1756. It all came down to a matter of cost.

Eventually, the advocates of militia reform prevailed. A reform bill of 1757 brought the Militia a big step closer to the Regulars. A ballot system was instituted for a "select militia" based on the precedent of levies and calls for volunteers, whereby men between eighteen and fifty years were selected by lot to serve in the Militia for three years.[23] The Englishman's temperament was so opposed to compulsory military service that the ballot led to rioting, both then and again in 1796, with the purpose usually of destroying lists of men eligible for service. There were already two ways troops were raised. "Local associations" or volunteer companies were raised by county lieutenancies, financed by local governments, and kept embodied for police duties; and (2) regiments were raised by noblemen in emergencies. When regiments were not embodied, officers continued on the rolls on half pay, a practice still observed in the nineteenth century. Militiamen were brought under martial law, although technically civil authority still was to administer justice in cases of corporal and capital punishment ("life and limb").

Provision was made also for the establishment of county regiments with companies and half-companies in towns and hamlets. This reform appealed to county sentiment by requiring the lieutenancies to form men into units appropriate to each county's quota; seven to twelve companies of forty men each in a county constituted a regiment, and fewer comprised a battalion. Weekly drills were required, and later annual two-weeks' regimental training camps were instituted. Each militia regiment was given an adjutant and sergeant instructors—one for every twenty men—from the Regular Army. However, the Militia too often was a dumping-ground for the least competent and conscientious Regulars.[24] On the other hand, there were many who, because of inheritance or marriage, left the Regulars and continued with the Militia through sheer love of soldiering. In addition, the Militia benefited from the military qualities and experience of regular junior officers who, commissioned from the ranks for merit, had reached the zenith of their careers and were no longer young.

Qualifications of property still dictated officer rank,[25] and a five-year compulsory retirement system was designed to ensure room for promotion, reduction of patronage and a relatively youthful officer corps. Moreover, pay, uniforms and arms were to be provided from Crown tax revenues rather than from local subscription. Thus, in theory at least the gentry and town corporations were relieved of a sometimes crushing burden, while their dependency on the Crown increased. County sentiment, loyalty to the Crown, government control, and the gentry's interests were all accommodated; and something like the modern system of county regiments was the result.

Practice didn't match theory, however. No system could adequately address the Englishman's dislike of the inconvenience of having to bear arms. Most gentry had a strong enough sense of *noblesse oblige* to accept their commissions and do their duty, but not much beyond the formal requirement.[26] Social prestige and patriotism were not enough to generate enthusiasm. As early as 1760 there was a shortage of officers willing to serve, because with the government's practice of embodying militia during wars, the gentry could not afford to risk their landed interests by absence. Among commoners fraudulent exemptions for family size, age, health, and other extenuating circumstances were epidemic. Multiple enlistments, enlistment for bounty, desertion, false lists and false muster—in fact, all the traditional dodges—gave a county the appearance of having met its obligations, when in fact the Militia had improved little.

The new organization and regulations nevertheless allowed for the embodiment of large numbers of militiamen in response to invasion scares in 1759, 1778, and 1783, and gave the Militia a status similar to that of modern citizen armies. So for the rest of the eighteenth century, the Militia achieved in the public mind a legitimacy and permanence which made it more a part of Britain's social fabric. National emergency had made the Militia respectable again. There still were large numbers of militiamen who were parliamentary electors, so that judicious recruiting and patronage might help an officer running for Parliament. Conversely, the many militia officers and county lieutenants in Parliament gave the Militia a strong lobby, evident in the founding of the Militia Club in 1789.

Still, so few gentry with the necessary property qualifications were willing to serve that anyone who was even barely acceptable might be commissioned. For such men, who might already have disqualified themselves from respectable civilian company through debts or misbehavior, and for men of the lower classes, the embodied militia became a means to gain social stature and privilege. These officers found their interests to lie with a militia strong in its own right, rather than in any other economic and political advantage it afforded. Unlike an army commission a militia commission did not have to be purchased; consequently many propertyless young men without other income or family influence used the Militia as a means of entry into the army by transfer. All the same, many officers shared a strong county and class esprit. They often exercised strong influence over promotions within their own ranks, and conspired to exclude professionals and men of low birth.[27]

The Militia came to be regarded as an adjunct of the Regular Army, and junior militia officers were treated as professionals by the government. Beginning in 1786, five years' service as a Militia lieutenant earned appointment as brevet captain.[28] (Brevet or "army" rank was independent of vacancy, and was held concomitantly with "local", or militia, substantive rank. This dual rank system was fraught with difficulties when regular officers served with militia and vice versa.) In 1796 the Militia came to resemble the Army even more, by being required to serve anywhere in the British Isles. Soon the militiaman's revulsion toward Irish service differed little from the attitude of regulars.

From 1808 the Militia became the Regular Army's main source of recruits for the Napoleonic wars, so that military service touched the British public as never before. The Militia was an important aspect of the first "total" war effort as the term might then have been understood, in the sense that the population and its resources, as well as its full-time soldiers, were enlisted in a national cause. However, although the Militia might serve as a mobilization and training base for the Army, its units could not be required to serve abroad, and since 1786 militiamen could be recruited only from their own or an adjoining county. By and large the regiments retained their regional character. Paradoxically, although property was both the main qualification and main cause of reluctance, a stipulation that half an officer's property had to be in the county in which he served strengthened the gentry's association of military allegiance with county interests.

Regular Army recruiting was only slightly less parochial, in that officers naturally sought recruits from their home county lieutenancies where they had influence. So, Regular Army regiments also had county identities of sorts, and vied with militia regiments for the same men. There remained a slight but diminishing distinction between army and militia recruiting, however. As the Industrial Revolution bred a teeming class of working poor, the army afforded escape for desperate youths from the manufacturing towns. The squalor and depravity of their origins which they perpetuated in the army became almost a military tradition. The Militia, although it too drew on town populations, remained more rural in character, because its officers and recruiters were sedentary folk of the countryside.

With a substitute system fostering all the old dodges money could buy, the ballot became an instrument of privilege, as in the past. The prosperous yeomanry were discouraged by the gentry from enlisting if they had a mind to, because they had the franchise and could vote against unpopular officers who stood for seats in Parliament. Therefore, as in the past the rank and file were from the least privileged classes, men who probably would have enlisted in the Regulars anyway, had there been no militia.[29] Despite all attempts at reform, the Militia remained poorly officered and trained through the rest of the eighteenth century.[30] The American and French revolutions ensured the Militia's survival in spite of public apathy, and the call of adventure brought ample volunteers to embodied regiments. It was only this sporadic enthusiasm engendered by threat of war that kept the Militia alive, and after Napoleon's final defeat the Militia all but disappeared until after the Crimean War.

Social conditions and the series of attempts at reform legislation produced a militia not much different from the regular army. The militia officer commonly was lazy, indifferent, and ignorant. The rank and file "were so badly led that it is doubtful if they could have faced seasoned troops with any hope of success."[31] In 1757 the government provided arms, accoutrements, and an ammunition ration for NCOs and men, and colors and drums for regiments. In theory, this should have meant that the soldier would have become less dependent on the gentry's largesse and more dependent on the Crown, and that the Crown acknowledged an obligation toward its Militia troops. The militiaman would therefore have had cause to transfer his first loyalty from his county masters to the Crown.

In practice, the government expected loss, wear, and even original defect, as well as transportation and storage of arms and equipment, to be made good by the regiments. Officers' ingenuity was taxed, sometimes at the expense of their own purses, and always at the expense of the men's pay. The government clothing allowance was scant, "enough only for a coat, perhaps a hat and some oddments, but not enough for shirts or breeches."[32] Naturally, there were complaints that commanding officers mismanaged funds for their own profit; but they also had to extract funds from miserly bureaucrats and cope with sharp-dealing suppliers. Not all officers were crooks. Many felt a nearly feudal obligation to their soldiers, and often their charity redressed low pay.[33]

Militia subalterns on full-time service, unlike senior officers with private means, had to live on their pay. They had to conduct and equip themselves according to their positions as officers and gentlemen, so they were usually in debt. Perhaps here was the origin of one of those whimsical traditions associated with the British officer. To be in debt to one's tailor became virtually a condition of belonging, and merchants had to be long-suffering before enlisting a commanding officers' sympathy to make the delinquent pay up.

The Crown's involvement in pay and supply contributed to the identification of regiments with their counties in an unexpected way. Because regiments had to maintain arms and equipment ready for use when embodied, in 1802 permanent central stores and armories began to be established at county expense. Here were the beginnings of permanent headquarters and depots for county regiments. This development contributed to the Militia's sedentary character, because even when a regiment was absent on active service, the county armory was the palpable expression of the regiment's regional identity.

In this respect the Militia was ahead of the Regular Army, which did not have regimental "homes" until the Cardwell Reforms of 1870–71 brought about a linking of battalions serving abroad with others in Britain. Even at that there was artificiality in the grafting of the system onto essentially nomadic regular regiments whose officers and men in many instances had no roots in the region that lent them its name. However, the imposition of regional identity on regular regiments may show the extent of the militia's influence on the army's ethos.

The Militia's identification with towns and villages did not make its men any more popular. Compulsory billeting in inns and public houses meant constant altercations with innkeepers; the publicans exploited the soldiers, and the soldiers brawled, drank, and abused their hosts. As the embodied militia grew during the 1790s because of the French threat, the problem reached such proportions that the government turned to the innovative measure of barracks. The earliest were squalid in the extreme:

Hyde Barracks comprised mainly an old malt house, divided into three storeys of which the lowest was only 5 ft. 9 in. high and had no floor but the bare earth, full of holes and often muddy. The middle storey had an even lower ceiling and the top one was a mere loft, stifling in summer and very cold in winter. . . . The drainage was bad, and the cooking had to be done in the dormitories. The men slept two to a bed, and the beds were packed so tight that it was often impossible to make them.[34]

Not only did barracks enhance and emphasize the separateness of military life and culture, but it also signified the state's acceptance of responsibility for every aspect of the soldier's existence. Barracks also meant a resident commissary who contracted with local suppliers, a practice first instituted for militia training camps in 1778. Company officers withheld a portion of the soldiers' pay and turned it over to the commissary for purchase of rations. In 1795 the government partially subsidized rations. Men were divided into "messes" of twelve, and each mess had cooking utensils and a fuel ration. As early as 1796 there was even something like a battalion field kitchen with cooks, but that sort of logistical sophistication was not the general rule.[35] In practice, barracks life was hellish; hunger and disease were the norm.

Officers lived in much better circumstances in inns where they established their messes. A sutler, civilian waiter, and soldier "mess-man" might attend the officers, and the officers would pay a subscription to the adjutant. A mess with drawing room and a mess-room with table-linen is on record.[36]

For unembodied militia annual training camp life was the somewhat more endurable equivalent to the permanent barracks life of embodied militia and regulars. Beginning in 1762 the unembodied militia was to train for twenty-eight days annually. In 1792 a standardized syllabus and reviews for testing were established, so that "the camp became a regular military academy, with a syllabus and a pass examination."[37] All this reflected the government's concern with a need for uniform instruction and standards, and perhaps most significantly, the government's practical authority to make demands on the militia. Life in camp was far from taxing, and for the officers it could even be a pleasant excursion. An officer might take lodgings with his wife near the camp, spend part of his day overseeing training, and the rest engaging in recreation and social duties.[38] Men also brought their wives, who often worked as washerwomen.

Camps afforded opportunities for exercises even of brigade size, although training consisted largely of arms drill and parade square evolutions which were the basis of tactical maneuver. By the late eighteenth century, the British Army's standards had fallen so low compared to that of the continental armies that the Militia had little difficulty reaching it. There was no official drill manual until 1792, so each regiment followed its own often baroque practices. While there was always a military lobby for simplifying drills, the ceremonial value of complicated evolutions was early advanced as a means of engendering martial fervor to sustain the soldier's resolve as an antedote to panic on the battlefield.

Perhaps the growth of light infantry and grenadier companies contributed to militia enthusiasm. Usually comprised of picked men, they initially had been used as flanking skirmishers in line units; now large training camps afforded opportunities for them to be grouped temporarily into special battalions. The prestige and sense of individual worth a militiaman might experience in achieving acceptance as a light infantryman or grenadier reflected current sentiments being fostered by French social theory. The citizen-soldier's initiative and enthusiasm were supposed to compensate for the Regular's discipline and training.

Militia discipline was more humane than that of the army, and officers were encouraged to "win the affection" of their men, who were "to be taught to think of themselves as gentlemen." Patriotism, county honor, and good citizenship were regarded as proper motives for taking up arms, so that older motives of profit and loyalty to the monarch's person were no longer adequate.[39] The development of this citizen militia and the professionalizing of its embodied component invested Britain's military ethos with a sense of social responsibility. The implication was of a "Constitutional" soldiery as distinct from a "mercenary" force, in the sense that the military as a whole came to owe loyalty to the Crown only as symbol of the Constitution.

Those high-sounding and dangerously liberal conceptions of the Militiaman's proper motives did not match practice. Desertion, theft, drunkenness, brawling, and abuse of civilians were still commonplace. While discipline was less vicious in the unembodied militia, flogging and more refined methods of inflicting pain were common in the embodied militia, those officers apparently were not much deterred by the "life and limb" provisions which marked the distinction between militia and army punishment.

Throughout most of the eighteenth century, the unembodied militia was generally ill disciplined and ill trained, and the embodied militia was generally ill led and incipiently mutinous. On the other hand, the militia and civilian society exerted mutually beneficial influences. The evolution of the militia from the Restoration to the beginning of the nineteenth century had a marked impact on Britain's military ethos. Starting as a pawn in the Crown's maneuvers for authority independent of Parliament, the embodied militia became almost a professional force with purposes free of political significance. In contrast, the unembodied Militia reflected social and political concerns. Although in the end the Militia almost ceased to be, it had enhanced the unique family character of the British Army, whose county regiments have ever since had internal bonds which have withstood the test of battle magnificently. Furthermore, military rank, no matter how titular, became associated with the gentility and sense of duty expected of the squirearchy. This somewhat military flavor in English society was evident in the prestige accorded to army and militia commissions during the nineteenth and early twentieth centuries. The army, militia, and society were all reflections of each other. A tradition of arms grew which has been military but not militaristic, and has drawn on civilian culture to produce such miracles as the Great War's Kitchener Divisions and the Pals' Battalions.

FROM CONTEMPT TO PITY

> [B]eing asked by a young nobleman, what was become of the gallantry and military spirit of the old English nobility, he (Doctor Johnson) replied, "Why, my lord, I'll tell you what is become of it; it is gone into the city to look for a fortune"....
> I admit that the great increase of commerce and manufactures hurts the military spirit of a people; because it produces a competition for something else than martial honours,—a competition for riches.[40]
>
> Let shame at length the state o'erwhelm,
> That knows he fought to save the realm,
> And lets the wounded soldier moan.[41]
>
> "The Soldier that has Seen Service.
> A Sketch from Nature" (Anon., 1788)

During the eighteenth-century, fear and distrust of the military were supplanted by contemptuous amusement, reflected in satirical lampoon and caricature, both in literature and in visual art. By the close of the century, literary interest was directed almost exclusively toward the common soldier as an object of pity rather than scorn. Changing conditions and the institution of universal militia service by lot after 1757 prompted these shifts in attitude. Throughout the Restoration period and the eighteenth century, Britain was embroiled in wars in India and the New World to protect its commercial interests and acquire more. The so-called cabinet wars involving British troops on the continent were limited dynastic squabbles. Not until the French and American revolutions would Britons feel any direct military threat. The army abroad soldiered in the interests of British commerce, decently out of public view, and the regulars at home and on the Continent were a separate breed, hardly fit for respectable company. Heroism itself was out of fashion, and the heroic epic form had become a medium for the bathos of John Dryden's and Alexander Pope's satire.

Britons had not yet assumed a proprietary attitude toward the Empire which they were inadvertently acquiring. There was as yet no class of colonial bureaucrats and army officers who felt an obligation to administer the "lesser breeds without the law," and the army abroad did not think of itself as defender of the realm. Rather, the army was seen, and saw itself, as part of a frankly profit-making enterprise. Soldiers continued to be thought of as mercenaries, whether individual itinerant officers selling their services to the highest bidder, or whole regiments contracted by one state to another to fill the treasury. They all seemed cut of the same cloth in this cynical age. As late as "1776, war was an art, soldiering a trade,"[42] and Britain both bought and sold military services well into the nineteenth century.

A clear expression of attitude equating military adventure with commerce and patriotism is Daniel Defoe's "Of Captain Misson."[43] Misson reports with approval the actions of a French ship-of-the-line's captain. The French have just captured a British armed merchantman, and the captain refuses to surrender the Englishmen's sea chests to the crew as spoils. He reminds his crew of the "Grandeur of the Monarch they serv'd; that they were neither Pyrate nor Privateers." It follows that the French king is himself piratical, and that state piracy has donned the uniform of military honor. Misson himself embarks on a career of benign piracy in the name of "God and liberty," holding always to his assertion that his men are righteous and principled, and therefore not pirates. Nowhere does Defoe hint at the ironic possibilities of Misson's words. By the same token, there was little to choose between the Royal regiments in India and their counterpart Company regiments of the Honourable East India Company. Both were engaged in state piracy and conquest which was seen as legitimate at home.

Although viewed as useful adjuncts of the nation's business, the marginal men of Britain's army were early regarded by some as neither dangerous nor necessary, and so were treated in print and picture with indulgent contempt as swaggering nuisances. Samuel Butler's *Hudibras* (1664–68) is a mock-heroic epic modeled on *Don Quixote*. A satire of the Civil War, it is a Rabelaisian quest by its clownish hero and his grotesque squire Ralpho. In the same way that *Hudibras* set the tone for later novels, the French author Alain Le Sage's *Gil Blas* (1715), a picaresque romance about an itinerant Spanish youth, served Tobias Smollett as model for his *Roderick Random* (1748). *Roderick Random* is an episodic tale of a young rogue who is pressed into naval service and later fights for the French army. A gambler and unsuccessful womanizer, he is a portrait of amoral youth, both exploiting and exploited by cynical self-servers.

The most skillful satirical essayists of the period, Joseph Addison and

Richard Steele, showed with eloquence and wit the soldier at his best and worst. Observing that an idle soldiery spoils for action in times of peace, Addison made the good-natured plaint:

[G]entlemen of the blade...seem to be generally of the opinion that the fair at home ought to reward them for their services abroad, and that, until cause of their country calls them again to the field, they have a sort of right to quarter themselves upon the ladies.

While Addison readily acceded that the "camps" nurtured in well-disposed men qualities superior to those bred at court, he pointed out that "a man who goes into the army a coxcomb will come out of it a sort of public nuisance."[44] There follows a collection of apocryphal letters from military officers who are self-preening braggarts and womanizers. Addison's attitude was Job-like; the military was a blight and burden to be borne patiently.

Richard Steele's essays are in the same spirit. Steele left Oxford in 1694 to join the Life Guards, and was a captain before he started the *Tatler* in 1709. So he knew the army at first hand and that perhaps explains why he was more indulgent of individual soldiers than of corrupt military institutions. Steele described a Captain Sentry who had not gone far in his profession despite gallant campaigning. Sentry is too modest, in a profession that requires a man to "get over all false modesty" in struggling through "crowds of toadies" to gain the "favour of a commander."[45] Yet Steele acknowledged in soldiers "a certain mechanical courage which the ordinary race of men become masters of from always acting in a crowd," and he recognized that officers were negligent of their own safety. He even found charm in the soldier's unpolished prose, bespeaking an artless and uncalculating mind: "a certain irregular way in their narrations or discourse, which has something more warm and pleasing than we meet with among men who are used to adjust and methodize their thoughts."[46] As an arbiter of morals, good taste, and good sense, the *Spectator* advanced views that were socially approved. Its blend of good-humored tolerance, condescension, and occasionally a hint of mild respect, reflects perhaps more moderate attitudes toward the military than were common. After all, polite society had to accommodate this curious and unbecoming breed with as good grace as possible.

In his condescending way, Doctor Samuel Johnson, who passed judgment on nearly everything, was reasonably accommodating about soldiers. Mr. James Boswell, his unctious biographer, in his *Life of Johnson* offers what he purports to be verbatim reconstructions of the great pontificator's views. Apparently officers were acceptable and men were not. Johnson holds forth to Boswell:

[T]he character of a soldier is high. They who stand forth the foremost in danger, for the community, have the respect of mankind. An officer is much more respected than any other man who has as little money. In a commercial country, money will always purchase respect. But you find, an officer, who has, properly speaking, no money, is every where well received and treated with attention. The character of a soldier always stands him in good stead. . . .

[A] common soldier is usually a very gross man, and any quality which procures respect may be overwhelmed by grossness. A man of learning may be so vicious or so ridiculous that you cannot respect him. A common soldier too, generally eats more than he can pay for. But when a common soldier is civil in his quarters, his red coat procures him a degree of respect.[47]

Boswell concludes this account by quoting a letter to the reader, written by Johnson to a friend about his godson: "He is weary, and rationally weary, of military life. . . . A soldier's time is passed in distress and danger, or in idleness and corruption."[48]

Henry Fielding's rollicking *Tom Jones* (1749) shows the same good humor and tolerance toward an ineffectual home army. In his travels Tom meets a sixty-year-old lieutenant who has made no headway in his profession because his wife has rejected his commanding officer's advances. The lieutenant commands an unruly detachment of hard-drinking rank and file and a couple of ensigns remarkable for their coarseness and ignorance, one of whom has "gone for a soldier" in preference to the only alternative, the clergy. The cursing and brawling crew are soon in their cups. When Tom bridles at lewd insults to his beloved's name he is laid out with a blow from a bottle. Later, his attempt to obtain a sword to defend his honor ends in his being cheated outrageously by the detachment's sergeant. To add insult, Tom listens to a sagely ironic lecture by the well-intentioned lieutenant on the importance of honor, a property which the lieutenant distinguishes clearly from virtue: "[B]e a good Christian as long as you live, but be a man of honour too."[49]

Published at midcentury, *Tom Jones* was a highwater mark for eighteenth-century satirical representations of the soldier. From here on a more sensitive and even romantic spirit began to appear in literature. The age of Rousseau was dawning, and the overcivilized British privileged classes were beginning to yearn for naturalness, simplicity, and innocence. A virtual cult of the "noble savage" in artistic and intellectual circles brought new interest in the plight of poor and simple folk who were held to be society's victims: the peasant starving or forced from the land by Enclosure, and like him the common soldier, were fit objects for genuine, if somewhat abstracted, pity. Not fully articulated as social theory, the intelligentsia's benevolent feelings were beginning to be expressed as belief that society collectively had a responsibility toward its members.

For the first time the common soldier was given a voice—not his own, but the voice of his poetic champions among the upper classes. Whether forced into military service by ballot, or beguiled by romantic fictions to enlist voluntarily, the soldier was being recast as victim. Throughout the century poetry echoed growing revulsion toward war's false glory. In 1701

John Philips may have relished his own disgust in "Blenheim," with descriptions of "hair scalps . . . whirled aloof," "mangled limbs," "brains and gore."[50] Britain's neglect of its soldiery also came in for heart-rending commentary. Verse by Mary Barber in 1734 needs no more than its title to tell its tale: "On seeing an Officer's Widow distracted, who had been driven to Despair by a long and fruitless Solicitation for the Arrears of her Pension."[51]

The luring of recruits prompted Isaac Bickerstaffe in 1770 to write "The Recruiting Serjeant . . . ," with the recruiter's air, "What a charming thing's battle!", and a list of its joys: "Shooting, stabbing, maiming, cutting."[52] When volunteers were being sent to fight a losing war against revolutionary Americans in 1776, an anonymous poet "M" penned "On the Frequent Review of the Troops," a complaint about the seductively "gaudy shows" which led to "all the people murdered."[53] Hatred of war led to pity for the returned soldier, and there is no shortage of minor verse on the theme: Into "The Soldier that has Seen Service . . . " an anonymous poet in 1788 poured his compassion for the "conquering hero" hobbling on crutches, with "two sickly brats" in tow, who "suck, for want of food, their thumbs."[54] John Scott's "The Drum" (1782) is about the recruiting party drum's "discordant sound" luring peasant youths to war. The poet contrasts the reality of "burning towns, and ruin'd swains" to the illusion of "tawdry lace and glittering arms."[55]

There were specific causes for this fresh attention to the rigors and miseries of military life. When the army expanded in response to unrest in New England, and later to the threat of a Republican French invasion, sons and brothers of townsfolk and the countryside's tenantry were dragooned by ballot into service with the embodied militia. The pathos of boys wrenched from their families' bosoms touched the gentry and upper-class townsmen. Already imbued with the ideas of the Enlightenment, many were revolted by the army's brutality. They had seen healthy young men leave, only to return broken by fever and hunger, and crippled from punishment and enemy shot. Moreover, some few literate soldiers were making their misery known. There is a record by one "Cobbett," who tells rather priggishly how he learned to read and write despite the "brawling of at least half a score of the most thoughtless of men" in a crowded barracks.[56] There is elegance of understatement, too, in an account by one "Sergeant Lamb" who recalls of his recruit days that "some of the old drill-sergeants were unnecessarily, if not wantonly severe."[57]

Life in barracks was only slightly better than the misery of the battlefield. The common soldier was quickly parted from the pittance he received. One recalls his extortionate recruiting sergeant: "I had to pay the drummer, for beating the points of war, and I must also buy a cockade for [the sergeant], and a suit of ribbons for his wife. . . . These same ribbons . . . were sold regularly to every recruit."[58] Another soldier recalls:

[M]any [recruits] deserted from sheer hunger. They were lads from the plough-
tail. . . . I remember two that went into a decline and died during the year, though
when they joined us they were hearty young men. I have seen them lay in their
berths . . . , actually crying on account of hunger. The whole week's food was not a
bit too much for one day.[59]

Even at the turn of the century men were being flogged mercilessly. We have
a scene of a soldier being given 229 lashes for sleeping at his post:

I saw the drum-major strike a drummer to the ground for not using his strength
sufficiently. . . . At length, the surgeon interfered, the poor fellow's back was black
as the darkest mahogany, and dreadfully swelled. The cats being too thick, they did
not cut, which made the punishment more severe. . . . [H]e died eight days afterwards.[60]

The art of cruelty was far advanced over the science of logistics for the
soldier's welfare in garrison and on campaign. In fact, by the end of the
century staff systems for the maintenance of fit troops and care of sick and
wounded were no better than, and probably inferior to, those of Marlborough's day. Campaigning in Holland, a soldier recalls the aftermath of the
Battle of Egmont, 1799:

The firing ceased sometime before sun-set. . . . We filled our canteens, and then went
to look among the dead and wounded for a comrade. . . . The dead were lying stiff
on the ground, in various postures; the groaning of the wounded was very afflicting;
for they were mostly bad cases, all that were able to walk or crawl having been moved
farther to the rear; and all the assistance, that could be given to those who were
unable to move, was to carry them from the spot where they had been lying, to a
place of greater shelter. . . . The universal cry of these poor men was for water. I
supplied them as far as I was able.[61]

It is to the credit of the English upper classes that as conditions like these
became common knowledge much of the mocking and the satire died away.
Besides, with a threat of French invasion in the century's closing decade,
the soldier was being seen as the defender of the nation, its values and its
institutions. The complacency on which cynicism feeds was being under-
mined by anxiety and compassion. The traditional view of the young soldier
of fortune as parasitic adventurer continued into the nineteenth century, but
even in novels about these lovable and not so lovable rogues the early
eighteenth century's literary sneering disappeared.

The major writers took up the cry in both verse and prose as the compassionate mood became general. A notable triumvirate of English letters,
Oliver Goldsmith, William Cowper, and William Wordsworth, expressed
these enlightened sentiments. Goldsmith's "The Deserted Village" (1770)

inveighs against the complacent wealthy who exploit the innocent poor. His list of victims includes old campaigners cast up by the tides of war onto the shores of an uncaring nation:

> The broken soldier, kindly bade to stay
> Sat by the fire, and talked the night away;
> Wept o'er his wounds, or tales of sorrow done,
> Shouldered his crutch, and showed how fields were won.[62]

Here is no swaggering braggart. This old soldier is the flotsam of national glory, whose martial strength is reduced to a crutch wielded in imitation of a weapon.

In his major work of prose fiction, *The Citizen of the World* (1762), Goldsmith gives a history told by a wounded campaigner, showing how he came to his low estate.[63] The "disabled soldier, . . . with an intrepidity truly British, leaning on his crutch," tells his tale to the Cantonese "citizen of the world" with simple dignity. His father, he says, was a country laborer who died when he was a child. Shunted from parish to parish, he earned a living in a workhouse, became a farmer's bondsman until the farmer died, and roamed from town to town working where he could. Jailed for poaching a hare on a justice's land, he was transported to the colonies. Returning to England, he was taken by a press gang and given a choice of service as sailor or soldier. As a soldier he served "two campaigns in Flanders, was at the battles of Val and Fontenoy, and received but one wound in the breast."

Discharged when peace was declared, he enlisted with the East India Company, fought the French "in six pitched battles," was denied promotion to corporal because of his illiteracy, fell ill, and returned to England "with forty pounds in my pocket, which I saved from service." This was at the beginning of the Seven Years' War. Pressed into service before he could "set foot on shore," he served next as a sailor, and lost his savings when captured and imprisoned by the French. A daring escape and recapture, then a further escape which the old campaigner recounts with such lack of self-concern that the tale's credibility flags:

I had almost forgot to tell you, that in this last engagement I was wounded in two places—I lost four fingers of the left hand, and my leg was shot off. Had I had the good fortune to have lost my leg, and use of my hand on board a king's ship, and not a privateer, I should have been entitled to clothing and maintenance during the rest of my life; but that was not my chance.

A poor man forced into military service, then cast aside and neglected because of a bureaucratic technicality, was the typical soldier of the late eighteenth-century literature. No longer was the literary emphasis on younger sons of the well to do, who took up arms for fame and fortune.

William Cowper's "The Task" (1785) shows the soldier as a vicious society's victim.[64] While Cowper's quarrel is with the military profession, his
sympathies are with the once innocent young men who were corrupted
morally by compulsory military service:

> The clown, the child of nature, without guile,
> Blest with an infant's ignorance of all
> But his own simple pleasures, now and then
> A wrestling match, a foot-race, or a fair,
> Is ballotted, and trembles at the news.
> Sheepish he doffs his hat, and mumbling swears
> A Bible-oath to be whate'er they please,
> To do he knows not what.

> He yet by slow degrees puts off himself,
> Grows conscious of a change, and likes it well.
> He stands erect, his slouch becomes a walk,
> He steps right onward, martial in his air
> His form and movement; is as smart above
> As meal and larded locks can make him; wears
> His hat or his plumed helmet with a grace,
> And his three years of heroship expired,
> Returns indignant to the slighted plough.
> He hates the field in which no fife or drum
> Attends him, drives his cattle to a march,
> And sighs for the smart comrades he has left.
> 'Twere well if his exterior change were all—
> But with his clumsy port the wretch has lost
> His ignorance and harmless manners too.
> To swear, to game, to drink, to shew at home
> By lewdness, idleness, and sabbath-breach,
> The great proficiency he made abroad,
> T'astonish and to grieve his gazing friends,
> To break some maiden's and his mother's heart,
> To be a pest where he was useful once,
> Are his sole aim, and all his glory now.

Cowper's argument is grounded on the pernicious effect on the individual
wrought by institutions created out of society's self-interest. "Man associated
and leagued with man/By real warrant, or self-joined by bond for interest-
sake" violates the law of nature, and the worldly knowledge men gain through
service in such contracts only corrupts. As a philosophical position, Cowper's
thought had its extension in social theory; men were a free association of
individuals, best left with their pastoral innocence. In the military context
the theory meant that corporate military enterprise, and the experience the
soldier acquired from it, made him unfit for peaceful occupations. This was
a strong argument against standing armies and military professionalism.

Wordsworth's poem "Guilt and Sorrow" (1791; revised and published 1842) is about poor and simple people who are casualties of war—not only by wounds, but by hardship and deprivation which has made them depraved and despairing.[65] They are turned from benign feelings to destructiveness by a society without love. Wordsworth gives as the source of his idea his view of the fleet off Portsmouth, which in 1793 was preparing for war against the French:

I left the place [the Isle of Wight] with melancholy forebodings. The American war was still fresh in memory. The struggle which was beginning, and which many thought would be brought to a speedy close by the irresistible arms of Great Britain being added to those of the Allies, I was assured in my own mind would be of long continuance, and productive of distress and misery beyond all possible calculation.[66]

The figure presented to the reader is a returned soldier-sailor, the debris of England's wars:

A TRAVELLER on the skirt of Sarum's Plain
Pursued his vagrant way, with feet half bare;
Stooping his gait, but not as if to gain
Help from the staff he bore; for mien and air
Were hardy, though his cheek seemed worn with care
Both of the time to come, and time long fled:
Down fell in straggling locks his thin grey hair;
A coat he wore of military red
But faded, and stuck o'er with many a patch and shred.

The old veteran plods through a desolate landscape, save for the single inn he passes, where he knows he will not be welcome. He has only the "wet cold ground" to look forward to as his bed, but here is nothing new, "for the chill night shower/And sharp wind his head oft hath bared." His history is hard:

A Sailor he, who many a wretched hour
Hath told; for, landing after labour hard,
Full long endured in hope of just reward,
He to an armed fleet was forced away
By seamen, who perhaps themselves had shared
Like fate; was hurried off, a helpless prey,
Gainst all that in *his* heart, or theirs perhaps, said nay.

After his pressed service at sea and his final release, the old soldier longs to see his wife again as due recompense for his torments; and he pictures himself laying "the prize of victory in her lap."* His hopes are dashed. In

---

*The paying of prize money to all ranks was customary.

a *variorum* edition based on another manuscript by Wordsworth, the sailor is shanghaied again, to serve either on land or at sea: "Even while in thought he took his rich reward/From his wife's lips, the ruffian press-gang dire/ Hurried him far away to rouse the battle's fire." The same *variorum* account tells of his having committed murder, perhaps to escape his tormentors. Now, "since phrenzy-driven he dipped his hand in blood," he is a fugitive "long hunted down by man's confederate power." Apparently, he has been goaded, for whatever reason, beyond endurance, for "till that hour he had been mild and good." Thus his "pangs" of guilt and remorse.

By the closing decade of the eighteenth century, Englishmen were not merely censuring and persecuting the disbanded and admittedly rascally soldiery, but were also beginning to examine the ills that drove many to desperation. The impetus for social reform was to gather momentum during the nineteenth century, but it still would be many years before much change would be seen in the army. The first manuscript of "Guilt and Sorrow" gives a typical account of the old sailor-soldier's crime. The state, that is the army authorities, have cheated him of whatever pittance in pay, prize money, or separation pay he had thought his due. Perhaps false exactions for rations, billets, replacement of worn equipment, or a dozen other contrived charges have lined his officers' pockets:

> [F]or fraud took all that he had earned.
> The lion roars and gluts his tawny brood
> Even in the desert's heart; but he, returned,
> Bears not to those he loves their needful food.

Filled with anger and dismay, he commits a crime of desperation: "He met a traveller, robbed him, shed his blood." Sheltering in the ruin of an ancient hospice, the weary traveler encounters a woman who tells her pitiful tale. Her husband, reduced to despair by poverty and unable even to feed their children, decided to enlist when "with proud parade, the noisy drum/ Beat round to clear the streets of want and pain."

She recounts how she and her children followed him to the coast, where with others in the same plight, they lived "long neglected" in squalor aboard ship, breathing the "pestilential air," Finally, the fleet set sail, and on reaching "the western world" the troops and their families suffered the familiar lot of their kind:

> The pains and plagues that on our heads came down,
> Disease and famine, agony and fear,
> In wood or wilderness, in camp or town,
> It would unman the firmest heart to hear.
> All perished—all in one remorseless year,
> Husband and children! One by one, by sword
> And ravenous plague, all perished.

Rescued, she still would recall the horrors of that distant campaign: "[G]roans that rage of racking famine spoke; / The unburied dead that lay in festering heaps, / The breathing pestilence that rose like smoke, / The shriek that from the distant battle broke." She concludes her tale, recounting how she contracted fever, recovered, and returned to England as a solitary vagrant.

The pair encounters a child-beater, and even this lowlife, when chided by the old sailor, sees men in red coats as objects of contempt, asking him "in scorn what business there he had; / What kind of plunder he was hunting now; / The gallows would one day of him be glad." Eventually, the old sailor and soldier's widow encounter a dying woman who turns out to be the old sailor's wife who has suffered horribly because of his flight. She dies blessing him, but his remorse drives him to confess to the authorities, and he is hanged.

This sad tale, told melodramatically, lays the blame for the nastiness of the soldiery at the feet of society's pernicious institutions. Certainly, soldiers and their families who followed them suffered extremes of deprivation and disease. The "yellow-jack" which ravaged the British Army sent to South America to wage the War of Jenkins' Ear (1739–41), and the cholera epidemics which struck down whole families in the cantonments of India through the next century are legend. Whether "Guilt and Sorrow" inspired Robert Southey's short lament, "The Soldier's Wife" (1797), or the complaint had become a commonplace is hard to say.[67] Either way, the theme of starving military widows seems to have been popular. Southey's "weary way-wanderer" carries a "cold . . . baby . . . , screaming its wretchedness":

"Thy husband will never return from the war again,
Cold is thy hopeless heart even as Charity—
Cold as thy famish'd babes—God help thee, widow'd One!"

"Guilt and Sorrow" comes at the end of a stage in the evolution of the soldier. The eighteenth century was full of crosscurrents and contradictions: mercenary adventurers, regular soldiers of the Crown, full-time militia volunteers, men forced or tricked into military service, and part-time militiamen prancing in peacock-splendor at country balls, or simply dodging full-time service. Some professed loyalty to monarch and nation, others frankly used military positions to fulfill political ambition, and still others made a cult of devotion to the profession of arms and military honor. With the civil war, ideological conviction and the responsibilities and rights of citizenship had become part of the military ethic. Yet both were rejected by a militia and a Regular Army which became increasingly secular and insular, placing themselves above civil law and apart from civil society. Soldiers of every rank were by turns admired, feared, despised, and pitied.

By the end of the eighteenth century the British Army had become culturally a state within a state, its members brutal and self-romanticizing. Rank and file were depraved and miserable, noncommissioned officers were corrupt and sadistic, and officers were ignorant and indifferent. Noncommissioned officers exploited their juniors for cash, while officers exploited the Crown for patronage and promotion.

The officer's duty to see to his troops' well-being and to his own professional education was hardly acknowledged. Belief in class obligation had declined with the lowering of social qualifications for officers, and education was hardly thought necessary when war was considered an art and not a science. It took "character" to be a practitioner of the art. "Knowledge" could be left to natural philosophers. The right and duty of soldiers to serve out of conviction had died, too. Back in 1642 zealous amateurs of the Parliamentary Army had trooped through town exhorting shopkeepers to keep the sabbath, but in 1796 a soldier on garrison duty in Gibraltar could say of the garrison chapel, "I was never in it."[68] This marginal military society, dedicated mainly to its own perpetuation and nursing distrust and resentment of a society that rejected it, was about to enter a century of new challenge. A military way of life which had thrived on its own corruption, ignorance, and misery would have to change to take on the little Corsican and to meet the demands of Industrial Age technology.

NOTES

1. From John Dryden's translation of Boccaccio's "Cymon and Iphigenia" (1700), ll. 399–413.

2. See Samuel Huntington's model for a Praetorian military in *The Soldier and the State* (Cambridge, Mass.: Harvard University Press, 1957).

3. From a sermon by Hugh Peter, "Mr. Peter's Message" (1646), in *Puritanism and Liberty: Being Army Debates (1647–49) from the Clarke Manuscripts . . .* , ed. A.S.P. Woodhouse (London: Dent & Sons, 1938), p. 387.

4. Thomas Collier, "A Discovery of the New Creation" (preached at the Headquarters, Putney, 29 September 1647), in Woodhouse, *Puritanism and Liberty*, p. 390.

5. Walden, 4 May 1647, in Woodhouse, *Puritanism and Liberty*, p. 398.

6. Woodhouse, *Puritanism and Liberty*, p. 396.

7. Ibid., pp. 401, 402.

8. Ibid., p. 404.

9. Ibid., p. 405.

10. "The Reading Debates" (A petition by the Agitators to Lord Fairfax), Woodhouse, *Puritanism and Liberty*, p. 409.

11. J. R. Western, *The English Militia in the Eighteenth Century: The Study of a Political Issue 1660–1802* (London: Routledge & Kegan Paul, 1965), pp. 7, 8.

12. Ibid., p. 8.

13. Ibid., p. 71.

14. Ibid., p. 54.

15. Ibid., p. 59.

16. Ibid., p. 60.

17. Ibid.

18. Ibid., p. 61.

19. See this section's epigram.

20. See Western, *English Militia*, p. 78n.; p. 95n.; p. 96n.; and Daniel Defoe's pamphlet previously cited.

21. Edward Hyde, "Of War," in *A Book of English Essays 1600–1900*, eds. Stanley V. Makowes and Basel H. Blackwell (London: Oxford University Press, 1912), pp. 24–32.

22. For example, Hippolyte de Guibert's *Essai Generale de Tactique* (1781). For a summary of Guibert's thought, see Cyril Falls, *The Art of War* (London: Oxford University Press, 1961), pp. 25–28.

23. Western, *English Militia*, p. 112. Cf. nineteenth-century France's "*mauvais numero*" and the recent U.S. Selective Service system.

24. Western, *English Militia*, p. 323.

25. Ibid., p. 130.

26. Ibid., p. 150.

27. Ibid., p. 335.

28. Ibid., p. 320.

29. Ibid., p. 188.

30. Ibid., pp. 194, 195.

31. Ibid., p. 339.

32. Ibid., p. 345.

33. Although there were allowances for families when the Militia was embodied, and although pay was not withheld for lack of state funds as it had been two centuries earlier, there was no change in Militia pay rates for a century after the Glorious Revolution, despite a continuous rise in living costs during the eighteenth century.

34. Western, *English Militia*, p. 383.

35. Ibid., p. 392.

36. Ibid., p. 393.

37. Ibid., p. 411.

38. Ibid., p. 397.

39. Ibid., p. 417.

40. James Boswell, *Life of Johnson* (1740), ed. R. W. Chapman (London: Oxford University Press, 1953), pp. 443, 513.

41. *The New Oxford Book of Eighteenth Century Verse*, ed. Roger Lonsdale (Oxford: Oxford University Press, 1984), pp. 751–52.

42. Theodore Ropp, "The Military Officer and His Education in the Next Quarter Century," *Signum* (June 1976):1–16.

43. Daniel Defoe, "Of Captain Misson," in *The History of the Pirates*, Vol. 2 (1728), reprinted in *The Augustan Reprint Society Publications*, No. 87, ed. Maximillian E. Novak (Los Angeles: Wm Andrews Clark Memorial Library, University of California, 1961).

44. *Spectator* No. 566, Monday, July 12, 1714, in . . . *A New Edition—Complete in One Volume* (Cincinnati: Applegate & Co., 1857).

45. *Spectator*, No. 2, Friday, 2 March 1711.

46. *Spectator*, No. 152, Friday, 24 August 1711.

47. Boswell, *Life of Johnson*, pp. 723–24.

48. Ibid., p. 927.

49. Henry Fielding, *Tom Jones* (New York: Signet, 1963), p. 324.

50. "Blenheim," *New Oxford Book*, ed. Lonsdale, pp. 8–9.

51. "[A]n Officer's Widow . . . ," *New Oxford Book*, ed. Lonsdale, pp. 233–34.

52. "The Recruiting Serjeant . . . ," *New Oxford Book*, ed. Lonsdale, p. 568–69.

53. "Frequent Reviews of the Troops," *New Oxford Book*, ed. Lonsdale, p. 640.

54. "The Soldier that has Seen Service . . . ," *New Oxford Book*, ed. Lonsdale, pp. 751–52.

55. "The Drum," *The Oxford Book of Eighteenth Century Verse*, ed. David Nicol Smith (Oxford: Clarendon, 1926), pp. 556–57.

56. From "The Progress of a Ploughboy to a Seat in Parliament" (1789), *Rank and File: The Common Soldier at Peace and War 1642–1914*, ed. T. H. McGuffie (London: Hutchinson, 1964), pp. 1–13.

57. Sergeant R. Lamb, "Memoir of his own Life" (1811), in *Rank and File*, ed. McGuffie, p. 7.

58. From Alexander Alexander's "The Life of Alexander Alexander" (1891), ed. John Howell (Edinburgh: 1830), in *Rank and File*, ed. McGuffie, pp. 13–17.

59. Cobbett, in *Rank and File*, ed. pp. 8–11.

60. Alexander, in *Rank and File*, ed. McGuffie, pp. 96, 97.

61. "G. B.," "Narrative of a Private Soldier in One of His Majesty's Regiments of Foot," in *Rank and File*, ed. McGuffie, pp. 307–8.

62. "The Deserted Village," *English Poetry . . .*, p. 214.

63. Oliver Goldsmith, *The Citizen of the World* (1762), ed. W. A. Brockington (London: Blackie & Son, undated), pp. 154–57.

64. William Cowper, "The Task" (1782), in *Poems by William Cowper, Esq.*, Vol. 2 (London: J. Johnson, 1785, reprinted in facsimile by London: Scholar Press, 1973), pp. 168–71. (Note: John Laffin in *Tommy Atkins* cites J. H. Stocqueler's use of Cowper's lines, and quotes them from Stocqueler's borrowing in *The British Soldier*, [1857]; however, Laffin has not identified Cowper as source.)

65. William Wordsworth, "Guilt and Sorrow," *The Poetical Works of William Wordsworth*, ed. E. de Selincourt (Oxford: Clarendon, 1940), pp. 94–127.

66. Ibid., p. 94.

67. "The Soldier's Wife," . . . *Eighteenth Century Verse*, pp. 707–8.

68. "G. B.," in *Rank and File*, ed. McGuffie, pp. 115–17.

3

THE DEVIL'S CODE: THE REGULAR ARMY IN THE INDUSTRIAL AGE

REGIMENTAL HONOR

Ben Battle was a soldier bold,
And used to war's alarms;
But a cannon-ball took off his legs,
So he laid down his arms.[1]

Unlike ideas of national and personal honor in continental armies, a uniquely military form of institutional honor emerged in the British Army. Certainly, regimental honor as an abstraction received lipservice by the rank and file of continental armies; but it never became a living reality except to commanders who associated the glorious victories of their regiments with their personal honor. For the British, the "honor of the regiment" became the overriding focus of loyalty and affection for every soldier from private to battalion commander.

Although the old argument as to whether the army was the property of monarch of Parliament continued as a problem for the army's senior command who wanted freedom from civilian control, it hardly concerned anyone at regimental level. The idea of a Constitutional monarchy allowed the soldier unity of loyalty. Although formally his loyalty to regiment did not take precedence over other attachments, he saw his regiment as the concrete expression of his God, monarch, and nation. Most chaplains, "more often tolerated than appreciated,"[2] represented the Anglican state church, and were expected to look after the solders' spiritual hygiene by exhorting them to the military virtues. Their role was rather like that of county parsons at home, who deferred to the local squirearchy. God was an Englishman, and on good terms with the regimental commander. Beyond the oath of loyalty to the monarch, politics was a forbidden subject. So the regiment had God, monarch, and nation on its side, and the proper object of loyalty was not in question. "Soldiers fought for God, Queen and Country. Of course they did. They also, and with more fervor fought for the credit of their regiments."[3]

While British officers honored their obligations as military gentlemen and brothers, the noncommissioned ranks found in their regiments a home and sense of brotherhood. As in both tribal and aristocratic cultures, the dead were felt to impose a debt of honor on the living, while bestowing the grace of their deeds on their successors. Through membership in their regiments, even the rank and file thought of themselves as a military aristocracy, superior to civilians.

The massive inertia impeding reform in the British Army was also a strength. Throughout most of the nineteenth century, there was no reasoned organization of the Army into divisions and brigades, and regiments were simply grouped according to the needs of the moment. Hence, the approved focus of loyalty for the common soldier was his regiment. After the abolition of purchase, the regiment became equally an object of affection for its officers, with an end to their gypsying and jockeying for rank and prestige from one regiment to another. A regiment, formerly about 1,000 tall ranks, became usually an organization with two battalions of about 1,000 each, when the War Secretary Edward Cardwell's reforms linked battalions at home with battalions abroad. A thousand men are a lot, but few enough that a soldier can feel a personal affinity with them because he wears the same badge and knows the same regimental customs. Further, soldiers felt a fratrnal bond toward another branch of the "regimental family" elsewhere. The idea of the regiment thus began to take on a quality of sentiment having little to do with its origins as a tactical unit. Indeed, a battalion in India was actually part of a *different army* from its regimental sister battalion in Britain! The Indian Army was responsible to the Viceroy, and was not under command of the British Army's Commander-in-Chief at the Horse Guards.

The regimental "family" which the recruit joined when he entered its depot was out to break him down and make him over in its image. Drill sergeants reviled and abused him, and made him feel worthless and insignificant; even after joining his battalion as a full-fledged soldier, a man continued to suffer brutal discipline and abominable conditions. The regiment was an unlovely home; yet curiously it *was* a home in which the soldier found a place which he had probably never had elsewhere. His honor depended on his keeping face before his comrades, for they were the living embodiments of the regiment; and the regiment's dead made their demands of honor on all of them. So the regiment bound together intimately ideas of personal and institutional honor. The phrase "the honor of the regiment" had real and personal significance for officers and men alike. Of course, it was rare that anyone gave voice to such sentiments; to do so would have been embarrassing and inappropriate. Soldiers cursed the regiment and their colonel, but only to each other. They would never malign their regimental cap badges, which had been worn as visible symbols of identity ever since their inception by royal warrant in 1751.[4] Many a pub brawl had its beginnings in regimental rivalry.

The British regimental system as it had evolved by the late nineteenth century was a paradox, because its strength was also a symptom of the army's organizational weakness. Other more efficiently and rationally organized armies seem to have lacked the special regimental spirit. The regimental idea was a key institution in British military culture, and the army's main source of strength. Long before the Victorian Age, the Regimental Idea had begun to assume the character of a secular religion. While each regiment had its own hoary traditions and customs, the underlying sentiment was the same everywhere.

In the idea of the regiment's honor, officers and common soldiers alike found expression for impulses which the rigors of military service usually suppressed. The universal need for love and sexual gratification, frustrated by conditions in barracks and on campaign, could be sublimated at least in part by fanatical devotion to the regiment and to the values of masculine honor it represented. Inviolable warrior bonds, once the special comradeship of pairs such as Achilles and Patroclus, and Roland and Oliver, became institutional demands, extending to all members of the regiment. The result was a sort of military feudalism in which officers and other ranks were "vassals" and "suzerains," each with mutual obligations of trust in ascending order. This notion of mutual obligation upon which an institutional idea of honor rested made extreme jealousy of personal honor inappropriate. Dueling ceased to be thought a morally acceptable convention, and in 1844 was outlawed in the British Army without difficulty.

The regimental spirit of the Victorian Age may well have been the purest soldierly sentiment the world has ever seen. That is, the soldier found his fullest realization of self in his devotion to his regiment. While that sort of loyalty required self-denial, it was not an exultant subordination of self in the German way, nor a Gallic celebration of the individual. Rather, there was a nearly mystical merging of the individual will with the general will. Toughness and capacity to endure became primary virtues for the rank and file. The regiment was an iron mistress, and soldiers even prided themselves on taking a flogging bravely.[5] Victorian regimental soldiers were after a fashion secular warrior monks. However, unlike their crusading forebears who mortified the flesh for spiritual purity, Victorian officers often were dandies and womanizers, and the rank and file were gluttons for drink and sex. As Kipling's Tommy reminds us, "young men in barracks don't grow into plaster saints."[6] Yet like knights of the *Militia Christi*, they were military ascetics who welcomed hardship, admired endurance, and despised weakness. What God demanded of the crusading knight, the regiment demanded of the Victorian soldier.

Unlike the soldiers of European armies, most of whom were temporary soldiers serving out their conscripted service under a nucleus of regular officers and NCOs, the Victorian British soldier was a volunteer regular. Especially after the reforms of 1870, shorter terms of service meant that many rank and file joined for a few years of adventure. No longer were the ranks filled only with men hopeless enough to sign their lives away for bare subsistence, but with men who wanted a part in the great game. The regiment satisfied that impulse for masculine warrior play as old as the victory games of the *Iliad* or the mythical Cuchulainn's beheading game.

The personal honor once found in those individual contests was transmuted as regimental honor. Like Charlemagne's team of Christians against Muslims, this was the regimental team against whoever got in the way, be he a soldier from another regiment in a pub or an overseas enemy. Although the rank and file may not have been conscious of the gaming element, officers found it hard to miss. Sent to public schools at an early age, they viewed life and the pursuit of honor as a game, and spoke in the lexicon of *homo ludens*. One mustn't "let the side down" even when it's a "sticky wicket." Not until World War I would the gaming sentiment fade for fighting men.

The presence of women, though only a very few, completed the regimental "family." A regiment's honor rested with the moral virtue of its officers' ladies. The sexual intrigues and infidelities which legend has it were common in British Army messes in India were therefore doubly dangerous, because their public exposure might reflect on the regiment. It remains a moot point whether there was more shame attached to an officer's being a seducer or a cuckold. The dependence of regimental honor on feminine honor is an important theme in Barry England's 1969 play about Victoria's Indian Army, *Conduct Unbecoming*. Officers are prepared to go to any length to conceal a sexual scandal for the honor of their regiment, even at the expense of their personal integrity.

In this masculine military society both the absence and presence of women had a lot to do with the Regimental Idea, so that women were seen ambivalently both as encumbrances and as objects of veneration. The regiment could not afford outside competition for the soldier's affection. The speed and mobility of nineteenth-century armies meant that wives and children no longer could be part of a cumbersome rearguard train as in the days of siege warfare. Nor were wives allowed in barracks, as they had been in the eighteenth century. The rank and file visited prostitutes, and usually contracted venereal disease. Few soldiers married, and then only with their commanding officers' permission.

Until 1857 an officer in India might well have had an Indian mistress, and regimental brothels were common. While these recourses provided release, they were not distractions from regimental devotion. After the Sepoy Mutiny, however, the arrival of senior officers' families as part of a program of military reform brought a wave of sexual morality. Moreover, the type of British officer in India changed from then on. From the incorporation of the Honourable East India Company's army into the British Army, officers were drawn from the public school-trained "leader class." Subject to more social shibboleths than common soldiers, the young officer was likely to have to remain celibate. In any case, a public school upbringing had deprived him of much social contact with the other sex. The regiment became all the more a focus of the officer's devotion, an extension of what the public school had been. Regimental competitions and ceremony, and a constant round of mess occasions—dining-in nights and lawn teas—all helped to sublimate impulses that might have been directed elsewhere if opportunity had allowed.

The ascetic military code, which reflected Victorian sexual mores, insisted on at least an appearance of sexual abstinence by all young officers. Commanders' approval of marriage amounted only to a grudging concession to human frailty. An officer was expected to find sexual release in marriage only after he had given all his youthful love to his regiment. Everybody knew the tradition that sexual indulgence made men weak and effeminate or confounded their purposes. Certainly, the least masculine virtue was better than feminine seductiveness. As Kipling's persona in "The Betrothed" put it, "A woman is just a woman, but a good cigar is a smoke." Unconsciously following in a warrior tradition as old as Greek drama, the typical regimental officer who was completely dedicated to his military ideals was hopelessly inept in the courts of love. C. S. Forester's Curzon (*The General*) affords a probably lifelike picture of a military bridegroom, who with his bride endures a wedding night of exquisite awkwardness. Unable to express natural feelings, he sets the pattern for a lifetime relationship devoid of any real intimacy or giving of self. His problem is that he cannot rid himself of his ideas about how a soldier should act, even in bed!

The idea of the regiment as surrogate wife and family has survived. John Keegan has described with feeling and insight the virtual "marriage market" at Sandhurst, where long before graduation there begins a process of choosing.[7] The officer cadet chooses his regiment, and his regiment chooses him. The process invites comparison to courtship. The selection criteria are in large degree complex and subtle matters of temperament and social suitability. Similarly, in *Bugles and a Tiger* (1958) John Masters describes autobiographically how as a subaltern in the interwar years he joined his chosen regiment of Gurkha Rifles for a trial period, during which he and the regiment decided whether they were suited for each other. (He was, and he rose to brigadier rank in World War II.)

As in the High Middle Ages, women represented a chivalresque ideal that gave men at arms spiritual strength. After all, Victorian soldiers took an oath to their Queen, and Kipling's phrase about "sons of the Widow" already had passed into the litany of Masonic military lodges. British soldiers saw in their Royal Lady an embodiment of the grandeur of the Empire. One of the two colors borne by a regiment, the "Queen's Color," had the aura of a lady's favor affixed to a squire's lance. Even when the monarch was male, the English nation remained female in grammatical gender, like "La belle France" and "Mother Russia." So there was a strong feminine element to masculine concepts of patriotism and honor, and it involved the idealizing of women.

There was a practical and social side to women's role in regimental life. In smart regiments at home, an officer who had reached marriageable age

and rank (say, thirty years at least, and major or senior captain) was expected
to marry a woman of social accomplishments and good family. His career
would be enhanced by whatever political influence and material advantage
her family might afford him, and she in her own right could exercise con-
siderable power by using her charm and intelligence judiciously at the many
social and regimental occasions. An officer's lady unquestioningly accepted
her place in the scheme of things as an asset to her husband's military
aspirations. She adopted his rank, as it were, and his fortunes were hers.

In the dominions and colonies, regimental officers' messes were the most
elite—and in many instances, the only—social institutions in garrison com-
munities. They were centers of social life, both for officers' families and for
local civilian dignitaries. In this milieu a feminine hierarchy of command
flourished under the Colonel's lady, the regimental matriarch to whom all
other officers' wives deferred and to whom awestruck young subalterns paid
court.

Especially for the young officer the regiment was a family. The battalion
adjutant and senior subaltern were elder brothers, ready to advise, chastise,
and guide; the company commander was a wise uncle and often a hard
taskmaster; the commanding officer was an august father, and his lady a
sympathetic and sometimes formidable mother. If the young subaltern were
fortunate, he was placed with an experienced and intelligent platoon sergeant
who protected him from himself while he learned how to command men.
In that way the regiment mirrored the public school, with its head, house
masters and their wives, perfects, upperclassmen, and hall porters. And like
the public school, the regiment reflected English society with all its unspoken
yet crystal-clear class distinctions and obligations.

All sorts of questions of personal virtue were mixed up with the idea of
regimental honor; an officer found cheating at cards was finished, because
his breach dishonored his regiment. Regimental honor could be compromised
by the rank and file's public lapses in virtue, as well. Kipling's Danny Deever
("The Hanging of Danny Deever" in *Barrackroom Ballads*) is executed because he "shot a comrade sleeping," thus becoming "nine 'undred of 'is
county and 'is regiment's disgrace." Danny's punishment must be made
public as an example, so the regiment is formed "in 'ollow square" to witness
his hanging. More important, the troops are to witness Danny's *military*
dishonor when "they've taken of 'is buttons off, an' cut 'is stripes away."
Danny has been ceremonially cast out of the regiment, and he has already
lost his "life" as the good report of fellow soldiers before giving up his soul.
In an earlier age Danny's act would have been criminal only in the sense
that murder always is, and his punishment would have healed the breech
of "good order and discipline." In the Victorian, however, a man did not
have to be a gentleman to have honor. The common soldier became the
repository of the regiment's honor, and he was charged with guarding it well.

Regimental ceremonies of execution and drumming out were appropriate for an age that made much of appearances. Understandably, this was also an age when visible symbols of military honor and royal favor were instituted. In the past, commemorative medallions had been cast for members of the upper classes who had performed some noteworthy and not necessarily military service to the nation. Queen Victoria extended a practice begun after Waterloo by awarding medals to all ranks for military campaigns and meritorious service. While she knew the worth of royal favor to her soldiers who adored her as a distant ideal, such external honors did not bear much looking into. Courage was courage, and cowardice was cowardice. The possibilities that "courage" might be fear of revealed fear, or that "cowardice" might be a higher moral utilitarianism were ideas better left alone, or else the whole Victorian notion of "honor" might have been rendered ridiculous. The kind of doubt-raising psychological questions posed by the American Stephen Crane's *The Red Badge of Courage* (1895) had no place in British literature or military culture.

Curiously, a world of appearances was able to create its own realities out of wishful thinking. Officers pretended to be fearless under fire; to take cover with undue haste, even to "bob," was thought unmanly.[8] So officers inwardly quaking with fear feared even more the loss of their honor. The result was that they often were magnificent inspirations for their men. The inward lie became the outward reality. Control of emotion, the "stiff upper lip," was founded in insistence that human frailty simply did not exist. Upper-class Victorians professed indifference to emotion and impulse. Aside from a flourishing underground in prostitution and erotic literature, society and its military reflection did not acknowledge promptings of the flesh which might have detracted from social or professional notions of honor. At all costs one had to "keep up appearances," and Britain held an empire in thrall largely because of that credo. District Commissioners (DCs) of the British Indian Civil Service dressed for dinner, even in the jungle without another Englishman for hundreds of miles. The punctilio of regimental gala affairs was scrupulously observed anywhere and under all conditions. Even in World War I officers were known to walk along the parapet, seemingly oblivious to a storm of steel. These were the outward forms that gave strength to credos of nation and regiment.

The learning of military honor was not in the nature of ethical education; it was moral training that taught the soldier what was done and what was not done. If an officer or man did not measure up in the little things, he was broken to the bit or cast out. An officer guilty of a real moral lapse might tacitly be expected to "do the honorable thing" by taking his own life rather than disgrace his regiment by continuing to live as a reminder of mortal imperfection. Although the British military code of honor never attained the extremes of the Japanese "Bushido," the Victorian officer corps in the century's closing decades made demands of honor as rigid as those for a Samurai. As with the legions of Rome, honor was inseparable from *bona fama*, which was intimately bound up with the regiment's "good name."

How rigid and mindless a value system had to be to produce such magnificence of spirit! Perhaps it is typical of a complacent culture that there seems to have been little sense of the contradictions posed by a morality of appearances. Perhaps if Victoria's soldiers had been culturally disposed to think much about their honorable sentiments they might have doubted more, and they would have been less effective in consequence. After all, they were knights errant for an adventurer nation engaged in imperial exploitation. However, the Victorian soldier was a Don Quixote who served his regiment, as in an earlier age he might have served his God or his lady. The chivalresque sentiment relied on a certain naiveté, or at least institutional self-delusion.

With endearing simplicity, British soldiers rarely looked beyond their regiments and the unwritten code of military honor. They accepted without much question what General Sir John Hackett has called the "unlimited liability" of military service.[9] These were men who never counted the cost. The officer's aristocratic ideal required complete outward disregard of remuneration. Money had to do with "trade," and that was supposedly beneath an officer's concerns. Admittedly, reward came indirectly through influence and patronage, but an appearance of fiscal negligence had to be maintained. It became customary, even, for officers to sign "chits" for their drinks in regimental messes, so that money need not change hands in public. By the same token, negligence of one's own life was part of the code, and in this, the rank and file could share as Gentlemen of the Blade. If officers and men had been bred to be more prudent, or even if they had been more roundly educated, they might not have been so exquisitely prepared to die well. British officers weaned on the classics would hardly have questioned Horace's "*Dulce et decorum est pro patria mori.*" In that resounding phrase was all the grandeur of Rome and the manly honor of her legionaries.

Unhappily, by the eve of World War I concern for the externals of honor had developed to such an extent that on occasion it was thought better to conceal breaches of the code or injustices in its application, than to risk compromise of social and military systems already showing cracks. Monarchies were crumbling, and social upheaval and political dissolution were imminent. The world of appearance was about to shatter like a looking glass, and with it the fragile appearances of honor to which the old aristocracies clung. Yet it would be the regiment which, as institutional repository of ideas of military honor, would have to withstand the shock of the Great War.

THE BRITISH OFFICER AS CONSERVATIVE AND AMATEUR

> He was only a captain in the Loamshire Militia, but to the Hayslope tenants he was more intensely a captain than all the young gentlemen of the same rank in his Majesty's regulars.

'I've written to him to desire that from henceforth he will send me no
book or pamphlet or anything that ends in ism.'

'But I don't think a knowledge of the classics is a pressing want . . . ; as
far as I can see, he'd much better have a knowledge of manures.'

George Eliot, *Adam Bede* (1859)[10]

Except in Britain, military education and organization flourished through
much of the nineteenth century, in response to the new demands of mass
warfare. Dispersion meant that subordinate commanders had to exercise far
more initiative than in the past to interpret orders and act in rapidly shifting
circumstances. Strategy grounded in national policy meant that armies daily
required more specialists in communications, transportation, administration,
and supply. Cavalry and infantry also had become specialized as light cavalry,
dragoons, light infantry, and rifle regiments. Large-scale road construction,
improved cartographic techniques, and greater effectiveness of small arms
fire, which rendered infantry less vulnerable on the move, resulted in an
army's becoming a group of little armies which had to be supplied, reinforced,
and redeployed as occasion arose. Unfortunately, the commanders of Britain's
armies remained mossbacked warriors cast in a heroic image. Bent on romantic notions of honor and glory, they were overfaced by the intellectual
challenges of mass society and technology.

First Napoleonic France, then Prussia after its humiliating defeat at Jena
in 1806, and finally Russia had developed military professionalism. In the
eighteenth century French military schools had concentrated on instilling
gentlemanly values and codes of conduct rather than on military instruction
as such, but from midcentury they had emphasized mathematics, sauced
with a highly theoretical treatment of fortification and gunnery, as a way of
training the mind. Prussian military education after 1806, in imitation of the
French, took on much the same aspect for most of the nineteenth century,
and so eventually would the British staff college.[11]

The theory that military education for infantry and cavalry officers should
develop facility of mind rather than just impart technical knowledge served
to justify curricula having little practical application. After all, so went the
argument, separate schools already existed for the technical training of artillery and engineer officers. The French army had had an artillery school
at Douai since 1679, and the British Army's Royal Military Academy at
Woolwich for Artillery and Engineer officers had existed since 1741. Officers
of infantry and cavalry were widely thought socially superior to technical
officers, so that *practical* military education seemed inappropriate, and amateurism was preferable, even if not by that name.

England's coasts were not in jeopardy, but the social order was showing
cracks from within. *Nouveaux riches* entrepreneurs and industrialists; advocates of labor reform and gas-and-water socialism such as the liberal-minded

Lord Shaftesbury and later the Fabian radical George Bernard Shaw; the so-called Peterloo Massacre of 1819; Karl Marx's Communist Manifesto of 1848—all were threats to the good order of the Realm. The last thing Britain's conservative gentry wanted was a system of selection and education for military officers which would further weaken the foundations of privilege and patronage on which the Empire rested. Until his death in 1852, Wellington opposed every attempt to dilute Britain's officer corps with men of brains and no breeding. Commission and promotion by purchase had a stranglehold on officer selection and education. Privilege and a "good name" played a vital role, and regimental commanders selected ensigns on their families' social merits.

Generals selected their staffs on similar grounds. Until the Napoleonic wars staffs had little to do with operations, which were left largely to the intuitive genius of commanding generals. After Napoleon's defeat, however, even Russia developed a general staff for operational planning in anticipation of future wars. Meanwhile the British army continued to rely largely on the skill of individual field commanders, assisted by favorites often selected for reasons of patronage. These "in" groups or "rings" were comprised of officers who shared their general's cast of mind, and not inclined to offer unpopular advice.[12] British staffs carried out little coordination anyway, because the Ordnance Corps (Artillery and Engineers) remained "virtually a separate Army" until the Crimean War.[13] The British could not get past making only a few belated adjustments to existing systems in response to demands for reform after military catastrophe. While the army of Prussia/Germany was continually educating its officers and developing its staff systems, the British Army remained backward-looking, and merely tried to redress the more obvious blunders of its last engagements.

Of all the armies of Europe none was more determinedly ignorant than Britain's. Prussia's Frederick the Great had founded the *Academie des Nobles* in 1765, the precursor of the *Kriegsakademie*, established in 1810 as rival and eventual superior of France's St. Cyr, founded two years earlier. Yet on the outbreak of war with revolutionary France in 1793 Britain did not have a single trained staff officer.[14] In fact, the Royal Military College (Sandhurst) had been founded precisely because of the incompetence of British officers in Europe through the 1790s.[15] The founding of the Royal Military College in 1802 had compromised upper-class privilege only slightly, because although graduates could be commissioned *gratis*, three-quarters of first appointments were still by purchase as late as 1860.[16] Wealth and influence were the major qualifications for commissioning in the fighting arms throughout the century.

At Sandhurst a "Junior Department" trained gentlemen cadets, and a "Senior Department" functioned as an embryonic staff college. The Senior Department produced some very competent officers for Wellington's staff in the Peninsular campaign,[17] but probably mainly because of Wellington's skill as a judge of competence in selecting his staff. The Senior Department withered after Waterloo for want of financial support, and graduates rarely received staff positions anyway.[18] With the Senior Department's parliamentary grant terminated in 1832, the annual enrollment was a mere fifteen officers. Each had to pay a fee which, along with money extracted from the gentlemen cadets of the Junior Department, subsidized their studies under only two professors, one of whom was nearly blind.[19]

Few staff-trained officers ever received staff appointments, and when absent from regimental duty on staff training they forfeited seniority for purchase of their next promotion. The system was hardly likely to attract men of intelligence and ambition. It is not surprising that for most of the century there was not a single book in English on staff duties, nor any one work on tactics recognized by the army as a basis for doctrine.

The British officer corps remained pretty much a closed shop, its class origins virtually unchanged until the eve of World War I. From 1849 applicants for Sandhurst were required to take an oral examination of general education, but unfavorable results were usually disregarded if they jeopardized the entry of stupid young men of good family. While successive reforms may have excluded some of the worst prospects, economic factors also excluded some of the best. Low pay meant an officer's reliance on independent means, except in the Indian Army, which made fewer financial demands on its officers. In home regiments, especially the "smart" ones, regimental custom demanded that vast sums be spent at the tailor, in the mess, and on the pastimes expected of gentlemen.

For all their military ignorance, however, British officers often were men of breeding who commanded with elegance. Theirs was not a cult of ignorance in the broad sense; they were often urbane and talented. Sir Charles Napier, who supposedly announced his successful conquest of the Indian province of Sind after the Battle of Hyderabad (1843) with the single word, "Peccavi" ["I have sinned"], wrote: "An ignorant officer is a murderer. All brave men confide in the knowledge he is supposed to possess; and when the death-trial comes their generous blood flows in vain. Merciful God! How can an ignorant man charge himself with so much blood?"[20] Fine words, but what sort of curriculum might the young officer seek to end his ignorance? How might one learn to war with Marathas and Sikhs when the only instruction available was battle itself? In Britain how might one learn the art of war when military life centered on the mess and parade square?

For the British, the incompetence of command which made the Crimean campaign a near disaster did little to ruffle a conservative and elitist military establishment. British officers still bought their commissions and remained obdurately ignorant. Their soldiers still were society's dregs. Officers found soldiering pleasant and romantic, something one did (when not on long leave) with a home regiment as fashionable as one's means would allow. Or it was a debilitating and dangerous life in India or elsewhere in the vast Victorian Empire, if neither name nor purse earned one a less distant and arduous post. For the redcoat, soldiering was sordid and brutal anywhere. Defenders of a nation that was pretty safe anyway and guardians of far-off exotic shores, British soldiers hardly existed for most nineteenth-century citizens at home. To the degree that they did, they were seen as "thin red heroes" in the abstract and in the flesh usually as brutes to be "chuck[ed] out."[21]

By the closing years of the century, the British Army resembled its continental counterparts; it was inward-looking and isolationist. On the other hand, unlike continental armies, it had not undergone stormy transitions caused by political upheaval. There was no real sense of grievance, because the army had not been given its head in the first place. It had never been a large citizen army like the continental armies, and it had not experienced the trauma of vast expansion and reduction. Since Waterloo it had not fought a major war against another European nation, and its men had been blooded only in irregular warfare against Zulu, Pathan, and Sikh.

The Briton's mystique of Empire blurred into his love of schoolboy stories of military expeditions on the Northwest Frontier. Yet in practice officers from the Indian Army were held in such low esteem that, even though they alone had battle experience, their advice was ignored by the clotheshorse commanders who botched the Crimean War. Whatever the event might have signified for the government and public, it made hardly a dent in military attitudes. Only through civilian movements for reform did anything improve.

Britain's sloth in developing a staff system and sound requirements of education is understandable. From the heady days after Waterloo and through Victoria's reign, British soldiers forged an empire and held it against native populations in India and Africa. The contest was uneven. Without European weapons technology, tribesmen could not hope to resist British arms. The British, in turn, enjoyed success without having to meet the challenges of education and staff organization which faced other European armies. Even at that, the British effort in the great game of Empire was not a string of victories. Incompetent leadership was all too often the cause of needless suffering, humiliation, and death.

In the meantime, the Junior Department's curriculum was designed more to produce acceptable gentlemen than competent soldiers, and "down to the Crimean War, the education provided at Sandhurst, and to a slightly lesser degree at Woolwich, resembled that at a second-rate public school."[22] During the winter of 1854–55, while the Army was suffering needless misery in the Crimea, a report by a "select Committee on the Royal Military College, Sandhurst" showed that what passed for a staff college, the Senior Department, still operated according to its 1808 Royal Warrant, and had changed not a jot over almost fifty years.[23] It was estimated that Britain spent "less than one-twentieth of the amount spent by Prussia" on educating its officers, "one-thirty-seventh that of France, and one-hundredth that of Austria."[24]

The grand romance of Empire obscured the less edifying realities shown in the Crimean War. Official inquiries demanded reform, but because Britain had won—no matter how inconclusively—not much was done about the system of patronage that could produce the likes of Lord Cardigan of Light Brigade fame, nor about the lack of staff procedures for maintenance of troops and care of the sick and wounded. Hunger, cholera, and every sort of neglect were accepted as part of the romance of soldiering.

After the Sepoy Mutiny in 1857, a number of reforms were instituted for the British Army in India. One result was that British public schools became recognized breeding kennels for the leader class which provided Britain's colonial armies and Civil Service with their officers. The public schools were held to produce young men of character, whose natural British superiority together with a sound knowledge of Horace and Virgil would fit them for "the white man's burden" in both peace and war. What need had they of military education? Officers who "swotted" at their books were suspect, and when finally examinations were instituted for entrance to the Royal Military College, "crammers" were hired to drill even the most stupid applicants so that they would pass.

The Staff College as successor to the Senior Department appeared only in 1858, after the British Army added the near loss of the Empire's richest jewel, India, to its commanders' poor showing in the Crimea. An entrance examination was devised, the curriculum was made more practical, and means were provided for an annual enrollment of thirty students, drawn from all branches of the army by quota.[25] However, all this took place in an atmosphere hostile to intellectual pursuits. Any regimental officer who showed interest in getting to the Staff College was thought peculiar by his brother officers, and senior commanders continued to favor regimental experience over study when selecting their staffs. Naturally, few officers applied for staff training; as before, those who did usually were not among the Army's best talent.

The aristocratic heritage which all British officers assumed upon taking their commissions required an appearance of effortless grace, without too much serious application to the profession. Only "games" and blood sports (in England cricket and the foxhunt, and in India pigsticking and polo) were fit objects for expressions of enthusiasm. Soldiering itself was thought of as a game. The closer a regiment to London, the more "fashionable" it was. The colonial regiments, which were the only ones actually engaged in campaigning, were socially beyond the pale, and officers of the Indian Army were virtually excluded from the high society game played at home.

The British Army's continued neglect of its officers' education was partly due to its limited numbers. European nations, faced always with threats to their border territories, had to develop plans for massive mobilization, including standing armies of reserves on active service for limited periods. By contrast Britain's army had remained a small body of Regulars, and large numbers of its manpower were not even in England. The need for a small and highly trained professional officer cadre to train and control a vast citizen-soldier organization was an exclusively continental phenomenon, and not part of the British experience. The Crimea was the British Army's last campaign involving other European armies, so that later in the nineteenth century British officers still saw military problems largely in terms of battle tactics rather than in terms of mass mobilization, organization, and movement, the stuff of military science and professionalism.[26]

Practical experience combined with good character was thought adequate by the authorities, so no doctrines of irregular warfare were evolved or taught to new officers destined for colonial service. Despite the expansion of military strategy to include social, political, economic, and ideological considerations, military thinking remained fixed in the eighteenth century. In consequence, the British Army remained what it then had been: a composite of dilettante officers proud of their military ignorance, brutal noncommissioned officers, and a rank and file of social outcasts, tough, durable, and superbly drilled. Military "education" for British officers consisted mainly of a public school upbringing to give backbone, followed by field experience. For the men, the childhood slums of manufacturing towns, the grog shops of garrison towns and cantonments, and the drill sergeants' canes were education enough.

Through the 1860s British officers learned little from the American Civil War and the Austro-Prussian War (1866). It was only France's swift and humiliating defeat by Prussia in 1870 which finally produced in Britain some reforms in military education and staff organization. In 1871 the Cardwell Reforms abolished purchase and brought about organizational and educational changes, but the intellectual sloth born of officers' contempt for theory altered little.

Not until 1873 did an Intelligence Department appear, as the closest thing the British had to an operations staff. Small and ineffectual, it simply gathered and collated information about other armies. Through the 1870s, 1880s, and 1890s, Britain's military doctrines fastened singlemindedly on home and colonial defense, in the belief that British troops' having to fight on the Continent was out of the question. This thinking was wholly a product of the government; the military had no function at all even to advise on national strategy. Only in the Intelligence Department was there any "original thinking about defence policy,"[27] and this miniscule body had no official cachet to advise the government on matters of national security.

Even after the events of 1870, no system of compulsory military education was established for officers in garrison. Although by 1877 mathematical abstractions at the Staff College were being replaced by reconnaissance exercises and staff maneuvers, lack of finances prevented much large-scale war gaming with troops. A continual depleting of home battalions to supply troops in Egypt, the Sudan, and India resulted from Edward Cardwell's linking of battalions at home and abroad, so that home battalions became little more than holding units and training cadres. In any case, units were garrisoned independently, and rarely came together for training in formations. The army clung stubbornly to drill as the principal means of training soldiers, so that the rounds of parades, ceremonial and inspections gave officers no encouragement to take their profession more seriously.

Because officers rarely, if ever, saw units functioning as coordinated parts of larger formations, they never understood the value of command and staff training.[28] At any rate, many probably would have found the intellectual challenge of large-scale maneuvers beyond them. By the turn of the century, many Sandhurst graduates—the bulk of whom went to the cavalry, Household Brigade, or Indian staff—had gained initial entry to the Royal Military College (RMC) only after a second try at the entrance test, thus displacing brighter first-time aspirants. Most other infantry officers had failed at university or had held militia commissions as a means of getting into the Regulars by the back door. (Because of the unpopularity of militia service, the standard required of officers was minimal.)

In the 1890s there were still only thirty-two Staff College graduates annually, and even they had learned very little about actual staff duties. It had only begun to dawn on a few military thinkers that the British Army still was not, but should be, a cohesive whole. Until that view of an army was understood, military education could not advance. Meanwhile, the Intelligence Department's warnings about the deteriorating situation in South Africa went virtually unheeded by the government, and the British Army entered the Boer War virtually unchanged since midcentury.[29]

Without a trained general staff, the British Army lacked commanders or coordinating agencies for an army that grew from 90,000 to 300,000 almost overnight. No attempt had been made to train soldiers for irregular warfare. Boer commando methods were thought unsporting and British troops should not stoop to their kind of game. The British Army's Chief of Staff, Lord Kitchener, lacked the brains the job demanded, and the entire campaign suffered from such elementary difficulties as lack of maps, inadequate reconnaissance, wrong reports of Boer dispositions, and vague orders by confused commanders.

The British Army's embarrassment by Africaaner farmers produced the customary spate of reform committees, as the British came to realize the inadequacies of an army with an inspired spirit and muscle but very little professional brain. In 1905 growing concern about German naval power made British military thinkers realize that Britons might have to fight on the Continent and that a coordinated policy for land and sea warfare would be needed. At last in 1906, a British Army General Staff was created, and steps were taken to educate officers in the dominions.

Reforms in military education were not enough in themselves. Most tactical scenarios were drawn from past battles, without much interest taken in new developments. To marvel at a classic maneuver by Napoleon at Austerlitz was fine, except that little account was taken of what modifications he might have made, had he been given a company of Maxim Guns. The commanders and senior staff officers of World War I were graduates of the Staff College classes of the 1890s. They were not as incompetent as we often hear, and they were thoroughly moral. But they were products of a conservative and backward-looking system of military education. Sir Douglas Haig, for example, an outstanding student in the 1896 class at Camberley, had a remarkable knowledge of American Civil War campaigns, and was convinced of the dominant role of cavalry on future battlefields. By the end of World War I he was a Field Marshal, having earned also the sobriquet "Butcher" Haig for his waste of British soldiers' lives.

Despite Edward Cardwell's admonition that "neither gallantry nor heroism will avail without professional training," the arbiters of British military education had continued to produce officers with little imagination but unbounded faith in the courage of British fighting men as the stuff of quick victory. Jingoism and complacency meant rejection of anything foreign as inferior, including food, languages, manners, and armies. Why study the methods of other armies or even give other nations the dignity of being analyzed as a military threat?

Symptomatic of the British military cast of mind was Kitchener's performance as secretary for war in the early stages of World War I. A hoary old warrior, once described as "not a great man, but a great poster," he was bewildered by the complexities of modern war.[30] He blundered over the Dardanelles campaign in 1915, and he ignored the plans and advice of his staff, which, if heeded before the "race to the sea" across Belgium, conceivably might have prevented four years of murderous deadlock.

Generals Haig and Allenby, and the others who were responsible for the later conduct of the war had better military education, but even theirs predated the Boer War, in which several had served but few had studied. Here is how one of their number, who perhaps was somewhat more objective than most, described his labors at Sandhurst:

The instruction (I avoid the word education) was the responsibility of three colonels, given the very unsuitable title of "Professors." Each was responsible for a collection of subjects—fortification, topography, and an oddly assorted group of tactics, administration, and law. These subjects were taught in water-tight compartments, and it was some time before I began to grasp the intimate connexion between them all. I cannot remember any lectures on military history, though there may have been some. . . . I spent many hours drawing plans of fortifications, and learning about scarps and counter-scarps, traverses, parados, parapets, trenches, ditches and glacis; curiously enough some of this proved useful to me, but not much.

I cannot recall learning anything about the siting of fortifications, nor of how fortifications are the servants of strategy and tactics. We did some useful practical work on the ground, digging, directing labour, bridging with trestle and pontoon, and demolitions. This certainly made us observant of ground, but again it was some time before I realized that the study of topography was intended to show how ground affected the application of tactical principles. The fact that tactics, administration, and law were lumped together, rather than grouping tactics with topography, is an indication of the muddled thinking behind the whole system for training officers.[31]

British officers were their own worst enemies in their struggle to maintain the separateness of the military profession. The Duke of Cambridge, Commander-in-Chief for almost the entire latter half of the nineteenth century, consistently objected to the establishment of a Chief of Staff and General Staff. His blind belief in regimental experience as the primary professional qualification for command or staff appointments played into the hands of politicians who feared the army's having a hand in formulating national strategy. The army thus was excluded from deliberations which might have produced a strategic doctrine to be understood, analyzed, and criticized. Without doctrine, there could be little progress in military education.

The nineteenth century brought general acceptance of other professions which by law could grant or deny licenses to practice, based on the testing of a body of knowledge and expertise. Yet opinions prevailed within the army that RMC education was unnecessary and even harmful, because its curriculum was adulterated with prevocational subjects not appropriate for a gentleman. It followed that by the army's own argument, anyone with a gentlemanly upbringing and public school education already was qualified to be an officer.

Paradoxically, education's vocational thrust was beginning to be felt in the public schools by the end of the century. "Modern Departments" were being instituted to provide a scientific and practical curriculum specifically for future colonial administrators and army officers. At Wellington a separate "Army Class" received a special "pre-professional" education in science, mathematics, and modern languages.[32] Yet despite this new legitimacy accorded to practical education, conservatives stuck doggedly to the view that preparatory education for officers should be directed toward development of moral qualities. Latin was associated in conservative minds with Rome's greatness, and like the Church of England was one of those cornerstones of the belief Britons had in themselves. As a "patrician field of study," it represented stability and discipline. Social status and professional seriousness were seen as incompatible; the officer ideal was that of the gentleman amateur, and practical training was thought of as "plebeian."[33]

The struggle between liberals wanting professional competence and conservatives seeking to preserve a determined amateurism reflected a larger debate about the purposes of education. Because of rapidly accelerating progress and specialization in all fields of practical endeavor, educational progressives were demanding career-oriented curricula, and conservatives saw "modern" studies as a threat to culture, erudition, and society's authority structure. According to the view that education had a higher moral purpose, it was better to be a useless gentleman than a capable lowlife.

The basic question, "What is a military education?" was a major focus of debate between conservatives and liberals in the army and government, and became part of a continual Constitutional tug-of-war between government and the army for control of military affairs. By and large, a conservative officer corps with strong representation among the upper classes made the army disturbingly independent of government. Educational policy was formulated at the Horse Guards (Army Headquarters) with little interference from the War Office, with the result that when legislated reforms were imposed on a reluctant senior command, their execution was usually desultory.

The elements of the ongoing debate about military education were essentially these: Should birth and character be qualifications for a commission? If not, should intelligence, competence, and general aptitude be tested before commissioning? Further, should a prospective officer be required to undergo and pass a program of military instruction before being accepted into the officer corps, or should he be accepted, then be required to measure up to the demands of either formal instruction or regimental experience? Once commissioned, should an officer be required to study further and pass examinations for promotion? If instruction and testing were necessary, then what was their purpose: to build and mold an officer's character to fit him for the various levels of command? To train his mind so that he might tackle military problems with intellectual discipline and facility of thought? Or to teach him the military art—strategy, fortification, ballistic theory, cartography, and the duties of command and staff? In other words, should an officer be an amateur or a professional, and if a professional, what did that mean?

If most British officers saw little point in their own professional education, even fewer saw much point in the common soldier's even being literate. If practical education were fit only for the lower orders, then the laboring classes were no better than they should be. However, the imperatives of the industrial age were being felt, and a caste system which rested in part on the ignorance of the laboring classes would have to bend. In the first half of the nineteenth century education for the rank and file rose hardly at all and, few were literate enough to record their miserable existence in letters and journals. But increasingly, execution of a commander's design would require elementary literacy as well as technical military skill.

Larger armies and wider dispersion gave much more importance to the written word. A flashing heliograph in the Khyber Pass might have to be read by a soldier in a detachment commanded by a sergeant, and relayed by flag semaphor to a message center whose corporal telegraphist awaited orders to send a further message to headquarters in Peshawar. As the Industrial Age gained momentum, weaponry became so sophisticated that literacy and knowledge of elementary mathematics became necessary. Even the breech-loading rifle, first on general issue in 1865, was sufficiently complicated that NCOs had to study manuals of instruction.[34] Also, the vast complexity of a mass army's supply, feeding, and transportation meant reliance on endless reports and returns.

Despite the need for learning, general and technical education for the rank and file lagged. The working class, from which the army drew its recruits, was illiterate throughout much of the century, and most industrial trades were learned through apprenticeship. But while little changed in the way of military trades education, the level of literacy from midcentury began a remarkable rise. This was in part because of a change in upper-class attitudes toward social responsibility. As a reflection of society at large, a part of the army's senior officer corps worked for education of the rank and file as "an important aspect of the army's transition from an earlier uncaring, fiercely-disciplined body to a more humane organization with greater provision for the welfare of its men."[35] In fact, there had been garrison libraries for the men as early as 1840, and shortly after the Crimean War many garrisons provided general interest lectures.[36]

The impetus for reform prompted by the Crimean campaign and the Indian Mutiny was the main cause of new policies for the education of NCOs and men. In 1857 only a handful had even an elementary education, and it was this lack that the measures prescribed by the Army's Council of Military Education in 1860 had to overcome.[37] In that year less than eight percent of the rank and file could do much more than write their own names.[38] By the turn of the century, however, at least minimal literacy was almost universal in the army, and almost forty percent of the rank and file had a rudimentary education.

The army had no cause to take much credit, though. Naturally, literacy rose in the army as it became more common among the working classes as a whole anyway. The success of attempts to make the soldier literate and at least able to do simple arithmetic was limited by the conservatism of officers who saw education for the rank and file as useless, dangerous, and probably impossible anyway. Their attitude is hardly surprising. The upper classes were already witnessing a groundswell of socialist unrest and demands for labor reform. The idea that intellect and character were determined by environment and not solely by heredity was unsettling and controversial. Education threatened to encourage the lower classes to get above themselves. When the Council of Military Education decreed compulsory education for the rank and file, many officers saw the move as "an unwelcome interference in regimental affairs."[39]

Whatever the discouragements, an educational system was nevertheless in place by regulation, along with complete machinery for teachers to be hired to conduct classes. Not much could be done about the apathy of unaspiring private soldiers, especially since few of their officers had any interest in seeing them learn. Of the four classes of certificate, the compulsory fourth class was so easy to pass that "an eight-year-old child might be expected to obtain it." Yet, as late as 1882 forty percent of the rank and file either could not or would not attempt it.[40] But the third, second and first class certificates had to be earned for promotion respectively to corporal, sergeant, and officer commissioned from the ranks. Proficiency had to be shown in reading, writing, mathematics, and one other subject (or British history and geography, after 1887).

While some progress was made in general education, trades training remained virtually nonexistent. Although the British Army needed to be self-contained with integrated services. little was done to nurture skills for the repair and maintenance of material, or for the myriad functions required of soldiers in a modern army. Despite repeated recommendations by government committees, there was constant opposition to training programs and establishments for military artisans. The grounds for opposition were characteristically fatuous. If soldiers were "employed as tradesmen they would cease to become good soldiers," and would be tempted to leave the army to use their skills as civilians."[41]

No doubt these beliefs resulted in part from the natural scorn which the upper classes had for manual occupations, in the same way that their tribal forebears whose pastimes were fighting and hunting left other labors to their women and children. So Tommy Atkins learned from his officers a contempt for military occupations other than combat and training for it. Even the lowest private had some sense of belonging to an aristocracy of warriors which separated him from other mortals. As a Victorian soldier he was one of a special breed who, in Kipling's phrase, warned all comers to "walk wide o' " them.[42]

Ironically, the Regular Army's spirit of professionalism as then understood worked against any improvement of professional competence in applied military technology. Patriotism, pride of regiment, masculinity, and selfhood were all bound up in the idea of fighting well, and left no room for the prudence and foresight that prompted later soldiers to look to their future and seek a trade. Nor was prudence encouraged; chances were that Tommy had no future, because disease or wounds would get him first. Soldiers who thought overly much about their prospects could not be relied upon to fight well. Therefore, officers were not likely to encourage education and training in the trades. The conservative view was that rational men with interests other than killing an enemy did not meet the irrational demands of battle as willingly as the ignorant.

There was some truth in that. The British had won the Empire with a tradition of command exercised by a leader class's courageous amateurism, and by the British Tommy's dogged capacity to endure the unendurable. British "character" had won battles, and knowledge was thought unimportant, even after it became grimly clear that courage was no armor against machine guns.

THE SOLDIER IN NINETEENTH-CENTURY LITERATURE

The young recruit is silly—'e thinks o'suicide.
'E's lost 'is gutter-devil; 'e 'asn't got 'is pride;
But day by day they kicks 'im, which 'elps 'im on a bit,
Till 'e finds 'isself one morning with a full an' proper kit.[43]

The nineteenth century was a heady time for the British soldier, as well as for those who wrote about him. In the background was the romance and tragedy of Europe's wars as seen through the eyes of Tolstoy, Stendhal, and Zola. Late in Victoria's reign, Kipling fired the British imagination by giving an Imperial glow to the common soldier's life and language.

Unlike the literature of peoples who had felt modern war, nineteenth-century English fiction portraying soldiers had little to do with war directly. Much of it included officers only incidentally as stereotypes in upper-middle-class society. Jane Austen's *Pride and Prejudice* (1813) is a novel of manners which assumes certain standards of social virtue.[44] Fittingly, the novel's title before publication was *First Impressions*; typically, English military officers were seen as handsome clotheshorses without inner substance.

Among other things, the novel is about the scoundrelly Mr. Wickham, who holds a commission in the Militia. An unprincipled adventurer, Wickham has subsisted on the kind patronage of his low-born father's gentleman employer, on the understanding that he is to take holy orders after a Cambridge education. Not suited temperamentally for the church, he wants to read law instead, and while at Cambridge he squanders his money in a life of "idleness and dissipation." This sort of background seems to have been almost a qualification for the stereotypical British military officer of the time. When Wickham's money runs out, he finds himself fit for the church after all, thinking to be given more money for a second chance. His ploy fails, and he sets about a series of courtships in hopes of marrying into money. All the while he lies, intrigues against his friends, and runs up debts with local tradesmen.

Darcy, the virtuous friend of Wickham's youth, has always known about Wickham's "vicious propensities" and "want of principle," but the scatter-brained Mrs. Bennet is infatuated with wealth and appearances, ambitious for her daughters, and easily duped by her own romantic nostalgia: "I remember the time when I liked a redcoat myself very well—and indeed so I do still in my heart; and if a smart young colonel, with five or six thousand a year, should want one of my girls, I shall not say nay to him." Mr. Bennet is less easily fooled by appearances. "He simpers and smirks, and makes love to us all," he complains when Wickham has run off with his young daughter Lydia.

Eventually, Wickham is "resolved on quitting the militia" after he has
been discredited a second time, and his bride's uncle uses his influence to
save the family name:

I think that you will agree with me in considering a removal from that corps as
highly advisable, both on his account and my niece's. It is Mr. Wickham's inten-
tion to go into the regulars; and among his former friends, there are still some
who are able and willing to assist him in the army. He has a promise of an en-
signcy in General ———'s regiment, now quartered in the North. It is an advantage to have it so far from this part of the kingdom. He promises fairly, and I hope
among different people, where they each have a character to preserve, they will be
more prudent. I have written to Colonel Forster to inform him of our present ar-
rangements, and to request that he will satisfy the various creditors of Mr. Wickham
in and near Brighton, with assurances of speedy payment, for which I have pledged
myself. And will you give yourself [Mr. Bennet, Lydia's father] the trouble of carrying
similar assurances to his creditors in Meryton [the seat of Wickham's Militia regiment],
of whom I shall subjoin a list.

A problem solved. The indigent blackguard, womanizer, and wastrel re-
signs his militia commission, has his debts settled by his bride's family to
keep up appearances, and leaves for a life of decent obscurity in the Regulars.
Quite a comedown for a young man who in the eyes of admiring young ladies
had "wanted only regimentals to make him completely charming."
    Austen's narrative reflects attitudes prevailing in the previous century, when
(in 1796) she had started writing *Pride and Prejudice*. Even in his days of
comparative grace as a militia officer, Wickham was the low-born beneficiary
of his father's master. Having proven unfit for the curacy and having betrayed
his benefactor's son, he already was an outcast. His fall from grace thus has
had two distinct stages: a loss of social cachet leading to his enlistment in
the Embodied Militia, then his betrayal of the Bennet family by his seduction
of Lydia, and his subsequent disgrace, ending with his commissioning into
the Regulars.
    When *Pride and Prejudice* appeared in 1813, Napoleon's armies were busy
in Europe and the English had yet to win glory at Waterloo. In the meantime,
the British reading public indulged its love of chivalry and romance with Sir
Walter Scott's poetry and prose. Scott's view of the British officer was un-
flatteringly typical. In his *Waverley* (1814), which appeared the year before
Waterloo, the central character Edward Waverley, a British Army officer, is
by Scott's account "a sneaking piece of imbecility." Commissioned in 1745,
Waverley joins his regiment in Scotland. He falls in love with a Jacobite's
daughter and a highland chieftain's sister, respectively. Too scatterbrained
to keep clear of Jacobite intrigue, he is imprisoned for inciting mutiny in
his own regiment. He joins the Jacobites, and at the Battle of Prestonpans
he saves a British colonel who is an old friend of his family. Only this stroke
of good luck procures Waverley a pardon when the rebel forces are beaten.

Between Waterloo and the Crimean War, the novels of William Makepeace Thackeray perpetuated already well-established attitudes toward the soldier through existing conventions of episodic satire and novels of marriage and society. The satires, notably *Barry Lyndon* (1844) and *Henry Esmond* (1852), have eighteenth-century mercenary officers as central title characters; the novels of society, for example *Vanity Fair* (1847–48), include army officers only as part of a larger tapestry of domestic love intrigue.[45] Thackeray's rendering of the Battle of Waterloo, though valuable in itself as a period piece, is not central to the novel.

Barry Lyndon's picaresque hero Redmond Barry is an Irish soldier of fortune who has fled Ireland, believing he has killed a man in a duel. He fights for the English and Prussians, owing his good fortune always to vice. He becomes prosperous through gambling, and marries a wealthy countess whom he abuses heartlessly. Through a series of reverses he ends his days in prison. Redmond Barry's swaggering and forthright rascality has had enduring appeal for Thackeray's imitators. He had a successor in G. A. Lawrence's Guy Livingstone, the central character of *Thorough* (1857). An officer of Household Cavalry, Guy is a belligerent hooligan without grace or morals.

Thackeray's *Henry Esmond* (1852) again draws on stereotypes of the military profession in the eighteenth-century. This time the hero is a virtuous victim of degraded conventions of honor and an innocent observer of depraved military conduct. Henry is one of society's marginal men by birth. He is the illegitimate son of a mercenary officer who is a drunkard, gambler, and despoiler of women. Raised by his father's family, Henry is sent to Cambridge. Morose and truculent, he has little liking for the clerical life, which the family assumes he will follow. His sense of loyalty combines with youthful rashness to embroil him in a duel. The minor "point of honor" over which the duel ostensibly is fought is really a shallow excuse for the graver matter of a lady's good name.

Like the dueling code itself, appearances mask ugly reality. The rich and titled get off scot free, and for the senior military officers involved, the incident is merely another episode in their roistering careers. Henry is imprisoned, and on his release he parlays his ruined prospects into a life of military adventure. He is thoroughly conscientious, and serves honorably in such illustrious battles as Blenheim and Malplaquet. Henry deplores the abuse of civilians and defeated soldiers alike by rapacious victors, and he tries to dispel romantic illusions by pointing up the ignorance of a public which covers its homecoming soldiery with brief glory. Little do they know that their heroes have robbed, raped, and murdered the weak and innocent.

Thackeray's strongest attack on war and illusions of military glory appears in *Vanity Fair*. Leaving the subject of the eighteenth-century mercenary, he concentrates on the nineteenth-century British officer at home during the Napoleonic Wars, and finally at Waterloo. Throughout most of the century, Army officers were apt to be social climbers of the worst kind, and the price of commissions varied with the social prestige of the regiment to which an officer was gazetted. Once an officer had attained the rank and regiment he wanted, there was no way to get rid of him.

Vanity Fair describes a domestic society in which military officers of this sort flourish. The colonel of the —th Regiment, to which the novel's officers belong, is "too old and feeble for command," and "his heart is with the tacticians of fifty years back." Captain George Osborne, an odious fellow who struts about "with hat on one side" and "elbows squared," affecting a "swaggering martial air," is dismayed at the prospect of having to live on his own pay when his father disowns him. Captain Crawley is a "clumsy military Adonis" whose marriage has tempered somewhat his "rude coarse nature;" his "delights" have been "turf, mess, hunting-field, and gaming-table," and his amatory "triumphs" have been "milliners, opera-dancers, and the like." In fairness, however, Thackeray does not deny the officer class some share of human decency; Captain Dobbin is a sound and conscientious officer, as is Major O'Dowd, who as an ex-Indian Army officer is more down to earth than the others.

The centrality of military officers to *Vanity Fair*'s society accurately reflects the place they were beginning to occupy in British society. With the growth of national romanticism in an era of empire-building, the officer corps was not as marginal as it had been. The dash and élan of the military officer could capture the imaginations of England's jingoistic population who, protected by the channel, had not suffered real war. England was taking on a martial spirit, although for Thackeray's upper-middle-class audience the rank and file still hardly existed.

Before Waterloo, Captain Osborne lionizes himself in his own romantic imagination. He places "military valour... beyond every other quality for reward and worship," and he is gratified at military service because it exceeds all other occupations for "speedy return of applause." He looks on war as "a great game," a "fierce excitement of doubt, hope, and pleasure, ... a game of chance." Brussels, thronging with British troops before the great battle, is described as "a perpetual military festival." The reality that follows, "the outbreak which was to drive all these orderly people into fury and blood," is signalled in the route of the Belgians and Osborne's death. The more impersonal and destructive war had become, the greater its capacity to touch ordinary lives.

For all the social pettiness Thackeray portrays, he allows its amateurish military officers their moments of greatness, gallantry, and sacrifice, and almost as if betraying a sneaking sentiment, there is romance in his descriptions. Dobbin and Crawley assure the well-being of their families before they march off to war, and their leave-taking is described touchingly. They are at least as decent as the scheming cynics they leave behind.

Thackeray treats the British soldier in the mass with respect, while condemning war: "[T]here is no end to the so-called glory and shame, and to the alternations of successful and unsuccessful murder, in which two high-spirited nations might engage." His respect for the soldier is compromised by his disparagement of all military honors as deceptive obscenities for which men will sell their lives. Soldiers pursue "the Devil's code of honour"; being "gazetted" for a decoration or promotion seems as important as life itself. Thackeray describes monuments to the dead erected in churches as "braggart heathen allegories," so that the inscription on Osborne's memorial, "Dulce et decorum est pro patria mori," prefigures the irony in Wilfred Owen's Great War poem.

Waterloo had brought a shift in British ideas about war. The sheer numbers of Englishmen sent to fight on the Continent, and the devastating effects of improved artillery and small arms, resulted in far more casualties and far greater losses to ordinary English families than ever before. With Waterloo Britons began to lose their innocence about war, and *Vanity Fair*, written in the decade preceding the miseries of the Crimean campaign, was prophetic.

Although the British Army's poor showing in the Crimean War and the Indian Mutiny two years later brought Parliamentary cries for reform, there was no real groundswell of concern for the British fighting man. If the public was shocked by Britain's military setbacks, the cause was more in the nature of indignation at military inefficiency than any real compassion for the soldier. Both events happened a long way from England, where prosperity and Imperial complacency reigned. Florence Nightingale's efforts at Scutari are notable mainly because they were the first decent attempt at medical care motivated by humanitarian interest. But they did not herald any large-scale reform in the welfare of troops, and she was heartily disapproved of by many conservatives. War photography, in its infancy at midcentury, was, like war art, properly patriotic. Crimean scenes show symmetrical lines of white tents, fortified gun emplacements with pyramids of cannon shot, and infantry reclining with classical grace, their arms neatly "piled" according to regulations. William Howard Russell, the first war correspondent to attempt realistic journalism about the grim realities of life on campaign in the Crimea, suffered every sort of abuse by the very army his pen might have helped.[46]

No literature of stature grew from the Crimean experience, save romantic paeans to the heroes and historical campaign accounts. Britain's complacency sailed on unchecked. Apparently without any sense of contradiction, Alfred Lord Tennyson expressed conventional sentiments in "The Charge of the Light Brigade" (1854). When 600 British cavalrymen died at Balaclava in a mad charge "into the jaws of death" because of the incompetence, petty spite, and obduracy of their commanders, Tennyson wrote history's most poetic praise of pointless death. Extolling unquestioning obedience as a military virtue overriding the criminal negligence leading to this disaster, he ends with the the rhetorical question, "When can their glory fade?." Perhaps Tennyson's appointment as poet laureate had something to do with his exalted tone.

As long as Britons were secure, and as long as they did not see the miseries of military life at first hand, there was little public indignation and a lot of self-congratulation. Britannia ruled the waves, Jack Tar kept the sea lanes open for the commerce of Empire, and Tommy Atkins looked after the places it came from. Despised in the flesh, Tommy as a collective abstraction was exalted as symbol of Britain's might and supposed racial superiority.

The romance of Empire came alive in Kipling's literature. Above all, his romanticizing of Tommy's squalid life in ballad and story captured the public imagination, and continued to hold it. The muscular spirit of *Soldiers Three* (1881), "*Barrack-room Ballads*" (1892), and a treasury of exotic tales of Eastern lore still evoke nostalgia for the Raj in military romantics.[47] Except for some of his minor works about World War I, Kipling's subject was the common soldier's day-to-day life in India, and the frontier skirmishes he fought against tribesmen. He invested with romance even the most banal and sordid subjects—a half-naked and limping regimental *bhisti* (water carrier) with a goat skin of stinking water, or a murderous thief being hanged. Even Kipling's representation of common men's speech seems like elevated prose as he heaps lavish praise on Gunga Din who would "tend the wounded under fire" and "didn't seem to know the use o' fear." Through a murmured exchange between men parading to watch Danny Deever's execution, he evokes a sense of muted grandeur in a recruit's fear and distress as a sinning comrade's departed soul seems to "whimper over'ead."

There is epic tragedy in Kipling's "Gentlemen-Rankers," a lament in the words of well-born black sheep who are "done with Hope and Honour," and live out degraded and drunken lives on the Empire's frontiers. In another age and in other hands, the poem's theme might have turned out as a badly conceived exercise in mawkish self-pity. Yet the refrain for this unpromising subject so captured imaginations that it has survived as the joyfully nostalgic Whiffenpoof Song.

In "Cholera Camp" dread disease takes on the color of a battle in which "the band's a doin' all she knows to cheer us; / And the Chaplain's gone and prayed to Gawd to 'ear us." The poem is full of "bugles calling," camp being struck, and rapid promotions "on ten deaths a day," all in a jaunty ballad meter which imparts a sense of martial urgency and excitement to a dreary account of epidemic misery and squalid death.

Much of Kipling's verse is about the military virtues admired by regulars, who otherwise were notoriously vice-ridden. The only measure of respect in this masculine military world was a man's fighting qualities: his courage, endurance, and loyalty. These qualifications for membership in a masonry of arms were seen to transcend even distinctions of race, religion, and ideology. "Fuzzy Wuzzy" in the poem of that title was a generic name for fanatical Sudanese Dervishes who, armed only with spears, "broke a British square" at Tamai in 1884. Yet there is condescension in Kipling's accolade to the Sudanese warrior as "a pore benighted 'eathen but a first class fightin' man." His Tommy Atkins persona can afford to praise warriors who gave a good fight, because in the end the British rallied and defeated the Sudanese. Still, Tommy concedes that perhaps the game had not been quite sporting: "[W]e sloshed you with Martinis, an' it wasn't 'ardly fair" (a punning allusion to the Martini-Henry rifle).

Kipling found the romance of military virtues in the most unlikely occurrences of garrison life. In "The Shut-Eye Sentry" a Battalion Orderly Sergeant and Corporal of the Guard guide their Orderly Officer through his paces when he has turned out the guard after overindulging in the mess. The narrator, "Privit Thomas A.," turns a blind eye in his sentry box, even though the Orderly Officer's conduct is swinish. (He urinates in his cap and kisses the sentry!) The NCOs "sluice 'im down" and make him presentable for morning parade, and his troops perform their drill perfectly by rote to cover up his garbled commands and keep him from detection by the colonel. This touching vignette celebrates the affection between junior officers and men which was as real as it was a conventional part of the regimental mystique. The long-service NCOs' motherly solicitude, the privates' stoic silence, and the punctilious performance of ritual "rounds" capture the essence of the regimental spirit.

"Belts" is a sad account of warrior exuberance and regimental pride spoiled because someone got serious. The poem recounts a brawl between "an Irish regiment an' English cavalree," which starts from a shouted insult to the English regiment. When the police appear, the soldiers join ranks "simultaneous," but the exultant cry of "belts, belts, belts," Tommy's traditional weapon in brawls, is soon muted. The soldiers disperse "like beaten dogs" when an Irish soldier is stabbed with a bayonet, "An' so we all was murderers that started out in fun." In "Cells" Tommy wakes up in the guardroom with a "head like a concertina" after being "drunk and resisting the guard." He seems exhilarated at the thought of "packdrill and a fortnight's C.B.!"

In keeping with the military convention of the time, Kipling returns repeatedly to the theme of marriage as incompatible with the military virtues. In "The Young British Soldier" an old sweat advises an " 'arf-made recruity" new to the East about the pitfalls of frontier soldiering. Along with staying away from local liquor, drinking in moderation during cholera season, and wearing a pith helmet in the sun, the recruit might marry, but "if you must... , / take care she is old." A wife's chastity is hardly a problem for a ranker's honor, it seems. "If the wife should go wrong with a comrade, be loth/To shoot when you catch 'em—you'll swing, on my oath!" The old sweat's solution is humorously utilitarian: "Make 'im take 'er and keep 'er: that's Hell for them both,/An' you're shut o' the curse of a soldier." Deserving of more respect and compassion is the soldier's rifle:

> When 'arf of your bullets fly wide in the ditch,
> Don't call your Martini a cross-eyed old bitch;

> She's human as you are—you treat 'er as sich,
> An' she'll fight for the young British soldier.

The responsibilities of marriage spoil the soldier's game by turning it into a serious job in "The Married Man":

> The bachelor 'e fights for one
> As joyful as can be;
> But the married man don't call it fun,
> Because 'e fights for three—

With home life as a distraction, the "married man" "wants to go 'ome to 'is tea." Chances are that he will be rather indecently prudent of his own life while more determined to kill his enemy:

> The bachelor pokes up 'is 'ead
> to see if you are gone;
> But the married man lies down instead,
> An' waits till the sights come on. . . .

> The bachelor will miss you clear
> To fight another day;
> But the married man, 'e says "no fear!"
> 'E wants you out of the way.

The British regimental ethos, inseparably bound up with jingoism and professional cultism, naturally lent itself to celebration of an exclusively male warrior spirit. In capturing this monkish sentiment Kipling shows how far it was from the feelings of citizen-soldiers in armies which fought in defense of hearth and home.

Whereas the citizen-soldiers of the twentieth century usually have sought an end to war and military service so that they can get back to a domestic routine, the regular of the late nineteenth century was addicted to a life of adventure and military routine in foreign climes. The army was mistress and mother. "Chant-Pagan" tells of a short-service irregular who returns from the Boer War to "awful old England again," with its depressing " 'ouses both sides of the street," and wondering how he can ever take it, "me that 'ave seen what I've seen." In "Back to the Army Again" another time-expired volunteer who reenlists revels as if coming home: "I smelt the smell o' the barricks, I 'eard the bugles go. / I 'eard the feet on the gravel—the feet o' the men what drill—." In brief, the British Regular's professionalism as understood by Kipling was expressed more as a love of soldiering than of war. All this would change within Kipling's lifetime, with the Great War's "War Poets," civilians in uniform who had no love of military routine, and who managed to record in verse the pity of war before they themselves died in battle.

A PASSING AGE REMEMBERED IN LITERATURE

> Life was not even tragic in those days; it was neither tragic nor comic;
> it was elaborately silly and vaguely dangerous. Flags, armies, national
> anthems, stuck upon my world like straws and paper gewgaws on the
> head of an idiot. But I did not conceive that this idiot could blunder
> into actual war.
>
> H. G. Wells, *The World of William Clissold*[48]

At the beginning of World War I the old Edwardian peacetime world for
a time continued to make the new. Citizen-soldiers came to the army with
their old beliefs about fair play, national honor, and love of Empire. Brought
up in the Imperial tradition and trained by regular army men, the men of
the New Army for a brief space lived the old dream and played the old
game. To grasp how great was the change to come, one may view the prewar
world through the hindsight of authors who had seen Edwardian England
vanish.

H. G. Wells's *The World of William Clissold* (1926) and Ford Madox Ford's
The Good Soldier (1927) capture the spirit of the time.[49] The triviality of
subject and the superficiality of the characters are typical of upper-middle-
class attitudes and concerns. In *Clissold* Wells's vacuous characters flit languidly
about Europe, dabbling in assorted pastimes for distraction, vaguely seeking
meaning in their lives, yet too world-weary to commit themselves to anything
much. Clementina speculates archly about becoming a prostitute. She has
been "rejected as a governess and as a companion" because she is "too
distinguished for one and too disrespectful for the other." She has "tried
dactylography" but cannot spell; she cannot abide the thought of marriage
"of the sufferable sort"; the stage is "beyond her" because she cannot act;
and above all she is "bored, and [has] ceased to attend to a task at once
difficult for her and inane."

The milieu Clissold describes is anaesthetized by its own pleasures; yet
a growing uneasiness underlies the frenetic pursuit of fresh sensation. He
senses a sinister quality in a way of life that had ignorant militarism as an
adjunct to a general decadence that drowned out prudence: "Amidst the
rhythms of jazz and the heavy blare of national anthems, what other voices
could be heard?" Clissold mentions military figures only incidentally, and
even then they are merely fashionable young officers who serve as objects
of sexual fascination for blasé young wives who relieve their boredom with
a succession of sexual infidelities. They are mentioned casually, as if by the
jaded women who used them. Clissold describes briefly a woman acquaintance's "scarcely ambiguous friendship for a young guardsman, Lord Had-
endower about whom I know nothing. I never met him; he was killed at
Soissons." Casual sex, casual death. The trivializing of the individual expresses eloquently an entire society's loss of capacity for feeling.

Ford Madox Ford's *The Good Soldier* is set against a similar background. The narrator Dowell is a lusterless *bon vivant* who recounts his and his wife Florence's association with Edward Ashburnham and his wife Leonora. Edward, a former Indian Army captain, has resigned his commission supposedly because of a heart condition. The narrator and his wife first meet Edward and Leonora at Bad Nauheim, where they come seasonally to take the waters. Edward ostensibly is still on sick leave, his heart weakened by "approximately, polo, or too much hard sportsmanship in his youth." In short, his affliction from his service in the 14th Hussars is socially and militarily correct.

Superficially, Edward is the ideal prescribed by good society, "so well set up, with such honest blue eyes, such a touch of stupidity." He and Leonora "look the county family, . . . so appropriately and perfectly wealthy; . . . so perfect in manner—even to the saving touch of insolence." Edward is "the cleanest-looking sort of chap; an excellent magistrate, a first-rate soldier, one of the best landlords." His sartorial taste is exquisite, his wardrobe the cavalry officer's ideal. Even his stance is impeccable as Dowell eyes "the immensely long line of his perfectly elegant trousers from waist to boot heel." Edward is reputed to have a DSO (Distinguished Service Order) and "his troop loved him beyond the love of all men." Supposedly, he has other decorations for gallantry as well, not to mention two recommendations for the VC (Victoria Cross) which were frustrated by technicalities. But these last testimonials are only according to Nancy, a young family friend and ward who is completely infatuated with Edward.

Other facts, sordid in the extreme, begin to emerge. Edward was named as the principal figure in a notorious scandal, for making improper advances to a servant girl, and only the intervention of his own country's magistracy kept him out of jail. Then there was Edward's seduction of Maisie Maidan, wife of a junior officer in his command. There is more. Apparently, Edward is being blackmailed by a brother officer, a colonel whom Leonora has taken as a friend. As the series of affairs and betrayals comes to light, Edward gradually appears in his true aspect—a compulsive sexual adventurer and deceiver, a hollow form without substance beyond his base impulses. Edward Ashburnham is a paradigm for the arid world of pretension, decadence, falsehood, and self-indulgence which Edwardian England's privileged classes had entered before World War I.

While the fictional Edward Ashburnham is too extreme to be typical of Edwardian military officers, regulars of the day might have seen something of themselves in him. Not a jolly whoring rascal in the tradition of Thackeray's soldiers of fortune, nor yet a scheming opportunist like Austen's Wickham, he has a weakness that Ford portrays with compassion and psychological insight. More than merely a fraud, Edward is victim of an overcivilized world in which lives are lived on the surface and everything is taken "for granted." Sentiment is stifled in obedience to bloodless convention that legislates even the minutest details of existence. When convention tyrannizes, healthy impulse finds expression in secret perversity. Beneath his impeccably conventional exterior, Edward is "passionate and headstrong," his sexual urges driving him to violate every social rule, and finally bringing him to suicide. By the outbreak of the Great War, the British regular officer was already a victim of desiccated ideologies and mindlessly rigid codes of conduct. The war simply killed less subtly and more violently than the neurasthenic existence so many led.

NOTES

1. The discharged veteran maimed in foreign wars remained a stock object of pity through the nineteenth century, but there was little serious concern. Thomas Hood's trivial "Faithless Nellie Gray" (c. 1843) was more bathos than pathos.

2. Byron Farwell, *Mr. Kipling's Army* (London: W. W. Norton, 1981), p. 216. Chaplains had been given military rank in 1816 and began wearing uniform in 1860. Apparently, little contradiction was seen between the chaplain's temporal and spiritual duties.

3. Farwell, *Army*, pp. 103, 104.

4. T. J. Edwards, *Regimental Badges* (Aldershot: Gale & Polden, 1953), p. 12.

5. Farwell, *Army*, p. 99. Restrictions on flogging increased until it was abolished in 1881. Its replacement, Field Punishment No. 1, entailing spreadeagling to cannon wheels, on a diet of bread and water, was hardly less brutal. Many major compromises of more humanitarian punishments are known; for example, the execution by cannon of mutinous sepoys in 1857, and floggings in Burma in World War II.

6. "Tommy," in *Rudyard Kipling's Verse: Definitive Edition* (London: Hodder & Stoughton, 1940), p. 398. [Ed. not cited.] (All subsequent quotations in this chapter of Rudyard Kipling's verse are from this edition.)

7. John Keegan, "Regimental Ideology" (Sandhurst: Royal Military College, 1982).

8. Farwell, *Army*, p. 106.

9. General Sir John Hackett, *The Profession of Arms* (London: Times Publishing Co., 1962), pp. 63, 64.

10. George Eliot, *Adam Bede* (New York: Airmont Publishing Co., 1966), pp. 53, 57, 136.

11. Brian Bond, *The Victorian Army and the Staff College, 1854–1914* (London: Eyre & Methuen, 1972), p. 59.

12. Gwyn Harries-Jenkins, *The Army in Victorian Society* (London: Routledge & Kegan Paul, 1977), p. 163.

13. Bond, *Victorian Army*, p. 51.

14. Ibid.

15. Ibid.

16. Ibid., p. 17.

17. Ibid., p. 52.

18. Although General Charles Napier was at the Senior Department in 1817, his breeding and natural talents, rather than his training, probably account for his successes.

19. Bond, *Victorian Army*, p. 59.

20. *English Letters*, Bodleian MSS, C236.

21. "Tommy."

22. Bond, *Victorian Army*, p. 17.

23. Ibid., p. 59.

24. Ibid., p. 65.

25. Ibid., pp. 73, 74.

26. Harries-Jenkins, *Army*, p. 134.

27. Bond, *Victorian Army*, p. 127.

28. Ibid., p. 157.

29. Ibid., p. 171.

30. D. Lloyd George, *War Memoirs of David Lloyd George*, Vol. 1 (London: Odhams Press, 1939), p. 450.

31. From the MSS and correspondence of General Sir Charles Bonham-Carter, GCB, CMG, DSO, in his son Victor Bonham-Carter's account, *In a Liberal Tradition: A Social Biography 1700–1950* (London: Constable, 1960), pp. 136, 137.

32. Harries-Jenkins, *Army*, p. 146, 147.

33. Ibid., p. 148.

34. Ibid.

35. Alan Ramsay Skelley, *The Victorian Army at Home* (Montreal: McGill-Queen's University Press, 1977), p. 98.

36. Ibid., p. 117.

37. Ibid., p. 93.

38. Ibid., p. 90.

39. Ibid., p. 92.

40. Ibid., p. 95.

41. Ibid., p. 100.

42. Rudyard Kipling, "The Widow at Windsor."

43. Kipling, "The 'Eathen."

44. Quotations are from Jane Austen, *Pride and Prejudice* (New York: Signet, 1961).

45. Quotations from *Vanity Fair* in this chapter are from the F.E.L. Priestley edition (Toronto: Macmillan, 1911; reprinted 1969).

46. Philip Knightley, *The First Casualty* (New York: Harcourt Brace Jovanovich, 1975), pp. 8, 9.

47. Works quoted from "Barrack Room Ballads" are in *Rudyard Kipling's Verse*.

48. H. G. Wells, *The World of William Clissold*, 2 vols. (New York: George H. Doran, 1926), p. 77.

49. Ford Madox Ford, *The Good Soldier* (New York: Vintage Books, 1955).

4

THE SHRIEKING PYRE: THE CITIZEN MARTYR IN THE GREAT WAR

THE OLD REGULAR'S LAST DAYS

"The type of boy we aim at turning out" the Head used to say to impressed parents, "is a thoroughly manly fellow. We prepare for the Universities, of course, but our pride is in our excellent Sports Record.
....

Indeed, unless you know how to kill you cannot possibly be a Man, still less a Gentleman.

Richard Aldington, Death of a Hero (1929)[1]

By the twentieth century, national interests had woven military life into the British social tapestry. Romantic nationalism, social Darwinism, and balance-of-power politics were dressed up in diplomatic ceremonial and military pomp. H. G. Wells's William Clissold complains:

The head of state is traditionally a fighting figure. Before the war the numerous royal families of Europe almost lived in uniform. They were ready, aye, ready. Their survivors show no disposition to relinquish the swaggering role. Wherever the remaining monarchs go the soldiers still turnout and salute, and every loyal Englishman ceases to be a rational creature and stiffens to the likeness of a ramrod at the first blare of the national anthem.[2]

In the opening decade of the century the main features of the British soldier's evolution since Waterloo became as complete as they were going to be, until World War I changed everything again. The growth of military corporate professionalism was accompanied by the officer corps' closing ranks against political institutions, which it sensed were hostile to the military's interests.[3] Claiming a monopoly on military education, knowledge, and competence, officers resented reforming efforts by government. Senior officers jealously assumed the right and responsibility as "sole judges of such critical defense issues as size, organization, recruitment and equipping of forces."[4]

Yet, of the professions only the military professed to honor an ethic of subordination to its client, the state. Antagonism between army and state was inevitable, however. Questions of size and organization hinged on conscription policy, which in turn involved Constitutional decisions and allocations of Britains's resources of manpower. Similarly, decisions about the army's weapons, equipment, and supply would have far-reaching effects on a nation's economy.

Ironically, the insularity of most senior commanders, determined to keep profane civilian fingers out of military affairs, assured that army staffs were unsuited to meet these new challenges to strategic expertise. The officer corps had made a virtue of ignorance of national policy. The reasons for this dogged intransigence were largely social and moral. Through the century just past it had been widely believed among Britain's upper classes that an officer corps not financially dependent on them would pose a threat to stability. Through the purchase system the military profession became intimately associated with upper-class interests. The commission was a mark of social acceptance, and, except in India, no officer was expected to live on his pay. On the eve of the first World War, the British officer corps remained largely amateurish:

[The] officer corps was still the preserve of young men of good social standing who had the outlook of amateurs and usually were. They were ill-paid, with "half a day's pay for half a day's work," and so had to be of independent means. This meant that most were hard to teach and many were unteachable. They were not well trained and were expected to be neither industrious nor particularly intelligent. From men such as these came the commanders of World War I.[5]

While the officer corps represented upper-class interests and the status quo, it also had incorporated a lofty conservatism into the professional ethic, as part of a concept of military institutional honor. This institutionalizing of military values, an "army honor" that had succeeded "warrior honor," had been developing since the seventeenth century.[6] "Army honor" was the property of every man under arms regardless of rank and imposed its obligations on all. Manifested as regimental mystique and the cult of "officer-and-gentleman," it reflected the values of the squirearchy and church. "Army honor" was seen as a trust, and the army saw itself as keeper of the flame, always in danger of being dimmed by profane political hands.

In the same way that the New Model army had brought pressure on Parliament by direct appeal to the protector, there were several instances in the late nineteenth and early twentieth centuries of senior British generals making direct representation to the monarch because they thought that the cabinet was not acting in the army's best interests. The professed aloofness from partisan politics and a religiously observed appearance of subordination to the state barely covered up unseemly factionalism.[7] The special bond between sovereign and vassal implicit in the relationship between government and the military, and symbolized in the officer's commission, was exploited and perverted by military traditionalists indignantly spouting old credos that linked cold steel and equestrianship with national pride and royal authority. If booted and spurred generals pouted and stormed enough, they usually intimidated the politicians and got their way.

No matter how much regulars professed to despise civilian values, and no matter the distance the officer corps tried to put between the army and the political process except when their own institutions were threatened, the British Army shared society's fortunes and reflected its attitudes. Classic military professionalism had grown along with the institutionalizing of other professions during the nineteenth century, and while the process seemed to many to set military officers apart from other species of mortal, it in fact linked military interests with national policy.

As the politicians found themselves drawn into World War I, they arranged for the recruitment of a vast army of civilians. This had happened in continental nations before, but not in Britain. These men's wartime experiences would forever change the character of the British soldier, as would the war he had to fight. Small arms technology had greatly increased infantry firepower. The magazine-loading rifle and the Maxim machine gun (1889) had been around since before the turn of the century, and resulted in an end to the fabled British square. No matter how spirited the troops who had formed up in open ground to withstand assaults by ill-disciplined natives, they could not withstand the devastating effects of automatic fire. By the same token, barbed wire rendered the cavalry charge useless. Yet British officers' tactical thinking was dominated by old doctrines relying largely on defense. Brought up on wars of Empire, they had a "small war mentality."[8] Offensive tactics had for a long time been pretty well limited to long approach marches from base camps to subdue insurrectionists, and little thought had been given to problems of offensive tactics against a modern army. Commanders continued to insist on the permanence of cavalry, and as late as 1907 troopers were issued lances in preference to carbines. Perhaps that gives some hint of the chivalresque fantasy into which British officers had withdrawn.[9]

In August of 1914 Britain as yet had no "Kitchener Divisions," no "Pals' Battalions" of "Temporary Gentlemen" and citizen-soldiers. There was only the old Regular Army, changed hardly at all by its South African experience, and with an officer corps scarcely more able than it had been before Cardwell's reforms had tried to legislate competence. In the early days of World War I, many of the old guard thought it unbecoming for troops to dig in, and men had to get shovels from local farmers. Officers still tried to stroll nonchalantly along parapets, blackthorn in hand and pipe in teeth, showing disdain for enemy fire.

It did not take long for the army to give up on those more obvious follies, but throughout the war the high command suffered a paralysis of tactical thought in the face of a technology they could not fathom. A trained infantryman with his Lee Enfield could fire an aimed round every four seconds, pausing only to recharge his magazine, and the Vickers medium machine gun (1915) rattled off belts of 250 rounds at a rate of 400 to 500 rounds a minute. From two machine guns per battalion at the beginning of the war there grew whole machine gun companies and a Machine Gun Corps. In

1915 light machine guns, the Lewis and the Hotchkiss, appeared. Artillery ballistic science had vastly improved. The invention of the dial sight meant that high trajectory weapons—howitzers and mortars—could be fired accurately from defilade, and death appeared as if from nowhere. From April 1915 poison gas was used on the battlefield; nerve, blister, and choking gasses, delivered at first on the wind from the enemy's positions, and later by cannister shells. As the war progressed the automobile, the auto truck, and then the tank came into use. Yet the generals still relied more on the British spirit than on their own intellects.

With Europe in convulsion, few British could comprehend the scale of events. The war would be over by Christmas, everyone said. The 70,000 Tommies who had been sent across the channel would sort out the Hun. This tough little army would become immortal in memory as the "Old Contemptibles." They fought a savage ten-day rearguard action against the Kaiser's lightning advance on Paris. Then, dropping with fatigue and hunger, they stemmed the German tide with a counterattack in the First Battle of the Marne. This was the British Regular Army's nova. An era was ending because this would be a citizen's war as ordinary Britons took up arms.

In the early days, even volunteers of the British Expeditionary Force and the millions of troops from the dominions and colonies could not grasp war's new realities. Their vision was great and their optimism unbounded; their idealism found expression in cant phrases: "war to end war"; "God, King and Country"; they were fighting another quarter in the Great Game. Until the summer of 1916, the spirit of British society was essentially what it had been through the Edwardian period, except that the war gave fresh focus for old sentiments. The British Expeditionary Force, vastly expanded with formations and units of citizen-soldiers, had been trained by the old regulars who had known another kind of war on the frontiers of the Empire. The new amateurs wanted so much to be real soldiers that they entered into the spirit of their training, hardly questioning the wisdom of the old sweats. Officers were fed on the traditional tactical doctrine espoused by General Haig and his contemporaries, that the first step was to break out into "open ground" where cavalry would come into its own as in the past.

Although "Temporary Gentlemen," the new officers at first were from much the same background as their Regular Army teachers. They had been to the same public schools and universities, and they were in "respectable" occupations. Although they otherwise would not have been soldiers, they were nevertheless members of Britain's leader class, and found little difficulty in adapting to regimental life. They looked well in their breeches and Sam Brownes, and they understood instinctively the relationships between ranks, which in the army paralleled equivalent relationships in civilian life. The other ranks were fed on a ration of discipline and usage handed out by old regular sergeant majors, as they learned to wind their puttees, take tucks in their tunics, form fours, and "sling the bat" like old sweats.[10]

The similarities between the new soldiers and their Regular Army mentors were superficial, however, and the old Regular Army discipline had little more than nuisance value for weary troops who came out of the trenches to rest areas. They had come to fight a war and get it over with, and not to play soldier, yet when they came out of the line they were greeted by nests of martinets who drilled and inspected them to get rid of their frontline slackness. Old regulars from general to junior NCO continued the only training methods they knew. Their ideas about discipline had been learned in an army of regular "Tommies" who had to be taught through endless repetition of drills and had to be maintained in "good order" with mindless tasks and punishment for minor omissions. But the Regulars' cardinal virtues had little meaning for the men of the New Army.

The new soldiers were of different stuff; they represented a cross-section of British society—farmers, factory workers, clerks who had come to do a job. Many brought initiative and intelligence, but they had to suppress them.

In a letter to his family from France in March 1916, Corporal James Parr, 16th London Regiment, wrote an account of routine in "rest" behind the line, after a day's exhausting route march:

Nowadays, the guards parade in full marching order with pack, boots cleaned, macintoshes to show under ground sheet in top of pack (an impossibility, by the way, if the pack is packed according to regulations), the fire picket for the night parade in belt and side arms—necessitating the taking to pieces of their equipment—all are inspected by the company orderly officer, and then marched to the orderly-room, where they are inspected again by the Adjutant and Batt. Sgt. Major; the bugle band meanwhile marches up and down playing furiously. . . . And the constant badgering about that it all means to the men and corporals, the cleaning up that has to be done, the packing and unpacking of packs, the alteration of equipment—it's enough to turn one's hair grey.[11]

Corporal Parr saw his last show and an end of "badgering" on the day of the first Somme offensive. He was listed as "wounded and missing."

At first, it was the old army that taught the new. But as the war grew old the New Army—the Kitchener Divisions, the Pals' Battalions, the University Companies, the Artists' Rifles—became the "real" army, officered by men like Robert Graves, and R. J. E. Tiddy, an Oxford Don, accomplished scholar and folklorist, who had scant patience with the military gods of Punctuality and Obedience.[12] Soon the few regulars remaining at regimental depots, training establishments, and rear area installations could no longer effect an air of superiority over men blooded in a worse war than ever had been imaginable in India, the Sudan, or Transvaal. To be sure, the first World War's citizen-soldiers called themselves "Tommies," but the "Tommy" Kipling had written about had gone forever.

The clearest description of distinctions between peacetime regulars and wartime citizen-soldiers, and their sameness as men, is Frank Richards's *Old*

Soldiers Never Die (1933).[13] Fusilier Richards, DCM (Distinguished Conduct Medal), MM (Military Medal), had been a regular for some seven years in India and Burma. When war broke out he had been a time-expired reservist in the Royal Welch Fusiliers for five years and a coal miner. He immediately answered the call "to the Colours" and was soon at the front with the Second Battalion, Siegfried Sassoon's unit. (The First Battalion was at first comprised mostly of regulars, and Robert Graves in his memoir *Goodbye to All That* gives some idea of the contempt with which "Temporary Gentlemen" were treated there.)

Richards's account has the good-humored, matter-of-fact, and unemotional tone of the old sweat, in contrast to the dramatic and often indignant prose of the more literate citizen-soldier who did most of the writing about the war. In the Second Battalion Richards was with both, all of them new to this kind of war. His commentary thus provides the remarkable perspective of a *pukka* old soldier spinning a hoary yarn. His common sense and simple pride in having been a good soldier is free of posturing and self-conscious martyrdom as he cuts through pretension and lies fed to the troops by the senior staff. When Richards tells his comrade the "Old Soldier" the contents of a message he is carrying about a French breakthrough, the reply is typical of then-current feeling: " 'Bloody B. S. ' " Richards comments, "[W]e had got so that we didn't believe anything." Not real indignation, this was merely skepticism born of long experience.

Richards was contemptuous of the religious sophistries by church and state to present dying in war as a Christian enterprise, and so he had little use for those who advocated war but who were too pious to fight it themselves. He reflects on the ambivalence of Christian and military values in his derisive commentary on the role of padres, who "prayed for victory and thundered from the pulpits for the enemy to be smitten hip and thigh, but did not believe in doing any of the smiting themselves." Regimental chaplains still administered the troops' spiritual welfare as their commanding officers required. But old regulars like Richards were uninterested in righteousness; for them, the military virtues of tenacity and courage were enough. Richards comments often about his "praying," by which he means damning to perdition officers who badger him. He shows wry humor in quoting a message from his corps commander berating officers for alleged pessimism: " 'Officers must eradicate this feeling from their minds and from the minds of the men serving under them.' " The message also contained the general's censure of the troops for profanity: " 'This practice must cease.' " Richards enjoys his company commander's reaction: "[H]is language for the remainder of the day was delightful to listen to."

The same general illustrates the prewar mentality of the army's senior commanders. Living in comfort far behind the lines, the corps commander has inspected Richards's battalion while it is out of the trenches. Although the battalion's standing order has been that brasses remain dull, the general demands that they be polished:

Many prayers were offered up for his soul. . . . [W]hen we marched down the main road, . . . the enemy in their observation balloons must have thought that hundreds of small heliographs were moving into action.

Richards tells another anecdote about follies perpetuated from the old army by a regular officer (nicknamed The Peer), who spots mud around the soles of Richards's boots during a field inspection. Richards tries to explain that he has been to the latrine dug in a muddy orchard, but The Peer will have none of it:

'Good heavens, Sergeant! This man is absolutely filthy!' I said: 'I beg your pardon sir . . . ' but I got no further. . . . He roared at me: 'Damn you! I'll run you in. How dare you speak to an officer before he addresses you?'

Richards and his friend Paddy are required to parade in full kit two hours after a stiff day's march. This trivial incident occurred when Richards's battalion had just been relieved in its trenches in High Wood and was on the march to the Somme.

Occasionally overkeen young officers attempted to emulate their Regular Army instructors. Richards recalls a brief rest halt on a long march:

[C]onsidering that we had ordered arms very slovenly, [our new officer] gave the command, 'Slope Arms!' This was also not very satisfactory, so we were soon doing a little arms drill. By the time he had given the command, 'Fall out!' it was time to fall in again.

By the summer of 1916, the army's character had changed radically. Richards reports that fewer than fifty men of the old Expeditionary Force were left in his battalion, and most of these had been wounded once or more. New values were growing in response to the war's realities. Describing a sergeant typical of the wartime variety, Richards writes:

When out of action his drilling of a squad of men may have not been up to the standard of a drill sergeant but he was highly skilled in the real arts of war and in an attack the best drill sergeant in the British army would have been a dunce alongside of him.

The real test of stamina was the constant shelling. Richards writes of men going mad, of new soldiers panicking and trying to run away down the trench, of older soldiers wounding themselves or making pacts to wound each other, or committing suicide. It was the waiting in the trenches for death or wounding that tested the soldier's mental toughness.

The kind of discipline that saw men through World War I was an inner control having little to do with the old prewar army's idea of discipline, which had been meant to force the submission of fractious men. But no sooner were hostilities over than the old regulars resumed their former practices. Richards reports a lecture by The Peer to the battalion's noncommissioned officers on the subject of discipline, a few days after the Armistice:

'[W]hile the War was on it was a case of every man for himself when in action, and discipline had become a little lax. They must remember that they belonged to a Line Battalion and discipline must revert back to its pre-War standard.'

THE SOMME AND A SHIFT IN FEELING

> What of us who, flung on the shrieking pyre,
> Walk, our usual thought untouched,
> Our lucky limbs as on ichor fed,
> Immortal seeming ever?
>
> "Dead Man's Dump," Isaac Rosenberg[14]

The problem in tracing a shift in attitude in World War I is that the enterprise is an attempt at charting in orderly fashion what is essentially a record of madness. Because of the complexity of this war as the sum of so many different experiences, feelings, and convictions, no two interpretations are the same. Nor is there general agreement about how, or even if, feelings changed. Belief in traditional forms of valor and heroism continued side by side with the cult of martyrdom; traditional patriotism existed alongside of disillusionment; trust in political and military leaders survived along with a sense of betrayal and alienation; deep religiosity subsisted with existential doubt; public optimism burned brightly together with private pessimism. Edmund Blunden (Royal Sussex Regiment, 1915–19, Somme and Ypres) consciously sacrificed literary coherence out of his need to record experience. In his *Undertones of War* (1928) he wrote:

[I]n this vicinity [Hooge] a peculiar difficulty would exist for the artist to select the sights, faces, words, incidents, which characterized the time. The art is rather to collect them, in their original form of incoherence. . . . I have not noticed any compelling similarity between a bomb used as an inkpot and the bomb in the hand of a corpse, or even between the look of a footballer after a goal all the way and that of a sergeant inspecting whale-oiled feet. There was a difference prevailing in all things. Let the smoke of German breakfast fires, . . . and the savour of their coffee, rise in these pages.[15]

Blunden's prose has the immediacy of direct experience, and that is what sets recorded memory of World War I apart from most accounts of earlier wars. The intensity of the war experience produced innumerable diarists, memoirists, and editors of letters by soldiers in battle, most of which were published years afterwards. At the time, the thing for most Britons was to win the war. The official position was that doubt did not exist, and private considerations were criminal if they weakened the will to win.

Early in the war a spirit of optimism was abroad, which, aside from "stiff-upper-lip" attitudes, would darken into pessimism, not simply about success, but about the morality and common sense of the enterprise. With the invasion through Luxembourg in August 1914, Germany took a first step toward implementing the Schlieffen Plan, to envelop France by way of Belgium while remaining in a defensive posture toward the east. Rather than face the German advance on the Belgian frontier, the French responded with the irrational "Plan Dix-Sept," to take back Alsace, occupied by Germans since the Franco-Prussian War. The strategic error was symptomatic of the French high command's obsessive need to restore French "*gloire*" on the slightest pretext. With fierce but futile opposition from the French and the handful of British Regulars later famed as the "Old Contemptibles," the *Reichswehr* advanced as far as Meaux, only fourteen miles from Paris, before running out of steam. A French counteroffensive forced the Germans back east of the Aisne River. It was autumn 1914:

So it was that, as the leaves fell and the ground turned to mud and the German howitzers with their twelve-horse teams plodded patiently up to the line, the British Army was poised over an abyss. It could be saved only by a reckless squandering of the virtues which, like its delusions, sprang from a background of peace and a stable, ordered society. Bravery, perfect discipline, absolute conviction of right and wrong and the existence of God; a whole code of behaviour that is now little more than an object of derision—these were to be pitted against the largest and most highly trained army in the world.[16]

France and England could be strangled if Germany could secure the French and Belgian seaports. The British, many still thinking of war in sporting terms, won "the race to the sea." Then came the first bloody Battle of Ypres in April 1915 as the Germans tried desperately to force the line, using poison gas for the first time. The British held on, and the war bogged down in muddy stalemate as winter set in. Through 1915 and 1916 there was strong pressure on the high commands of both sides to break the dead-lock. The British tried at Loos and Neuve Chapelle, but the Germans had prepared even a defensive third line with Teutonic thoroughness.

Much of the early optimism was expressed publicly in printed material that was purported to be without official sponsorship, when evidently it had originated with the government's psychological engineers to keep up public

morale. At least some of the published material may have been from the
rank and file, but it had been carefully culled and edited to represent only
approved attitudes. A book entitled *Made in the Trenches*, published to raise
funds for a home for disabled veterans, claims to be "composed entirely
from articles & sketches contributed by soldiers."[17] There is no evidence in
it of any real bitterness toward authority, and even in the best of conditions
that alone would make it somewhat suspect as a true voice of soldiers. The
daring punch line of an exchange between two privates about another's
winning the DCM is, "Blimey, why ain't I got one too? I hid in the same
dugout." Not a bad cut at the inequities of the awards system; yet no such
humor appears relating to officers, when the distribution of honors to senior
command and staff was becoming a notorious joke among the troops.

This book includes a reprint from the *Daily Mail* entitled "The 'sure-to-
be-hit' Feeling." Examples are given of men whose presentiments of death
have proven unfounded, and the irrational cause is given:

Being "off colour" is accountable for some of them, and the losing temporarily of
one's grip over oneself for the remainder. It would be easy to be miserable and
depressed. Cheeriness is mainly a matter of spirit.

If that little apothegm failed to boost a "windy" reader out of the doldrums,
he could read about "The Moaner," a poem dedicated cleverly to the "A/
Adj. to the 1st Moaners Battalion." A sample of its lines: "He'd moan at
the sergeants and wish them in H—l. . . . He'd moan at the mud and he'd
moan at the dust,/He'd moan at his rifle and leave it to rust." No good for
the frontlines, the bad soldier is given "the run of the Q. M. store" to finish
out the war in ignominious safety with other grousers.

In a nobly tearful tale entitled "The Padre," a chaplain during a field
service asks his soldier congregation if they would like to sing another hymn.
"A . . . tough nut, . . . whose very presence at a voluntary service is a source
of wonder—suggests 'Abide with Me' " as the German artillery strikes up
a counterpoint. If the reader knows what's good for him, he will find refuge
from fear in army-dispensed religion. The tale proves the point with a vignette as the padre tends a dying soldier:

"Don't trouble, padre," the words come in fitful gasps. "I'm done in; my number's
up. I've been a bad lot, but I tried to do my little bit."
"God knows," and there's a world of pathos in the tone; "and He is more merciful
than man."

Not to worry, then. Death in battle is virtuous, and in exchange for soldierly
services rendered, God will turn a blind eye to earlier transgressions.

Then there is "The Winged Hun," a witty commentary about the continual summer war against flies in the trenches. To win against them is im-

possible, because "a policy of attrition is futile. The armies of the Allies could never 'attrite' the armies of General Fly." The lighthearted inference is that attrition *is* a sane and practical military doctrine for war against the *human* Hun, whose numbers are finite. With what good humor does the writer accept the premise that the winner of the Great War simply will be the general with men left alive!

The most popular of this genre, the work of Bruce Bairnsfather, creator of the "Old Bill" cartoons, exemplifies the soldier's vitality and simple faith early in the war. Captain Bairnsfather's military life was itself a paradigm of the cast of mind he both possessed and portrayed. A major's son born in India, he served in France as a machine gun officer before being "blown up by a shell" at the Second Battle of Ypres and evacuated as a shell-shock casualty.[18] Bairnsfather's accounts and cartoon collections—*Fragments from France, The Better 'Ole, From Mud to Mufti*, and *Old Bill, M. P. I.*—abound with jollity, vigor, and keenness about his duties. Even descriptions of the wet and cold and fatigue of trench warfare show a man living his war intensely, his morale shored up by certainties yet unshaken:

Having rapidly realized that there was not the slightest prospect of sleep, and that the morrow looked like being a busy day, we commenced with characteristic vigour to carry out our nefarious design. . . .
The nervy Boches had spotted our sap as something new, and their bullets, whacking up against our newly thrown up parapet, made us glad we had worked so busily.

Bairnsfather's account of the fraternizing between opposing armies at Christmas 1914 is revealing of the then-prevalent attitudes:

It did not lessen our ardour or determination; but just put a little human punctuation mark in our lives of cold and humid hate. . . . [H]ere were these sausage-eating wretches, who had elected to start this infernal European fracas, and in so doing had brought us all into the same muddy pickle as themselves. . . . It was just like the interval between rounds in a friendly boxing match. The difference in type between our men and theirs was very marked. . . . [O]ur men, superior, broadminded, more frank, and lovable beings, were regarding these faded, unimaginative products of perverted Kulture [sic] as a set of objectionable but amusing lunatics whose heads had *got* to be eventually smacked.

Here is little of the common sympathy that later grew from shared misery. For Bairnsfather the Christmas camaraderie is a brief suspension of "hate," yet contradictorily the war is still a "friendly boxing match." Boche soldiers are shown as different beings, morally and militarily inferior to the British. They are not portrayed as victims of a rotten war foisted on them by rotten politicians. Rather, they collectively are naughty loonies who have got out of hand.

Their straightening out was to be done by stock characters: "Our Bert,"

"Alf," and "Old Bill," comic figures created out of old assumptions about the tough, uncomplaining, and doggishly loyal lower classes. Presumably, they were thought to have enough imagination to find humor in discomfort, but not enough to suffer like their betters. Whether many regarded themselves in the same light is hard to say, because the literature of the period was still largely by officers and civilians. In Bairnsfather's cartoons Old Bill is the happy warrior of the trenches—in balaclava helmet, sporting a walrus moustache, stumpy pipe stuck in his mouth, bundled in a bulky greatcoat, his legs and boots like puttee-bound tree trunks growing out of the mud.

His mates' and his own captioned one-liners are the wryly understated wit of dugout domesticity: [Huddled over a brazier on a cold night] "Chuck us the biscuits, Bill. The fire wants mendin' "; [Sitting on outpost near the putrifying corpse of a horse] " 'Ow about shiftin' a bit further down the road, Fred?"; [In reading a letter in a trench filled with water to the waist] "Poor old Maggie! She seems to be 'aving it dreadful wet at 'ome;" [Sprawled under sandbags after a near miss by mortars] "They're devils to snipe, ain't they, Bill?" The soldiers in Bairnsfather's cartoons have neither steel helmet nor respirator, the soon-to-appear symbols of the impersonality and randomness of war technology, and the powerlessness of strength and will to succeed in fair combat. War and the soldier were still being thought of in traditional ways, although already there had been massive artillery bombardments, gas was being used, and the New Army was being readied in England to fill the thinning ranks.

An almost quantifiable shift in focus and tone occurs in material written after the early great battles had been fought and when the war had become a stationary slugging match. Attitudes did not change overnight; but if we were to seek a seminal date symbolic of a change in war literature as reflections of the soldier's altered view of war and his relationship to it, it would be 1 July 1916.

The background of events was this: The early engagements destroyed the old Regular Army and more. Yet the Allied high command seemed incapable of any strategy but that of repeating the same mistakes by throwing more men against machine guns and barbed wire. From the perspective of regimental officers and men, the high command committing these crimes was remote, incompetent, stubborn, and uncaring of life. The hated staff was a glimpse of motor cavalcades in rear areas, polished Sam Browne belts, cavalry boots, and red tabs.

Through 1915 the British had been learning painfully that the traditional metaphors of blood sport and field games did not fit the inglorious processes of this war. By 1916 Germany was suffering too, with food rationing and *ersatz* coffee as effects of Britain's sea blockade. Germany was trying to break the stranglehold at sea by stepping up submarine warfare, and on land by trying another big push. This was a concentration of force on Verdun, France's best fortified part of the line. The French held on through April and May of 1916 under continual shelling and attack, while the French government and high command were showing their exasperation with the British, and exhorting them to save France by opening another major offensive.

This was to be the disaster of 1 July, remembered now simply as "The Somme." Paul Fussell writes, "Before it took place the Battle of the Somme was referred to as The Big Push. Afterwards, it was known, at least among the survivors, as 'The Great Fuck-Up'."[19] Already having had to take over much of the French front because of France's awful losses at Verdun, the Empire's forces were now to undertake a mass offensive of vaster proportions than anything hitherto imagined on an 18-mile front. How does one write about a battle when its scale means rounding off individual souls to the nearest tens of thousands? We can only recount the common experience that affected so many so deeply, that ever since it has been seen as a major turning point in attitudes toward the war, and thus to the British soldier's self-conception.

Frontline preparations for the big push began on the night of 30 June/1 July, as parties worked silently and feverishly with wire cutters, clearing gaps in the wire in front of their own trenches. During the early hours of 1 July, troops in support trenches, rear area villages, and tented camps roused themselves and moved off to assembly areas in the forward trenches, where they awaited their moment to go "over the top." By decree of the General Staff, the soldiers were dressed in "battle order," or should have been.[20] Battle order consisted of rifle, bayonet, webbing, haversack, respirator, and full waterbottle. The basic ammunition load was 150 rounds of .303 ball, and the day's ration issue was hard tack and canned bullybeef. The official total weight was sixty-six pounds, not conducive to sprinting, but not unmanageable either. The problem was in the additional stores and equipment that troops were required to carry: Mills bombs, shovels, picks, sandbags, field telephones, knife rests, ladders, Lewis gun drum buckets, "Bangalore torpedoes" for breaching wire, and so on. So convinced was the General Staff that the assault would succeed, that the order for the bearing of these unreasonable burdens was in the belief that there would be an immediate need for the troops to consolidate the positions they overran.

At 0625 hours in gray dawn, the Allied artillery began its softening-up barrage, although the Germans were so well dug in that it had little effect. At 0728 hours the assault began in broad daylight. All along the line men struggled up scaling ladders propped against fire steps, and advanced through the gaps in their own wire, lurching and staggering under their burdens across the cratered no-man's-land, unable to advance much faster than a walk or slow double. The German machine gunners emerged from their deep dugouts as the barrage lifted, and British Tommies fell like harvest wheat. By the time the attack ended, the Allies had advanced only six miles at the most anywhere, and in many areas, not a yard. Casualties were staggering on both sides. The German army lost about 600,000 men, only 65,000 of whom were made prisoners; the French lost about 200,000, and the British about 450,000. Once more the opposing armies settled down to their massive duel of attrition.

Aside from the cast of mind that brought about this horror, the high command had blundered in even the most basic of planning. Haig had placated Joffre, the Allied commander-in-chief, and France's Marshal, by delaying the attack until full daylight because the French liked to see the effects of their artillery. As if that were not bad enough, Haig's staff had caused troops to be so encumbered that there was little chance of them getting clear of machine gun fields of fire before they were cut down. The enormity of the slaughter and the needless waste of life through the blindness of generals who hardly knew what the frontline looked like was not lost on the survivors. If the soldier had not listened before, now he learned a lesson about the way his leaders regarded him in the grand scheme: he was expendable flesh.

From this point, the sporting metaphor vanished from serious war literature, surviving only in officially "sanctioned" publications. One such, an artful book called A "Temporary Gentleman" in France, appeared in 1916 by "permission" of the War Office.[21] Its cover shows a Bairnsfather cartoon of a New Army lieutenant contentedly sharing his lunch with a giant rat that looks more like a fugitive from a Beatrix Potter book than a hideous creature of the trenches, fattened on corpses.

The expression "Temporary Gentleman," referring to citizens commissioned as "Temporary Officers" for "the duration of hostilities," bore the assumption that they otherwise either never would have thought of joining the army, or would not even have been acceptable socially as officers. Yet it also bore the assumption that Temporary Officers accepted for a time the old army's traditional strictures, values, and standards of gentleman officership. The book purportedly is a collection of letters from a typical Temporary Gentleman, and to make sure that the reader does not miss his touching ordinariness, the editor includes a short biographical epigram. He comes of a suburban London family, his deceased father a conscientious small businessman who has left his widow with modest means. The Temporary Gentleman has attended a day school (not a public school!) and has become an auctioneer's clerk, played cricket and football, and bicycled. Stirred by a "recruiting song" he has joined up, and through his training has become "magnified, developed, tuned up, brought to concert pitch."

The editor exults in "those great middle classes which have given us so many thousands of officers of the type which the writer of these letters represents." Ironically the editor has referred in his introduction to the "argument our officers, and the inimitably courageous men they lead, have been presenting with some emphasis since July 1" to the Germans. He concludes, "If anything in the race is inexhaustible, the supply of these types is." More realistically, the toll on Britain's leader class had been so great by the summer of 1916 that the War Office had to reach into the commercial classes for men whose family and even accent would have excluded them from commissioned rank in the prewar army. The collected letters of this "Temporary Gentleman" probably were fabricated to pass off the Somme as a victory justifying appalling losses and to reinforce traditional attitudes in officers who before the war were not army "types" at all: "though their Commissions may be 'Temporary,' [they] are not only fine officers but, permanently and by nature, gentlemen and sportsmen."

A few excerpts from these probably apocryphal letters indicate their purpose: "It really was a wonderful journey from Salisbury Plain, with never a hitch of any sort of kind. . . . Someone with a pretty good headpiece must arrange these things." [Translation: Trust the Authorities and don't question. We are looking after you.] "I think the French are glad to see us. The people in the town are quite keen on our drums and bugles. . . . It makes you 'throw a chest.' " [Translation: Never doubt that you are heroic and loved.] "Our noble company commander . . . [is] keen on knuckle-duster daggers. . . . It's his spirit that's made 'A' Company what it is." [Translation: Your commander is always fine and right. Cultivate your aggressive urges, then get out there and kill!] "[W]hen the ration-wagon's late and a man drops half his whack in the mud, he grins and says, 'The army of today's all *right*.'" [Translation: It is un-British to be discontented with your lot. If your officer corrects you or if things get you down, save up your frustrations and take them out on the enemy.] "God bless all the sweet brave waiting women of England and France, and Russia." [Translation: The Allies are beautiful because they are right. The personifications of their national ideals are the women waiting for you to do your duty before you come home. You mustn't disappoint them.] "[T]he Boche has rather shut the door on chivalry. . . . [Y]ou cannot possibly treat him as a sportsman, because he'll do you down every time." [Translation: If you have to violate the decencies of civilized combat, it's not your fault.] "And I take it as evidence of the moral superiority being on this side of the line, that we see very much more of their trenches than they ever see of ours." [Translation: You cannot lose, because your cause is right.] "Great and glorious news! The push is a fact." [Translation: Nothing is more exhilarating and worthwhile than a jolly attack.] "[I]f the entire casualties in the whole advance are weighed up against the position won, I believe I am right in saying that the cost was remarkably low." [Translation: If your son died at the Somme, or if you were wounded there, never mind. That was a small price to pay for such a grand victory.]

With the failure of the Somme, offensive war on the Western Front settled down to murderous "artillery duels" and suicidal frontal assaults. Success and failure could be measured only in yards of trench held and lost, and the numbers of dead and wounded left after "strafes." In any one of several massive bombardments and assaults, more British soldiers died than all the casualties of both sides on D-Day, 1944. There was little glory even for the romantic, in a war of attrition. Meanwhile, ignorance of war and militant jingoism were as strong as ever at home, and the more that war-weary soldiers saw of it when they returned—on leave if they were lucky and mutilated if they were not—the greater became the gulf between citizens who fought and those who did not. In frustration at his hero's welcome the soldier knew that it was hopeless to try to describe to the innocents at home a war defying description.

How could you describe drowning in the din of a bombardment that seemed to last an eternity, then left you gasping and trying to hold onto your wits, or watching claustrophobically through a respirator's fogged eye pieces as a mate strangulated in a green sea of chlorine vapor, or waiting for the barrage to lift as the signal for the advance, the SRD: ("Service Rum Demarara") grog a hot ball in your gut, but not touching the awful falling feeling, or shamble-running loaded down with gear, across torn-up soil past sickly-smelling bundles of blue-white meat in crumpled grey cloth caught up on your own wire, or cowering with trembling jaw and heaving chest in a crater and listening to the measured hammering of the machine guns' traversing fire, joy at still living spoiled by fear of being found out a coward.

If you were lucky, you got a "blighty" that would put you out of commission honorably just for the "duration of hostilities." If you were less fortunate, you would be permanently maimed, or if you were less fortunate still, you would recover and be sent back to live it over again. And through it all you might never meet a "Hun" face to face. He was a sufferer like you, bearing his own cross to Calvary along with you. So who was the enemy? The War Office politicians who fed you lies, your own commanders and staffs, the "brass hats" and "red tabs" who fed you false hopes and tinned bully beef, then sent you out as burnt offering, and the patriots at home, who kept spewing hatred and cheering you on to your Golgotha. Well, if it was your duty to stand by your chums and die for them, you would—but not for the cushy hypocrites who oozed Christianity and lied to you that the Fritzes bayoneted Belgian babies for sport. The old lies just wouldn't wash any more.

The stalemate continued through 1917. The French and British kept trying to force the German line, at terrible cost of life. Passchendaele and Cambrai, the first mass tank attack, brought only minor success. France was desperate for food, and its army was mutinous. Russia was in revolutionary chaos. The United States finally declared war on 1 April 1917, and not a moment too soon for the Allies. America's vast conscripted army needed time to train, and would not take the field until the following spring. Meanwhile, British troops hung on wearily and fearfully.

GAMESMEN AND VICTIMS

> If you could hear, at every jolt, the blood
> Come gargling from the froth-corrupted lungs,
> Obscene as cancer, bitter as the cud
> Of vile, incurable sores on innocent tongues,—
> My friend, you would not tell with such high zest
> To children ardent for some desperate glory,
> The old Lie: Dulce et decorum est
> Pro patria mori.
>
> Wilfred Owen, *Dulce et Decorum Est*[22]

World War One's citizen-soldier became a self-acknowledged victim and martyr, with pride in his strength to endure the unendurable. "In the three lines of trenches the main business of the soldier was to exercise self-control while being shelled."[23] In the mind of the new breed of warrior the old grandiose notions of military honor—dashing cavalry charges, pomp and ceremony, escapades in the Khyber Pass and on the South African *veldt*—belonged in the pages of the *Boy's Own Paper* or as tales told round campfires to Lord Baden-Powell's shiny-faced Boy Scouts. World War I soldiers felt they had honor enough if they could simply survive and not commit suicide or try to run away in a "funk."

To be sure, the late Victorian and Edwardian years had seen the flourishing of neochivalric sentiment among the English upper classes. Any number of stained-glass knights in public school chapel windows attest to the pressure on young gentlemen to grow up to be England's new Sir Galahads and Saint Georges.[24] For many, that early indoctrination would not withstand the reality of modern war. Men who had a taste of trench life were ready to agree with Shakespeare's Falstaff that honor of the glorious Hotspur variety "is a mere scutcheon." Their visions of soldiering and battle soon contracted to the few feet of mud they occupied with one or two chums; all the high idealism and love of regiment shrank to the immediate, personal, and nearly inexpressible comradeship of men who had nothing left to hold onto but faith in each other. After 1916 that basic human value was the line soldier's common experience.

The citizen-soldier may have started out on what he thought would be a chivalresque quest of arms, but once in the trenches he came to understand that his mental stamina was being tested without the opportunity of quest. Of course, there were night trench raids and large-scale assaults which usually bogged down in slaughterous machine gun fire. But by far the most common experiences were seeming eternities of dozing in "funk holes," shivering stand-to's on fire steps at dawn, and the nightly tedium of carrying party duties, sloshing blindly over submerged duck boards and through suckin-gooze, loaded down with munitions and rations needed for living through another day of waiting to die.

If the realities of World War I made nonsense of the traditional myths of honor and chivalry, neither were many soldiers prepared to believe that their lives and deaths were without meaning. Ultimate meaning was seen to lie in death itself. This altered view of military honor was not simply antimilitarism; on the contrary, it was incorporated into the military ethos. The idea of Christ as ancient precedent for the warrior winning his victory by participation in his own death was shared enthusiastically by young English Gamesmen-Galahads. Officers of a generation trained in the rigorously Christian public school traditions established by the renowned Doctor Arnold of Rugby were ideally molded to their view of themselves as Christian martyrs. To die unwillingly and by accident as mere passive victims could happen to animals. There was no grace in that; so many of the Great War's soldiers found comfort in a conviction of active martyrdom.

For others, the sacrificial view seemed a mockery of faith. Like Wilfred Owen, whose poignant poem "Dulce et Decorum Est" bears grim testimony to the folly of jingoistic sentiment when it wastes young lives, many men at the front were disillusioned about their dying martyrs' deaths for a noble cause. If dying was the way to grace, there was something wrong. For most soldiers, it seemed obvious that doctrine should celebrate living. They had seen the ugliness of death, and they had felt the beauty of life. Yet, those who sent them to die seemed to have it backwards. They were victims of the illusions of others, by being told to think like martyrs. The martyred soldier as a Christ figure became a commonplace symbol. Kipling's poem "Gethsemane," about a soldier drinking from the bitter "cup" of poison gas, the ubiquitous references throughout the letters and literature of this war to roadside crucifixes, and legends of miraculous visitations, all became part of the self-conceptions held by many soldiers.

Many at home who had never experienced the fear and fatigue of life in the line indulged in maudlin regret at soldiers' deaths, while reassuring each other that they had not died in vain. In *War Letters of a Public School Boy* a proud and loving father presented correspondence by his son Lieutenant Paul Jones, Tank Corps, killed in action in July 1917.[25] The "Memoir" by Paul's father gives a portrait of an ideal British youth, typical of the Great War's junior officers: a Dulwich College boy, matriculant from London University with honors, cricketer, football captain, and winner of the "Victor Ludorum" shield. His single flaw seems to have been defective eyesight, and he had to settle for a commission in the Army Service Corps. The father's jolly description of Paul's first unit, the 9th Cavalry Brigade, shows complete ignorance of conditions at the front:

[The] Brigade . . . took part in the severe fighting of the early months of the War and was now waiting eagerly for a fresh opportunity to display its prowess. Our Cavalry officers are a distinct type, with traditions and modes of life and thought of their own. . . . He [Paul] found them gay-hearted, chivalrous gentlemen, and soon shared their enthusiasm for horses.

That the writer's enthusiasm seems not at all tempered by events shows the impenetrable wall of conviction set up by those at home, and a good thing too in a way. It must have made acceptance of a son's death easier than belief that it was simply a waste of life.

The "Memoir" tells of Paul's discontent and sense of guilt at not being in a fighting unit. Paul eventually engineered a transfer to the Tank Corps, and wrote home:

Had I remained in my post of Requisitioning Officer, . . . I would have been moderately content. But in my heart and soul I have always longed for the rough-and-tumble of war as for a football match. . . . It is not only my own desire and my own temperament that influence me, but the example of others. . . . Why, that a fellow that sat in the same form-room as I did two years back has won the V.C., paying, it is true, with his life for the honour. But what a glorious end! . . . The effect on me is as a trumpet call. All my old Welsh fighting blood comes surging up in me and makes me say, "Short sight or no short sight, I *will* prove my manhood!"

Paul finally saw action at Arras in April 1917. In the final letter before his death in July, his new first-hand taste of war tempered his attitudes only slightly. A note of doubt creeps in: "Of course, the other side of the picture is bound to occur to the imagination. But there! I have never been one to take the more melancholy view."

Before the Somme and even afterwards the public indulged a failure of imagination hovering somewhere between cynical commercialism and mawkish sentimentality. The *London Times* for 10 March 1916, just three months before the slaughter at the Somme, contained an advertisement for a " 'Lest we forget' Memorial Medal" commemorating the fallen, and describing the medal's pictorial representation of "Death upon the Battlefield" as more noble and beautiful even than life. The obverse represents Britannia crowning with a wreath of laurel the fallen Hero who in his dying moments still clasps the Union Jack . . . ; The reverse . . . [is] indicative of our mighty Empire, to die for which there is no comparable sacrifice."[26] Such effusions became obscenities for men at the front, nor would it be lost on them that someone was making a profit from the glorious dead.

Cynicism was not universal, however. Many young men imbued with the old public school values, and those close to them who grieved when they died, were touchingly certain of the sanctity of their nation's mission. *A Student in Arms* (1917) is one of the most moving expressions of self-conscious hagiography. Although its publication for motivational purposes cannot be discounted, the account has a ring of conviction. It contains the observations of Donald Hankey, an infantry officer who was killed going "over the top" in October 1916. J. St. Loe Strachey writes in his introduction to the Second Series:

Six days after this [from the date of Hankey's last letter] the Student [Hankey] knelt down for a few seconds with his men—we have it on the testimony of one of them—and he told them a little of what was before them: "If wounded, 'Blighty'; if killed, the Resurrection."[27]

Whether we are to believe this uncommon display of spontaneous and unembarrassed religious devotion by a whole platoon is not the point. The sentiment is true.

By and large, the citizen-soldier lived neither with ecstatic visions of death sanctified by sacrifice, nor in a state of constant near-mutinous complaint. He resigned himself to what had to be, and put up with it as cheerfully as he could. A chaplain in France in 1918 wrote in *A Soldier's Calvary*:

He [the soldier] is going out to be mutilated or die. That is his standpoint whatever may be the general's or the war-correspondent's. He goes for his country's sake and the right,—It is his duty, and there is an end on it. Most of the killing in modern war is done by the artillery and machine-guns. Comparatively few men have seen the face of an enemy they know themselves to have killed. A regiment goes out to be shot at, rather than to shoot. Until this simple fact be grasped, the mentality of the soldier cannot be understood.[28]

Motives for carrying on were both simpler and more complex than the chaplain's attribution of traditionally approved ones. Yet, there is psychological insight in his description of a state of mind arising from a need to accept the inevitable. As introduction to a collection of "War Letters of Fallen Englishmen,"[29] Laurence Housman describes two "voices":

A large majority, though firmly convinced that what they do is right—or right in the sense that it is inevitable—show their detestation of war in its operation. Yet some of these express the keen satisfaction it gives them as an individual experience—mainly as a test of themselves, of their power to conquer fear, to live at the full push of their energies, mental and physical.

But alongside of this standpoint there are others equally worthy of respect—representative of other types of mind and character, of men who are not born fighters, men who have had a hard struggle to conquer their individual fears, temperaments, and disgusts, and have not come through with elation, or even with conviction.

In essence Housman describes the distinction between martyr and victim. Lieutenant Harry Sackville Lawson, Royal Field Artillery, ex-headmaster of Buxton College, was self-consciously a martyr in a letter he wrote to his former pupils in 1917:

I've got one thing in particular to say to you all—just the main thing we've talked about together in its different bearings in the past—just one important thing which keeps life sweet and clean and gives us peace of mind. It's a Christian thing, and it's a British thing. It's what the Bible teaches—its what the Christian martyrs suffered in persecution for. It soon found root in England and began not only to fill the land, but also to spread abroad and become the heritage of the Empire. It's the story of the Crusaders, of the Reformation, ... The thing is this: Playing the game for the game's sake.

Lieutenant Lawson, Christian martyr, English Crusader, and gamesman at arms, was killed the following year, by his own lights triumphant.

In the same vein, a letter from Private Roger Marshall Livingstone, 44th Battalion, CEF (Canadian Expeditionary Force), to his mother in October 1917 set her straight about the soldier's role:

It is evident that you do not understand, but I shall put it to you this way; Do you realize that Christ was the first one to fall in the present war? How? Well, simply this: The very principles for which Christ gave His life are identically those principles for which Britain is to-day giving her life-blood.

Private Livingstone died of wounds the same month.

Then there was the voice of the victim, who saw no purpose at all in the suffering and death. A letter by Captain William John Mason, Gloucestershire Regiment, written in the autumn of 1915, is full of despair:

I don't know how anyone can "glory" in war except perhaps during the actual heat of an attack, then you cease to be yourself, and are released from all ordinary cares and associations. . . .
And what can you think then except of the crass stupidity of mankind in waging war. . . .
What a cruel and mad diversion of human activity! Food indeed for pessimism if ever there was.

Captain Mason was killed just two days after the first Somme offensive.

A letter from nineteen-year-old Second Lieutenant William Henry Ratcliffe, South Staffordshire Regiment, to his parents shows the wisdom of early experience of war:

I was reading a story in one of the magazines that you sent out which was trying to prove that this war had a good effect on men's minds and made them more religious than they were before. Whilst I was in Jersey I really thought that this was the case. . . . But now that I am out here, I must confess that I . . . think that war has an almost degrading effect on the minds of soldiers. What is there out here to raise a man's mind out of the rut? Everywhere one sees preparations for murder; . . . Everywhere the work of God is spoiled by the hand of man.

Lieutenant Ratcliffe was killed the next month, on the day of the first Somme offensive.

Many of the soldiers of World War I died as victims of outworn values they understood imperfectly but believed in implicitly. They went to war consciously as martyrs to defend the status quo, and unconsciously as victims, because the status quo in many ways was not worth the dying. Soon many caught on to this bitter joke. They began to see beneath the hypocrisy, and to view themselves as victims of geriatric political and social systems subscribed to by old men who sacrificed their own young. Yet, at home few ordinary British citizens doubted the rightness of war, and they could not conceive that their warrior sons were dupes of the establishment and its profiteers.

Few citizen-soldiers were martyrs in a way that those at home could understand properly. War comrades died for each other, and not for anyone or anything else; not for nation, regiment, or any such abstractions as "freedom." Until the Great War, British and European monuments to soldiers and battles commonly had been stone and bronze effigies of generals on horseback, or heroically posed figures symbolic of the nation's martial prowess, draped in flags and holding aloft wreaths of laurel. After the Armistice of 1918 monuments appeared figuring common soldiers—somewhat idealized to be sure, but much as they were in life—and on the pedestals the names of the war dead. No longer the pomp of ceremonial to commemorate the glories of Waterloo and Sebastopol. The dead of the Great War remembered by fellow citizens in two-minutes' silence between the mournful bugle notes of the Last Post and Reveille were the archetypes of a new idea of soldier: martyred citizen in uniform.

VERSE AND FICTION OF THE FIRST WORLD WAR

> [A]ll things that lived and moved and had volition and life might at any moment be resolved into scarlet viscosity seeping into the earth of torn fields. . . . Nay, it had been revealed to you that beneath Ordered life itself was stretched, the merest film with, beneath it, the abysses of chaos. . . .
>
> Ford Madox Ford, *It Was the Nightingale*[30]

The poetry of the war's early stages had the stamp of all the old moral certainties, absolute conviction in the righteousness of England's cause and the propriety of war as the means of its achievement, and at first complete ignorance of its potential destructiveness. In "The Fourth of August" (1914) Laurence Binyon idealized Britain's soldiers as a collective abstraction, the

spirit of England, "ardent-eyed," and "purified," going "in their splendour."
In "Men Who March Away" (1914) Thomas Hardy advanced the old medieval doctrine of trial by combat, that "Victory crowns the just." The poem
has that same sporting public school spirit of *Tom Brown's School Days*, as if
this war were to be simply a larger version of Tom's thrashing the bully
Flashman, for braggarts "Surely bite the dust." In "Happy is England Now"
John Freeman exulted over the wonder of Britons moving towards "the deep.
Of an unguessed and unfeared future." Sharing England's happiness in "the
brave that die," he seems to have been oblivious to the possibility of a
nation's grieving at the waste of life. In W. N. Hodgson's "England to Her
Sons" England hears youth "thrilling/To the trumpet call of war;" and ex-
horts them to "gird" for battle.

These early war poets' thoughts had been molded in the passing age; they
could not know or feel what soldier poets were soon to learn. Laurence
Binyon was forty-eight years old when World War I began, Thomas Hardy
was seventy-four, and John Freeman was a thirty-four-year-old businessman
who never went to war. W. N. Hodgson was a mere twenty-one, a public
school product, and an early volunteer. In France, with the Devonshire
Regiment in 1915, he was mentioned in dispatches and awarded the Military
Cross. He was killed at the Somme on 1 July 1916. The tone of his verse
might have darkened had he lived to ponder the meaning of all that dying.

World War I poetry and novel fiction by those who fought has the quality
of a memoir given only a thin skein of imagination. Siegfried Sassoon had
lived the experience he wrote about in his persona as George Sherston (*The
Memoirs of George Sherston*). Indeed, his fictional friend David Cromlech was
his real-life friend Robert Graves (*Goodbye to All That*). Much of the war
poetry has the same subjective directness. While most of the novel fiction
was written as emotion recollected in tranquility during the '20s and '30s,
much of the poetry was jotted on field message pads, letters, and cigarette
packets in the trenches. Not only were the writers articulate, but many were
accomplished classicists with rich cultural backgrounds and creative skills.

The verse of the war poets reflects their suffering where there can be no
victor. In "Nightfall" Death wears a crown, for "no emperor hath won, save
He."[31] One is struck by the dawning of a new understanding that this war
ran counter to God's creation, to nature itself. In "After the Salvo" the poet
contrasts a trench rat and "a skull, torn out of the graves" with an iridescent,
azure butterfly. A poppy grows at a crater's edge, and while men destroy their
own dwelling places, "the spider lives."

This common theme, the poets' joy in creation and living things, inten-
sified in the presence of man-wrought destruction and death. The poetry
tells of men who went insane, "mowed" and "raved," up to their necks in
mud,[32] and of a man maimed horribly with "Both . . . legs shot away."[33] There
was a worse fate for the deserter, the "shameless soul" of a "nameless man"
going up in "cordite smoke."[34] Soldier-poets wrote of resignation at the

prospect of death, "for some go early, and some go late;"[35] and one poet mourned the deaths of the "beautiful men" of his company, whom he had led and loved.[36] Robert Graves wrote of the randomness of death in seeing two soldiers killed by the same shell, "Together tumbling in one heap."[37]

Verses told of old verities shaken, of a smiling general who greeted troops on their way up the line, now "most of 'em dead," and of the general's staff whom those still living curse for "incompetent swine."[38] As faith grew dim soldiers wondered about the glory of death in battle, whether the dead "found everlasting day," or were "sucked in by everlasting night."[39] Even the fond belief that the warrior's death might have a meaning was shaken. There were no "passing bells" for men who died like "cattle," their only requiem "the monstrous anger of the guns."[40] A soldier, aching for an end to a seeming eternity of psychic pain, begged of his Lord to know how long before the "crimson-welling carnage" would abate.[41] The soldier-poets' plaint reached its fullest voice with Siegfried Sassoon's cry to Jesus to "make it stop,"[42] a plea for time itself to cease its destructive race.

In March of 1918 Germany was able to rally briefly when Bolshevik Russia bowed out of the War with the Brest-Litovsk Treaty. Germany brought troops from the East to the Western Front, and with Ukrainian oil and wheat available, this was the moment for a final big effort before the Americans got into the war. A German offensive split the French and British armies, and the German army broke out across the Somme. But the German advance bogged down. At the Marne, Ludendorff's desperate "Friedensturm" shattered itself on the French artillery, despite the capture of Chateau Thierry. From here on the allied counter-offensive with massive American participation steam-rollered over the German lines. The Argonne Forest, the pursuit to Mons, and on 11 November 1918 it was all over.

Counterpoint to the victory madness in Trafalgar Square of "banging drums, tootling penny trumpets," and "a blare of tin mouth organs"[43] is a solemn note by poets seeing by turns meaning and meaninglessness in the warriors' sacrifices. Personified Victory is cautioned to "lift not thy trumpet," but to go "over hollows full of old wire" where "the long-dead lie." If sacrifice had done nothing else, it had revealed a truth about hypocrisy and war. Even Kipling's sentiment towards England and her soldiers had been altered by the holocaust; speaking for the dead he gives the reason for their sacrifice: "because our fathers lied."[44] No longer was the soldier a tough old regular playing out his own destiny by facing his enemy head on in a desperate game. Now he was a citizen victim of the very people who ordered him to war to protect them. Dying, he martyred himself to an ideal of love and justice that they never understood. By 11 A.M., 11 November 1918, the British soldier, once seen as purposeful hunter had become the hunted.

Whereas the War Poets' vision was limited in the main to the immediate horrors of the battlefield, much of the later fiction affords a broad view of the war in its cultural and social context. The Great War was the first in which Britons of all classes were compelled to serve, at first by conscience and later by law. So while some educated young officers changed their minds about their great adventure after it had started, there also were gentlemen rankers who were disaffected from the beginning. Many of them were victims not simply of the coercive democratization of military service, but of an entire social and political system. They saw the technology of destruction as merely part of a larger corrupting process which destroyed minds as well as lives. A new generation was being sacrificed to the worn-out ideals, and even greed, of the old.

The Patriot's Progress (1930). Spokesmen for their generation, the literary veterans wrote about the soldier as a military Everyman in his final days and hours. In a pathetic little account of John Bullock, Henry Williamson in *The Patriot's Progress* created a composite universal Great War soldier from his own experience.[45] The naive John Bullock's path is a grim parody of the road John Bunyan's Christian travels to his salvation. Full of newspaper rhetoric about supposed German atrocities, Bullock hurries to enlist, anxious lest the war might end before he sees "some fun." From then on, his life is a descent into a slough of degradation and "slavery."

The only vestige of Christian decency is fraudulent; a padre goes about cheering up the troops, believing "that Christ had come again to the world, arising in the comradeship of men crucified on the battlefields." Williamson concludes drily, "He died of nervous exhaustion soon after the Armistice." The only German soldiers Bullock sees are his prisoner stretcher bearers after his leg has been blown off. They are fellow victims, and one's "Good luck, Tommee" is the warmest human gesture in the novel. On Armistice Day in London, a Hun-hating old gentleman chides his son for noticing the embarrassing absence of Bullock's leg:

"This good man is a hero. Yes," he went on, "we'll see that England doesn't forget you fellows."
"We are England," said John Bullock. The old gentleman could not look him in the eyes; and the little boy ceased to wave his flag.

Journey's End (1929). Under the sustained stress of trench life, personalities could disintegrate even in healthy bodies. Many officers coped with the strain of command with whiskey, to dull the senses and strengthen the will. Robert C. Sherriff's three-act play *Journey's End* focuses on the spiritual killing in war.[46] Himself an infantry officer wounded in 1917, Sherriff had lived what he wrote about. Entirely staged in a dugout, the play is about a rifle company commander Captain Dennis Stanhope, who has been in France for three years. His nerves are shot, and he keeps going on drink. When Second Lieutenant Jimmy Raleigh, a young friend from school who has idolized Dennis, arrives as a replacement, Dennis suffers acute inward shame at his own degeneration. He has been about to become engaged to Jimmy's sister, and expresses his dread of exposure by his compulsively paranoic persecution of Jimmy. When Jimmy is mortally wounded, Stanhope briefly becomes his old caring and compassionate self. However, there is no resolution at the play's close. Dennis will have to go on facing the war and himself alone.

Death of a Hero (1929). In Richard Aldington's *Death of a Hero* the sensitive, artistic nonhero George Augustus Winterbourne has an urge to break away from the strictures which keep him from being himself.[47] He finds the conventional ideas of manliness, national pride, and military honor repugnant. For him they are mere "Cant" to justify destructive social codes and political doctrines. A "Quixotish" young man without artifice or pretension, George is victim of Victorian parents, public school instructors, women, his martinet commanding officer, and the stress of battle.

Winterbourne's life is an Aeneid of alienation. He is driven to find work he loathes, to leave home, to join the army where he is "bullied and driven" by Regular Army NCOs, and finally to suicide. His journey ends without revelation or triumph. For Aldington there was no national ideology, political doctrine, social theory, or chimera of military glory that could justify war. These were only delusions the old fostered in the young so that they would suffer and die willingly. Yet if youth had to die for an idea, the idea itself had to be false because it was a betrayal of the individual's right to life. If men's loyalty to God, King, and Country was returned only in demands for military sacrifice, then surely there had to be a larger and better conception of justice.[48]

Aldington sets up an opposition between faith in the old abstractions embodied in Winterbourne's platoon commander, the unimaginative Evans, and rebellious questionings by the Winterbourne-victims of sterile convention. Evans, an ingenuous and thoroughly indoctrinated ex-public school boy, thinks him subversive. The only enthusiasm Winterbourne shows is when he has to fill shell holes and take down wire. He explains to Evans, "We're making something, ... not desecrating the earth." Evans, who finds the sentiment dangerously "republican," has "a superstitious reverence for War":

He believed in the Empire; the Empire was symbolized by the King-Emperor; and the King—poor man—is always having to dress up as an Admiral or a field Marshall or a brass hat of some kind. Navydom and Armydom thereby acquired a mystic importance, and since armies and navies are obviously meant for War, it was plain that War was an integral part of Empire-Worship.

The Evans's were staunch soldiers, but a dying breed, and more soldiers began thinking like Winterbourne. If there was such a thing as honor in war, it lay only in avoidance of hypocrisy. Aldington comments bitterly on General Sherman's "War is hell" cliché, "Thanks for your honesty. You, at least, were an honourable murderer." The new breed of soldier took no pride in killing, and if for a time he exulted in battle ecstasy, he might later be heartily ashamed, as Siegfried Sassoon professed to be.

Hating war and the army, Winterbourne nevertheless respects soldiers as "men." They have endured hardship by forming deep comradeships rather than by hating other soldiers who they are told are the enemy; "their manhood existed in spite of the war, and not because of it." The only real enemies were "the sneaks and the unscrupulous, the false ideals, the unintelligent ideas imposed upon them, the humbug, the hypocrisy, the stupidity." The credo of the new soldier was hatred of pomp and pretense, and pride in how much misery he could take and still help his comrades to survive. When his sphere of action contracted to his small circle of fellow-sufferers, his moral sphere grew infinitely to transcend patriotic creeds.

Winterbourne's prewar life shows him as natural victim of a system that killed nonconformists. His parents are typical of late Victorian middle-class culture—guilt-ridden, conventional, and obsessed with an appearance of propriety. Winterbourne Senior's profession as lawyer is more a status qualification than occupation, and his wife Isabel is "poor army," her father a retired Regular Army captain. Each had thought that the other would bring financial ease to the marriage, but they have outwitted each other by appearances. Their lives are grinding poverty, sanctimonious piety, and sexual repression.

George's finer feelings, expressed in his attempts at poetry and painting, are assaulted by brutalizing social norms. He endures a public school life in which development of "character" is thought to be education's most important function. Fondness and aptitude for "games," readiness to conform and subscribe to convention, a hearty blood instinct, and enjoyment of militarism in the school's OTC (Officer Training Corps), are designed to make George "manly." Early a victim of an economic system that starved talent, George prostitutes himself as a hack journalist. He leaves home when his sex-obsessed and paranoically suspicious mother accuses him of visiting prostitutes.

Like his mother, the other women in his life "neither want nor understand Quixotic behavior and scrupulousness." George breaks free of old moral strictures with his first love Elizabeth, and later in obedience to a doctrine of free love, he has another lover Fanny. He is hopeless in trying to understand either of them. Elizabeth and Fanny's competition gets in the way of their Free Love doctrines, and George is victim of their sexual tyranny. Like World War I which made victims of warriors, this is *amour courtoise* inside out. George is the hunted and never the hunter. Valuable to both women as a quarry to be "bagged," he joins the army because he is "fed up" with the sexual war.

Winterbourne's sexual difficulties are analogues of war. The war to end war was merely one tyranny replacing another. The victory of conventional mores when George marries Elizabeth because she fears she is pregnant prefigures George's death when he is ground down by forces which bring him to despair. Their union is ill-fated because "they were adventurers in life, not good citizens." In a broader sense, George's inability to be an unimaginative "good citizen" and "good soldier" kills him.

Aldington fulminates against the Cant which insists that war was a healthy "bloodletting,"a cathartic for the poisons that supposedly accumulate during a long peace. In keeping with the then-current perversions of Darwinism as social theory, the sort Siegfried Sassoon immortalized in verse as "red-faced majors" were convinced that war was natural and necessary.

Ironically, all such beliefs in the rightness of war brought about their own destruction. So new were the values which rose from the ashes, that it would seem by hindsight as if "before the war" had been another dimension:

[S]uch a wholesale shattering of values had certainly not occurred since 1789. . . . 1914 was greeted as a great release, a purgation from the vices supposed to be engendered by peace! My God! Three days of glory engender more vices and misery than all the alleged corrupters of humanity could achieve in a millenium. *Les jeunes* would be amazed if they read the nauseous poppycock which was written in 1914–15 in England.

How different "before the war" had been is apparent in Aldington's description of a London mob on the eve of hostilities chanting "We want war!" The mindless optimism contrasts with George's "giv[ing] up hope" for peace at the news that Belgium has been invaded. There is irony in a staff officer exhorting men to resign themselves to death in a war supposedly being fought for civilization:

'You are the War generation. You were born to fight this War, and it's got to be won—we're determined you shall win it. So far as you are concerned as individuals, it doesn't matter a tinker's damn whether you are killed or not.'

The regular's idea of himself as a species bred for war had in the past been a source of pride, and it had earned him by turns the public's admiration, contempt, and fear. The new sort of warrior was different, however. Aldington sees his generation of soldiers as creatures "born for the slaughter like a calf or a pig."

Winterbourne's disgust with traditional values is manifested in his desire to stay "in the ranks and in the line, take the worst and humblest jobs, share in the fate of common man." He eventually agrees to a commission, only because he succumbs to the "sore temptation" of officer training as a way of getting out of the line and back to Elizabeth. Fear and misery have so degraded him that he has sold out to his persecutors.

Back in the trenches as a lieutenant, Winterbourne experiences the nerve-grinding weight of responsibility for other lives when everything conspires to make him doubt the importance of his own. His nerve is eroded by unremitting stress, fatigue, and harrying by his commanding officer, "an ex-regular Corporal." Winterbourne's mother's reaction to his death is a telling commentary on its lack of meaning. She derives sexual stimulation from indulgence in melodramatic self-love with her latest lover, a stupid second lieutenant of the public school variety.

Winterbourne the anti-hero has been too weak to withstand war's degrading effects. He has given in at every stage: joining the army to escape sexual conflict, returning to Elizabeth to escape the war, and choosing death as a final hiding place when he stands up in a hail of bullets. For Aldington there was a miraculous quality in the way that love, comradeship, and convictions of duty flourished where otherwise there was nothing but the moral and physical squalor of inhuman processes:

The soldiers just "went with the business," hating it, because they had been told that it had to be done and believed what they had been told. They wanted the War to end, they wanted to get away from it, and they had no feeling of hatred for their enemies on the other side of No Man's Land. In fact they were almost sympathetic to them. . . . The fighting was so impersonal as a rule that it seemed rather a conflict with dreadful hostile forces of Nature than with other men.

The Middle Parts of Fortune. Frederic Manning's *The Middle Parts of Fortune*'s first public edition (*Her Privates We*) was an emasculated version of the 1929 limited edition, which did not cater to linguistic squeamishness.[49] Only in 1943 was the full text restored and the author's name made known. Manning gives his characters' speeches in soldiers' argot. A soldier accounts for a comrade's absence from muster parade after an attack: " 'e were just blown to buggery, . . . I seen 'im blown into fuckin' bits." Public morality can turn truth into pale euphemism, yet the obscenity of fact far outstripped its description.

The novel is from the common infantryman's point of view. Its hero Private Bourne is a gentleman ranker. Among his comrades he is the focus of Manning's insights into the psychology of men in battle. Yet set apart from them by class, he is also a lens affording a perspective on war. The novel begins after the first Somme offensive, when the army had settled down to periodic "shows." Fortune seemed arbitrary, selecting its victims as randomly as the fall of the dice thrown by Bourne, and his war comrades Shem and Martlow.

Men had been reduced to creatures of instinct: "They had been through it, and having been through it, they had lapsed a little lower than savages, into the mere brute. Life for them held nothing new in the matter of humiliation." War itself is seen by Bourne in animal terms; mule transport is for him "symbolical of modern war, grotesque, stubborn, vindictive." There is a hint of Bourne's return to a primordial state which elevates as it casts down, because it removes corrupting thought and fear. "Floundering in the viscous mud," he is "at one the most abject and most exalted of God's creatures." Finding "some strange intoxication of joy" in attack, Bourne's mind focuses on "one hard point of action," wherein "pain and pleasure [have] met and coincided, and fear becomes indistinguishable from hate." In fact, all moral and intellectual distinctions about human conduct are rendered meaningless and dualities disappear: "the extreme of heroism, alike in foe or friend, is indistinguishable from despair."

Some youthful subalterns have still to lose their illusions. The young Mr. Cross thinks of war as a rugby scrum, and harangues the blooded veterans on the "value of team-work": " 'You want to get the ball out into the loose, an' keep it movin'.' " Even his reduction of the final syllable is a public school affectation like a prewar cavalry officer's fashionable lisp. Lieutenant Rhyss is full of war's romance. Speaking to the men "of patriotism, sacrifice, and duty," Rhyss "merely cloud[s] and confuse[s] their vision," because they have come to know war in the individual case, and not as an abstraction. For them a soldier is simply "a man against a world, a man fighting desperately for himself, and conscious that, in the last resort, he stood alone." For self-reliance lies at the very heart of comradeship.

Manning's point is not that true chivalry in war had ceased to exist. Cross and Rhyss indulge in some self-delusive posturing because they are still virgin warriors. Captain Malet as model of the leader class bridges the old regular officer's professionalism of character and the Temporary Officer's dedication:

It was his expression, his manner, something in the way he moved and spoke, which made one feel that only an enormous effort enabled him to bridle the insubordinate and destructive energy within him. . . . He would not have gone into an attack with a hunting-horn, or dribbled a football across no-man's-land: probably he would have thought anything of the kind a piece of sentimental levity.

When he walks the parapet to encourage his men before an attack, and when he returns to a captured trench for the ash-stick he has left behind, he is not playing to an audience. He is simply doing what he thinks he has to. Malet is evacuated with both legs broken, signifying the fate of the noble spirit in an ignoble age.

According to Bourne, "honour . . . is only an elaborate refinement of what are the decent instincts of the average man," not the old regular's cult of regimental glory or a false notion of national glory. This war had ended illusions:

War, which tested and had wrecked already so many conventions, tested not so much the general truth of a proposition, as its truth in relation to every individual case; and Bourne thought of many men, even men of rank, with military antecedents, whose honor, as the war increased its scope, had become a fugitive and cloistered virtue, though it probably would renew its lustre again in more costermonger times.

Before World War I the illusion of war as honorable had remained intact for regular soldiers. The destruction of distinctions between citizen-soldier and regular also destroyed institutional notions of military honor. The only common denominator was belief in *living*:

[T]his conventional notion of honour, . . . obligations of loyalty, . . . may have been very well as long as it had been possible to consider the army as a clan or a profession, but the war had made it a world.

It is the elemental life-sustaining virtue of comradeship transcending codes of class and profession which a well-meaning but superficial chaplain misunderstands. Urging Bourne to take his commission, he points out that as an officer he would have friends of his "own kind." Bourne admits that there is no one in the ranks whom he "can call a friend," but he says that comradeship "takes the place of friendship":

It is different: it has its own loyalties and affections; and I am not so sure that it does not rise on occasion to an intensity of feeling which friendship never touches.

Without the old regular's military codes, love of regiment, and class notions, the elemental bond between wartime soldiers turned out to be an urge for survival. Such abstractions as the "officer corps" paled beside the brotherhood of adversity:

At one moment a particular man may be nothing at all to you, and the next minute you will go through hell for him. No, it is not friendship. The man doesn't matter so much, it's a kind of impersonal emotion, a kind of enthusiasm, in the old sense of the word. . . . [W]e help each other.

The reality filling the void of belief in moral abstraction is the comradeship between Bourne, Shem, and Martlow, "the spiritual thing in them which lived and seemed even to grow stronger, in the midst of beastliness." After all, it is only in comradeship that one may have any trust when death is "a machine gun, searching for possibilities with a desultory spray." At least "they could help each other . . . to that point where the irresistible thing swept aside their feeble efforts, and smashed them beyond recovery."

This war changed the men who fought it. Bourne meditates that it is "useless to contrast the first challenging enthusiasm which had swept them into the army, with the long and bitter agony they endured afterwards." The steadfastness of the martyr at the stake had become the soldier's only measure of conduct. Characterizing the soldier as an imitation of Christ, Manning describes troops "who had known all the sins of the world" marching past a crucifix and lifting their eyes "to the agony of the figure on the cross, eyes that had probed and understood the mystery of suffering." Manning rails against the stubbornness of old regulars who still insisted on the old values:

Regular officers as a rule didn't understand the new armies, they had the model of the old professional army always in their mind's eye, and they talked of the fire-discipline of the old army, and rate of fire they were able to maintain in repelling counter-attacks, saying that reliance on bombs had ruined musketry. They forgot how the war had changed since 1915, ignoring artillery developments: and it never occurred to them that if one Lewis gun could do the work of ten men, it was rather foolish not to prefer it. . . . The majority of them, though there were brilliant exceptions, did not understand that the kind of discipline they wished to apply to these improvised armies was only a brake on their impetus. Then again, as a rule the regular officers did not get on with the temporary officers of the new army; but the regular army, perfect as it was, was a very small affair; things were now on a different scale, and in these new conditions the regular officer was as much an amateur as his temporary comrades.

If World War I reduced distinctions between regulars and citizen-soldiers, it also exaggerated the difference between those who had lived it and those who had not. With cavalier attitudes at home, and with evidence of an insensitive staff playing with men's lives, a feeling grew among the troops that they were victims of a great hoax, as if their hypocritical generals were in league with an arbitrary fate. A sense of existential futility grew, seen in destructiveness for supposedly exalted ideals.

Manning's citizen-soldiers are ordinary folk, trying to do what they think they must. He shows officers, warrant officers, and NCOs as reasonable, conscientious, and imperfect, each dealing with the stress of war in his own way. There is very little philosophizing. Rather, the novel sticks to describing men who did not philosophize much. In war philosophy leads inevitably to a weakening of resolve. "Weeper" Smart's lachrymose revelations are derided, and Corporal Hamley's admonition to the others to "put a sock on it" meets with no opposition. It is better to believe in what you have to do, because it makes the unreasonable easier to bear.

In Parenthesis (1937). Almost on the eve of another war David Jones published his poetic Great War novel *In Parenthesis*.[50] Jones describes the meaning of the novel's title as a stopping-out for the citizen-soldier:

This writing is called "In Parenthesis" because I have written it in a kind of space between—I don't know between quite what—but as you turn aside to do something; and because for us amateur soldiers . . . the war itself was a parenthesis—how glad we thought we were to step outside its brackets at the end of '18.

The soldier is caught between "each salvo" which "brackets more narrowly," trapped between his first going "up the line" and his sacrificial death.

The particular victim is an every-soldier figure, John Ball, whose interior monologues evoke the feelings, sounds, and smells of military life in and out of battle. He poetically describes Recruit Training under regular NCOs at a regimental depot:

Knobbed nickel at under arm thumb at seam smart cut away from the small (and hair on upper lip invests him with little charm) re-numbering re-dressing two inch overlap pernickety poshers-up, drum-majors gnashing in their Blancoed paradises, twisted pipe-clayed knots for square-pushing shoulders, tin soldiers, toy soldiers, militarymen in rows. . . . the unnamable nostalgia of depots.

War stands out in stark contrast to soldiering. The Tommy becomes the soldier eternal—the scapegoat, the lamb, mankind who through fear comes to "hate [his] own flesh" when he faces his enemy. Crucified and self-crucifying, the soldier sees in his enemy a reflection of himself like a day-sentry viewing mirrored images of enemy positions in a trench periscope.

There are no clear-eyed heroes in *In Parenthesis*—only the morally blind leading their brothers through fields of chance, some "the goat on which the lot fell." Pot Saunders is sheer parody as a Christian postfiguration. "One of three" huddled under a ground-sheet, he is called away as a headquarters runner. The others lament his parting because it breaks up their "bivvy," "for such breakings away and dissolvings of comradeship and token of division are cause of great anguish when men sense how they stand so perilous and transitory in the world."

The last major episode commences with an allusion to Good Friday as the troops prepare to attack, to assault their Golgotha, "the place of the skull." War is the business of "properly organized chemists" who with lethal gases can make a soldier "more blistered . . . than painted Troy towers/and unwholer, limb from limb, than any of them fallen" in ancient battle. There is not even the consolation of worldly honor, for there is "no maker to contrive his funerary song." Ironically, in the midst of chaos officers like latter-day Fluellens maintain "the Excellent Disciplines of the Wars."

Throughout the novel Jones shows the difference between the old regular's love of his craft and the new amateur's hatred of it. John Ball remembers his musketry instructor's erotic idiom praising the rifle: "Marry it! Cherish her . . . , coax it . . . , fondle it. . . . You've seen her hot and cold. You would choose her from among many." Yet for the dying Jones his rifle is "like the Mariner's white oblation," humankind's curse for neglecting to love living things.

Memoirs of an Infantry Officer (1930). Between 1929 and 1936 there appeared a chronicle of a British Infantry officer George Sherston's coming of age, from a country childhood and fox-hunting youth to his first flush of idealism in war, his growing disgust, and finally his wounding and evacuation from the front. *The Sherston Memoirs: Memoirs of a Fox-Hunting Man, Memoirs of an*

Infantry Officer, and *Sherston's Progress* are the pseudonymous memoirs of Siegfried Sassoon.

Memoirs of an Infantry Officer (1930)[51] is complete in itself as a record of Sherston's progress from innocence to experience. At first he thinks of war as a fine test, like "winning races." Patrols in no-man's-land were "entertainment," a "concert," and Sherston describes his men with blackened faces aping minstrels. War was still a game, and Sassoon and his men felt important and in control: "None of us could know how insignificant we were in the so-called 'Great Adventure.' "

As Sherston comes to understand his place in this war, he learns to face an uncontrollable fate by giving up hope of living: "I had more or less made up my mind to die because in the circumstances there didn't seem anything else to be done." Yet his fatalism is accompanied by a poignant love of life. He has only contempt for the deliberate inculcation of hatred in soldiers, and relates sardonically his experience of an officer who wins a DSO for his "homicidal eloquence" in teaching the "Spirit of the Bayonet."

Sherston comes to recognize in himself the "egotism" that makes heroes. Commenting that "books about war psychology ought to contain a chapter on 'medal reflexes'," he notes clinically that his own Military Cross only increases this "blindness to the blood-stained future," a view less simplistic than that of nineteenth-century Regulars. He recalls his love of the game when, venturing into no-man's-land against orders, he finds the illicitness exhilarating. On another occasion while he cuts wire preparatory for an attack, excitement and pleasure blunt his sensations of danger, and he becomes temporarily oblivious to the "tragic slaughter" to follow.

Sherston's fever when he has come down with dysentry seems a physical analogue for the onset of war madness induced by news of a friend's death. While in hospital, and released from the immediacies of survival, he hears that "young Allgood" (a name of some meaning) has been killed. Sherston's innocence is drowned in feeling as he hears a mortally wounded invalid deliriously reliving battle: " 'Curse the Wood. . . .' " There were so many "woods": Belleau Wood, Moreuil Wood, Mametz Wood (where Sassoon won his MC), places of death, like the heart of darkness in every soldier. A physical parallel to a crisis of conscience, his fever breaks the following morning. The dying patient's bed is empty. Sherston is morally sane.

Repatriated to England, Sherston discovers a fool's paradise where everyone "jog[s] along much as usual," believing like the clergy that killing Germans is a "Christian act," and still hunting foxes to keep the sport alive "for the sake of the boys at the front." All the fatal attraction and repulsion bound up in the soldier's sense of self is implicit in Sherston's wry recollection, "I was armed with my uniform and the protective colouring of my Military Cross, and no one could do enough for me. . . . I wanted the War to be an impressive experience—terrible, but not horrible enough to interfere with my heroic emotions."

Back in France, Sherston's intellectual rejection of war is complex. He takes perverse pride in belonging to a fraternity that understands; increasingly alienated because of the disparity between war and its heroic image, he becomes contemptuous of noncombatants. In a fleeting moment he even finds the war "a friendly affair and. . . . much better than loafing at home." Ironically, his thoughts are accompanied by the sight of his men resting in warm sunlight under an old apple tree by a crucifix, the curse and its price. But Sherston imparts no sense of grandeur to the sacrificial lottery with its "blundering doom." Resentful of noble newspaper sentiments supposedly held by young officers, Sherston is disdainful of romanticized reports of suicidal assaults. Although he admits to his anticipation of going over the top as a "religious experience," he knows that what he feels is really "self-deceiving escape from the limitless malevolence of the front line."

Sherston's end of belief, and his hostility to those at home because they cannot understand, leave him with a need for something to hold onto. The old regular's regimental tradition is no help; only the men around him matter:

[T]here was nothing left to believe in except "the Battalion spirit" [which] meant giving oneself into comfortable companionship with the officers and N.C.O.s around one; it meant winning the respect, or even the affection, of platoon and company.

Even with such solace as this, the impermanence of any mortal object of faith is borne in on Sherston with the regular passing of comrades killed in action. So Sherston continues to play a game, to "play at being a hero in shining armour . . . ; if I didn't I might crumple up altogether."

Finally, Sherston decides to quit the "sausage machine" and its "ant-like armies." He has arrived at an intellectual position by which his belief in living takes prior place over "the idea of sacrifice and disregard of death." He makes his "grand gesture" by publishing his protest in a pacifist journal and refusing further service. His friend David Cromlech saves him by arranging for a medical board to declare him insane. In recounting his encounter with the board, Sherston recalls that " 'Fighting on religious grounds' sounded like some sort of joke about the Crusades." Sherston agonizes that his dual identities as warrior and pacifist present a "conundrum." This was the temporary soldier's dilemma, not resolved by the old regular's regimental loyalty.

Parade's End (1926–28). Ford Madox Ford's *Parade's End* tetralogy: *Some Do Not . . .* , *No More Parades*, *A Man Could Stand Up—*, and *Last Post*, is about a vast change in the British class structure "under the stress of blind necessities."[52]

Precise details of Ford's own military service from 1915 to 1919 are not known. Already forty-two years old when he enlisted with a commission in the Welch Fusiliers, he served in France and may have been evacuated as a shell-shock case. Ford tended to embellish his past; however, he was close enough to war that his fictional rendering may be said to be based on first-hand knowledge.

Ford's tetralogy captures a society's final stages of decay. The noise of human absurdity had been rising, like the paradox of a shell's tumultuous descent to a "crescendo" for two centuries, so that men could not hear their own thoughts. Ford dwells on the impossibility of communication, shouts unheard over strafes, blocked communication trenches, voice-muffling respirators, even a garbled and interrupted phone call at a girl's school on Armistice Day. The cacophony is an analogue of a vaster chaos which has drowned out Order. The central figure Tietjens's initial complacency in *Some Do Not . . .* gives way to nearly intolerable self-doubt in *No More Parades*. In *A Man Could Stand Up*— his alienation and longing for stability are replaced by his acceptance of himself as flawed man in a flawed world. Ultimately, in *The Last Post* he finds peace for his shattered spirit in the countryside.

The war is merely a continuation of a survival game among members of a society divided into victims and predators. The mad Captain McKechnie,[53] the Colonel, an alcoholic ex-regular battalion commander, the ludicrous little subaltern Aranjuez, and Tietjens himself are victims. McKechnie lacks the emotional controls to withstand the shock of war, the Colonel's personality is eroded by the stress of command, Aranjuez is seriously wounded, and Tietjens is the object of everyone's spite.

In *No More Parades* the early setting is a hut in a rear area in France, where Tietjens administers a "draft finding unit." Tietjens is confined here with the paranoic Captain McKechnie, while others arrive and depart for the front like transient asylum patients. The hut is like Tietjens's mind. He wearily does his duty within its confines, imposing order on all who enter like unbidden thoughts from the surrounding chaos. Like his mental control, the thin walls are slim protection.

The theatre of war Ford describes often in metaphor is a wasteland where men are hemmed in by corruption and neglect. As the world descends into anarchy, Tietjens's doubt deepens toward despair. Charlatans, incompetents, and hypocrites people a canvas that broadens to include Britons of every class and background at war. The world seems at the mercy of a capricious God, and "Order" has receded. Clinging grimly to his sanity and even his sense of identity, Tietjens continues futilely to pit his intellect against chaos.

Believing it his "military duty to bother himself about the mental equilibrium of this member of the lower classes," Tietjens finds himself drawn unwillingly into an absurd game with McKechnie, having to do with the writing of Latin sonnets. A symbol for the war, the game forces Tietjens to acknowledge his common humanity with the likes of the mad captain. Tietjens has no use for the old military "games" mentality:

The curse of the army . . . was our imbecile national belief that the game is more than the player. That was our ruin, mentally, as a nation. We were taught that cricket

is more important than clearness of mind, so that the blasted quartermaster...
thought he had taken a wicket if he refused to serve out tin hats.... That's the
Game! And if any of his, Tietjens', men were killed, he grinned and said the game
was more than the players of the game.

For Tietjens the folly of the "games" mentality is a sign of intellectual and
moral decay, with war as the final stage. At the end of the war, he laments,
there will be "no more Hope, no more Glory, no more parades for you and
me any more. Nor for the country... nor for the world."

The caprice seeming to govern the war is symbolized in a draft of soldiers
commanded by "an obscene subaltern too drunk to halt them." As with
subalterns, so with God; as with the draft, so with nations. Tietjens feels
"an intolerable depression" knowing that they and millions of others are
merely "playthings of ants busy in the miles of corridors." With insight
comes compassion. Tietjens learns that his responsibility for his soldiers
living and dead is more than a bloodless obligation of class: "your dead...
yours... your own. As if joined to your identity by a black cord."

A Man Could Stand Up— is set against the background of trench warfare.
Survival is unpredictable, and like those he once thought of as lesser mortals,
Tietjens has to make the best of a life that depends on staying below ground
level. The idea of being below ground also bears the connotation of an
acknowledgment of the animal self. Germans in gas masks remind Tietjens
of "goblin pigs," and all men in dying look "collapsed inwards. Like the
dying pig they sold on trays in the street." He assumes command when
nervous exhaustion and alcohol render his colonel unfit. An underground
charge buries him, and he is nicked by a sniper's bullet. Moments later he
encounters General Campion, a prewar officer, who dismisses him con-
temptuously for his untidy appearance and sends him to the rear.

Tietjens's stripping of his London home of furniture when he returns from
war is symbolic of his stripping his mind of the bric-a-brac of a past life. The
empty room with only a camp cot is a stark backdrop for the frenetic gaiety
of Christopher's Armistice Day celebration. Here are gathered the mad
McKechnie, the dying colonel, the one-eyed and half-blind Aranjuez—all
brief visitors soon to leave, like ghosts of the past leaving his mind forever,
because "today the world had changed. Feudalism was finished; its last
vestiges were gone. It held no place for him." In *The Last Post* the healing
begins.

THE GREAT WAR AND A CHANGING TRADITION

> They tried to get the tone of the old time-serving N.C.O. They couldn't;
> all the same, you couldn't say they weren't creditable achievements.
> Ford Madox Ford, *A Man Could Stand Up—*[54] (1926)

In 1916 a sententious novel entitled *Hospital Days* appeared. [55] Showing
how jolly a wound can be, it probably had been officially inspired for mo-

tivational purposes. However, the book's closing argument in favor of the recently instituted gold "wound stripe" as a mark of honor reflects the altered military ethos which destroyed distinctions between regular and citizen-soldier:

The feeling among officers who were in the army before war broke out was, on the whole, opposed to the stripe. It was . . . directly contrary to the traditions of the British Army. . . . However, they are all wearing the stripe now because orders are orders and must be obeyed. . . .

The fact is, the difference nowadays between a Regular and a Territorial or Reserve officer is immaterial. Each have to face the same conditions; each must, if need be, lay down his life for his country.

It is here that we come to the crux of the question. . . . [T]he Army of to-day is not quite the same as the Army that was composed of long-service soldiers. The men in it now really represent the country in arms. . . . We are to-day making tradition—perhaps the greatest in our country's history—and our habits must change in the process.

For the wartime volunteer or call-up, "soldiering" was an interlude, some-times remembered in after years as a great adventure lived more intensely than any other part of his life, and sometimes recalled as a ghastly and chaotic disruption of an otherwise serene and ordered existence. His military *raison d'être* was war, and nothing else. Training and preparation for battle were mere preludes, and to him the idea of "soldiering" was inseparable from war itself. All else, ceremonial training and barracks routine, were something other than "soldiering," something artificial, an imitation or substitute. Like the militiaman who hangs his uniform in a closet after parade night, the returning wartime soldier stowed his warrior's clothing in an attic trunk and resumed his "life" where he had left off.

Although war obviously was the regular soldier's *raison d'être* as well, it spoiled his "soldiering" for him hardly less than it intruded on the civilian's existence. The regular was an ardent aesthete, sustained more by the sat-isfaction he derived from the beauty of an often tedious round of duties than by ethical aims. His love of order, symmetry, uniformity, and routine that he nurtured to help him cope with confusion and fear were affronted by modern war. The regular saw his sacred craft invaded by philistine temporary soldiers, some inspired amateurs and others not, some ferocious zealots and others reluctant warriors. Either way, although many played at being regulars, they did not truly subscribe to the regular's military values. They had scant respect for his traditions and customs, and less patience still with the stoic obedience and minute attention to detail that shaped him.

It was only modern European war that spoiled the regular's professional life. In eighteenth-century European conflicts, and in nineteenth-century campaigns in Africa and Asia, regulars had fought using essentially the same formations, arms drill and maneuvers they had learned on the barracks square. There had been something as satisfyingly ceremonial about battle as there had been about preparation for it. War had not been a state of being distinct from peace; nations and armies competing for empires, then building and holding them, had been in a constant state of war; and until the mass levies for nineteenth-century continental armies, battle had been fought by the same soldiers who spent their lives preparing for them. Short-term volunteers had been in a minority, and had conformed in sentiment to their regular masters.

Until 1847 a regular had signed on for twenty-one years, and from then on, for ten years in the Infantry or twelve in the other arms. There were few time-expired men, then, as a reserve to share their values with the militia. Even after Cardwell's reforms, when regulars could sign on for six years, men like Frank Richards, the old regular who remained in a reserve battalion of the Royal Welch Fusiliers, were too few to impart the Regular Army's ethos until World War I. Anyway, traditional parade ceremonies and maneuvers and the discipline instilled by barracks routine bore little resemblance to battle in World War I. The intricate parade square maneuvers by shifting ranks to "Form Two Deep," "Change Direction," and "Form Close Column" demand a kind of precision having little connection with "Advance to Contact" calling in fire coordinates, and crawling through the wire with cork-blackened face.

Although the early drafts of temporary soldiers were barely drilled and taught, they brought imagination to modern war. Unfortunately, static warfare gave it little scope for use. Conversely, some regulars had almost ceased to regard battle as their proper purpose, because it was a chaotic affair best dealt with by stark utilitarian methods and often best derived by devilishly imaginative civilians in uniform. Of necessity, the regular learned to accept the inevitable with good grace, and in war even managed grudging admiration for his new comrades in arms as each regiment of the New Army was blooded at the front.

In turn, the wartime soldier learned to temper his peacetime contempt for the regular. In its place grew admiration, admittedly tinged with resentment, for the professional's qualities and skills. The temporary soldier zealously aped the regular, until the regular became lost in hordes of amateurs, all trying to keep up with events that outstripped the knowledge and inventiveness of both. Yet, at the outset the regular gave the temporary actors lines to mimic imperfectly and work variations with, until the altered version of the soldier's calling took on a life of its own. When the war ended, the wartime soldier enjoyed a brief glory as savior of his nation. Some of his number remained as the regular soldiers of a new peace, and soon peacetime society's contempt, or at best a grudging regard, was theirs.

With World War I, a distinction between wartime and peacetime soldiers replaced the older distinction between regulars and Volunteers or conscripts. As regular regiments were decimated in battle, their ranks were filled with soldiers who were in for "the duration." Soon nobody could tell regulars from anyone else. The only distinction of any importance was whether or not a soldier had been at the front. The Territorial regiments which mobilized for war won as many battle honors as those in the regular Order of Battle. In any case by the end of the war, no "regular" regiment had any more regulars than the New Army battalions. After the war, many temporary soldiers stayed on in a vastly reduced army to become the new generation of regulars. They brought with them their wartime values, traditions, and sentiments, and arbitrary definitions of the soldier as professional and amateur ceased to mean much.

NOTES

1. All quotations are from Richard Aldington, *Death of a Hero* (London: Chatto & Windus, 1929).

2. H. G. Wells, *The World of William Clissold*, 2 vols. (New York: George H. Doram, 1926), pp. 567–68.

3. This theory is central to Samuel P. Huntington's *The Soldier and the State* (1957) and Amos Perlmutter's *The Military and Politics in Modern Times* (1977).

4. Gwyn Harries-Jenkins, *The Army in Victorian Society* (London: Routledge & Kegan Paul, 1977), p. 270.

5. General Sir John Hackett, *The Profession of Arms* (London: Times Publishing Co., 1962), p. 52.

6. Andre Corvisier, *Armies and Societies in Europe, 1494–1789* (Bloomington: Indiana University Press, 1979).

7. Robert Blake, "Great Britain: The Crimean War to the First World War," in *Soldiers and Governments*, ed. Michael Howard (London: Eyre & Spottiswoode, 1957).

8. Harries-Jenkins, *Army*, p. 197.

9. By contrast, America's Union Army gave up its last attempt to introduce lances into the cavalry in May 1863, when the 6th Pennsylvania Cavalry was issued carbines! (See "Tradition," Vol. 65, London: Belmont-Maitland Publishers, 1972.)

10. "Sling the bat" was soldier slang derived from Hindi, meaning "use the lingo." Much of the regular soldier's lexicon consisted of corruptions from Hindi; for example, "cushy": comfortable and easy go; "buckshee": gratis, or extra (from the beggar's whine, "*baksheesh*"); "dhobi": laundry; "chitty" or "chit": a note (from Hindi "*chitthi*": letter). For further examples, see Chapter 5.

11. Laurence Housman, ed., *War Letters of Fallen Englishmen* (London: Victor Gollancz, 1930).

12. See R. J. E. Tiddy's introductory digressions in *The Mummers' Play* (Oxford: Clarendon, 1923).

13. Frank Richards, *Old Soldiers Never Die* (London: Faber & Faber, 1933). [Although Robert Graves's name does not appear, Richards's narrative is as transcribed by Graves. See Robert Graves's introductory note to Frank Richards's *Old Soldier Sahib*.]

14. Isaac Rosenberg's "Dead Man's Dump," in Brian Gardner, ed., *Up the Line to Death: The War Poets 1914–18*, (London: Eyre & Methuen, 1964).

15. Edmund Blunden, *Undertones of War* (1928), rev. ed. (London: Cobden-Sanderson, 1930).

16. Alan Clark, *The Donkeys* (New York: Universal Publishing & Distributing Corp., 1961), p. 17.

17. Sir Frederick Treves, ed., *Made in the Trenches* (London: George Allen Unwin Ltd., 1916).

18. Bruce Bairnsfather, *Bullets and Billets* (Letchworth: Garden City Press, 1916).

19. Paul Fussell, *The Great War and Modern Memory* (London: Oxford University Press, 1975).

20. See Brian Gardner, *The Big Push* (London: Cassell, 1961). Photographs show some troops in "Marching Order" and others going over the top without any webbing at all.

21. Captain A. J. Dawson, intro., *A "Temporary Gentleman" in France: Home Letters from an Officer in the New Army* (London: Cassell, 1916). "Temporary Gentleman" is not necessarily a pseudonymous signature for a real writer. The "letters" are more likely a contrived manuscript authored at the instigation of some ministry of "information."

22. Wilfrid Owen, *Dulce et Decorum Est* (1916) Gardner, *Up the Line to Death*, pp. 141, 142.

23. Paul Fussell, intro., *Siegfried Sassoon's Long Journey: Selections from the Sherston Memoirs* (New York: Oxford University Press, 1983), p. 74.

24. See Mark Girouard, *The Return to Camelot* (New Haven, Conn.: Yale University Press, 1981).

25. Harry Jones, ed., *War Letters of a Public School Boy* (London: Cassell, 1918).

26. *London Times*, 20 March 1916, facsimile reprinted in Fussell, *Siegfried Sassoon's Long Journey*.

27. J. St. Loe Strachey, ed. and intro., *Donald Hankey: A Student in Arms* (Toronto: McClelland, Goodchild & Stewart, 1917), p. 31.

28. Thomas Tiplady, *The Soul of the Soldier: Sketches from the Western Battle Front* (New York: Fleming H. Revell Co., 1918), p. 192.

29. Laurence Housman, ed., *War Letters of Fallen Englishmen*, p. 2.

30. Ford Madox Ford, *It Was the Nightingale* (1933) (Philadelphia: J. B. Lippincott Co., 1933), p. 64.

31. Phrases from Herbert Asquith's "Nightfall" and other verse quoted in this chapter are contained in Gardner, ed., *Up the Line to Death*.

32. Wilfrid Gibson, "Mad."

33. Wilfrid Gibson, "In the Ambulance."

34. Gilbert Frankau, "The Deserter."

35. R. B. Marriot-Watson, "Kismet."

36. Herbert Read, "My Company."

37. Robert Graves, "The Leveller."

38. Siegfried Sassoon, "The General."

39. Siegfried Sassoon, "To Any Dead Officer."

40. Wilfred Owen, "Anthem for Doomed Youth."

41. Robert Palmer, "How Long, O Lord?"

42. Siefried Sassoon, "Attack."

43. Wilfrid Gibson, "Bacchanal."

44. Rudyard Kipling, "Common Form."

45. Henry Williamson, *The Patriot's Progress* (London: Sphere Books, 1930).

46. Robert C. Sherriff, *Journey's End* (New York: Brentano Press, 1929).

47. Aldington, *Death of a Hero*.

48. Geoffrey Best's *Humanity in Warfare* (1980) establishes this thesis. The contradictions between political notions of "just war," "peace with honor," and human justice had later parallels in the Vietnam War.

49. Frederic Manning, *The Middle Parts of Fortune*, intro. Michael Howard (London: Granada Publishing Co., 1977).

50. David Jones, *In Parenthesis* (London: Faber & Faber, 1937).

51. Siegfried Sassoon, *Memoirs of an Infantry Officer* (London: Faber & Faber, 1930, 1965).

52. All quotations from Ford Madox Ford's *Parade's End* tetralogy are from the Vintage Books edition, 1979, intro. Robie MacCauley.

53. Apparently, "MacKenzie" of *No More Parades* and "McKechnie" of *A Man Could Stand Up—* are meant to be the same character. Both are madly resentful of Tietjens, and the sonnet duel begun by MacKenzie is carried on by McKechnie.

54. Ford, *A Man Could Stand Up—*, p. 56.

55. Anon. ("Platoon Commander"), *Hospital Days* (London: T. Fisher Unwin, Ltd., 1916).

5

A JUST CAUSE: THE INSTITUTIONALIZING OF AMATEURISM SINCE THE GREAT WAR

AFTER WORLD WAR I

.... This poor dust
Ranked soldierly, these veterans salute
The promise; the old guard presenting arms
Trusts to the new, and gives it all it can.

. . . .

Thus a dim music every step I tread
Connotes the living purpose of these dead.
Edmund Blunden, "War Cemetery"[1]

There were differences between the postwar regular and his prewar counterpart. The new soldier, whether officer or man, was not as easily identifiable by social caste. Sheer attrition had accounted for so many upper-class public school boys who became platoon commanders, that military authorities had had to reach down to those without "proper" accents and backgrounds to find enough officers. Battlefield commissions and selection of officer trainees from the ranks did much to end the upper-class monopoly on officership, and in any case "good" families were no longer as anxious to see their sons well placed in the army. A stint in the Brigade of Guards still served a young man as a credential for public or corporate life, but fewer public school boys aspired to military careers. While family connections continued to play a part in acceptance and promotion, officers received pay adequate to live on, and they were expected to display sufficient competence to earn it. Wartime amateurism had at last made the army more professional.

After the war, the government recognized that England would have to use similar mobilization policies in any future European war. The Territorial Force was reconstituted in 1921, and the role envisioned for it included overseas service. Significantly, its new title was the Territorial *Army*. For the first time Britain's part-time soldiers bore the same title as the regulars. From 1936 onwards, when Hitler's intentions were becoming clear, the Territorials were almost solely responsible for coastal defense. Between the two world wars, however, revulsion toward militarism took the form of strong disarmament policies. Equipment was allowed to become obsolete, some regiments of Territorials had become little more than social clubs, and soldiers again found themselves shunned by decent folk. On the eve of the Second World War the Territorials numbered 212,000, a woefully small and tragically ill-equipped force, considering the rumblings from abroad. There are many accounts of conditions like those described by one writer as "battalions at home with a strength of two hundred or less, carrying out maneuvers with wooden machine-guns and flags representing non-existent troops. Sometimes there seemed to be as many flags as men."[2]

Similar accounts appear in General Horrocks's *Memoirs* and in Evelyn Waugh's novel of the "phoney war" in 1939, *Put Out More Flags*. By the time of the Dunkirk evacuation shortly after war was declared, the years of deliberate neglect had reduced the British Army almost to impotence.

There is reason, then, to marvel at the miraculous dedication and resilience of regulars and Territorials alike, in building a new citizen army while "the few" waged the Battle of Britain overhead. From the beginning of the war the backward-looking "military mind" bound by class custom and military tradition was little in evidence. Since World War I sweeping social and political changes had taken place, and the regular army knew also that it was presiding over the disintegration of the Empire. No longer was there cause for military complacency, or serious conviction among senior officers that the civilian leadership should be excluded from military planning. From the beginning, Montgomery, Auchinleck, Wavell, Slim, and other talented commanders deferred with good grace to the Cabinet's direction of the war. There would be no sulking Kitcheners.

As for battalion-level officers and rank and file, there was little of the old regulars' sneering. Many a regular's civilian father could claim the name of "soldier" because he had been "in the war," and no longer was the idea of "citizen" seen as a dilution of "soldier." It was accepted that peacetime soldiers "soldiered" in the tradition of those who had fought, and wartime soldiers trained and fought in the spirit of competent regulars. The new volunteer didn't bother learning to "sling the bat" to imitate prewar regulars. Instead, volunteer and regular alike sang "Mademoiselle from Armentieres" and "It's a Long Way to Tipperary," the songs of an amateur army.

Certainly, many of the old mistakes were made in the early days, as a new generation of soldiers trained for the war their fathers already had fought. They learned to dig trench systems in preparation for a stagnant war that would not occur, and they route marched endless miles as if troop transport had not been invented. On the other hand, there was constant experimentation and invention by civilian and military staffs alike, indicative of an innovative cast of mind. British commanders displayed an intellectual élan not seen since the spirit of Napoleon and Wellington had flickered out a century earlier. Although Montgomery was a professional, he was no conservative when it came to fundamentals; he was as tactically aggressive as he was psychologically astute in his appeal to citizens in arms. His unorthodox attire and speeches delivered with troops clustered around him bore little resemblance to the behavior of the commanders of World War I Haig, Gough and French, who never understood the difference between wartime soldiers and peacetime regulars.

Operation Overlord, the Normandy invasion of 6 June 1944, was a testimonial to the death of military conservatism and narrow professionalism. Troops and supplies launched out from the great Mulberry floating dock; paratroopers dropped from the skies; Commandos scaled cliffs and headed for targets inland. Troops stormed the beaches and raced up the shingle in conventional fashion, but the whole operation was the result of exhaustive intelligence analysis and coordinated planning beyond the capabilities of earlier staffs.

On the North African, Italian, and Northwest European fronts there was little of the alienation experienced by troops in World War I. The issues were more clearly drawn. Always there would remain the sentiment that the soldier is a martyr; but whereas in the Great War the state, church, and society had been the persecutors, this time the menace seemed less equivocal. Aside from state propaganda, enough became known of Naziism's institutionalizing of military atrocity that the soldier's ideological motives were clear. He could not easily view the German soldier as simply a fellow victim.

Divisive sentiment caused by entrenched political and social privilege had ceased to be a major factor in military morale. Further, the soldier on foreign battlefields could not readily believe that he was not understood at home. The bombing of London and the seaports, the leveling of Coventry, the early rumors of an expected invasion, the Spitfires and Messerschmidts wheeling in dogfights over the Channel, and finally the rain of V–1 and V–2 Rockets made the war everybody's property. In fact, soldiers in remote training centers on the moors were less at risk than civilians in industrial centers. Everybody endured food rationing, carried respirators, and observed blackout regulations. Soldiers on home leave had worked beside air raid wardens, digging bodies out of the rubble in their own neighborhoods, and while soldiers on foreign battlefields sheltered from shelling in dugouts, they thought of their own families huddled in Underground tunnels waiting for the All Clear.

In April 1918 when Field Marshal Sir Douglas Haig had issued his famous "backs to the wall" memorandum, he had been addressing only his army in the field; in 1940 when Winston Churchill vowed that Britons would "fight them on the beaches" he spoke to everyone. The soldier of World War II had no monopoly on martyrdom, and he knew it. At least he had the feeling that he could do something this time, and did not have to wait endlessly in static positions to be slaughtered. The rapid advance across Europe was his chance to fight. If he was angry at the army, it was not so much that he had to be in it, but that so many opportunists both in and out of uniform profited from his sacrifice. His anger was not directed towardhis government or mil-

itary high command for committing him to war, as much as it was toward
petty betrayers.

WORLD WAR II AND THE LITERATURE OF THE CITIZEN-SOLDIER

'Use them,' he repeated dreamily, 'spend them. It's like slowly collecting
a pile of chips and then plonking them all down on the roulette board.'[3]

The poetry and prose inspired by World War II reflected differences from
World War I. Even in this new war's early stages when, except for the bloody
Dieppe Raid, Allied troops had yet to set foot in Northwest Europe in any
numbers since Dunkirk; there was an awareness that the scope, if not the
intensity, of war had increased. An introduction to a 1943 anthology of war
poetry first comments:

In this war, so far at least as Europe is concerned, everyone, because of raids and
invasions (actual or possible) is some sort militant . . . , [T]he assumption that a poet
on active service must reveal war more sensitively than his unenlisted fellow is hardly
sound.[4]

If in World War I the idea of the combatant as martyr and victim achieved
maturity, it grew in World War II to include the civilian population. The
citizen-soldier's uniform no longer set him apart from the civilian population
even as much as it had in World War I.

The poetry of the World War II reveals this new sentiment, and much of
it was written by civilians or by men in uniform still on home service sharing
the same experiences as civilians. Much is domestic in tone and setting, and
it does not show the self-consciously tragic knight-errantry of the Great War's
gentleman subalterns. The reasons for changes in authorship and tone were
as much social and economic as military. The Great War had decimated a
generation of prewar public school boys, and officership was less class-bound.
Industrialists had made fortunes from the war, and during the 1920s and
1930s their sons and daughters were achieving social prominence and en-
tering universities and the professions. School curricula were changing to
accommodate the realities of industrial society; no longer were upper- and
upper-middle-class youth the sole repositories of a body of classical knowledge assumed to be appropriate to a leader class. Poetics, once the common
property of a broad social and cultural elite, became the province of a se-
questered intellectual elite. Eliot, Auden and Spender were the new proph-
ets; but except for some of the early verse, Auden's "Yes, We are Going to
Suffer," for instance, they wrote little about World War II. To outsiders
these poets appeared obscurantist, rarified, academic. Neither was there an
audience of literary dilettantes like the Great War's subalterns, who went
to war with copies of Horace and Virgil in their packs.

With World War II, "the privacies of the nineteen-thirties poets—forever writing and dedicating poetry to each other, and their exclusive if bitter squabbles—were left to the past."[5] The poetry would become more diverse in authorship, style, tone, and subject, reflecting the sentiments and experiences of men and women of all classes, in and out of uniform. The early poetry had little of the epic jingoism of early World War I verse. Except for the natural exuberance of many a youth anticipating a great adventure, 1914's blindly blithe elation at the prospect of war was absent. In the fall of 1938, an advertising copywriter complained in his poem "England" of a press that "suppresses truth and twists it," the "inward snigger" of some politician, and of the "cant and smug discretion."[6]

When the bombs began falling, the poetry of war belonged to civilians as much as to soldiers. One poet—unfit for military service, but finding that the front line suddenly was everywhere—wrote how "earth opens" to "squandered bombs" on a "burning countryside."[7] It was no different for servicemen. An airman expressed the general "wild pity" of violation at seeing his battered hometown, where every stone contains some "history of its own."[8] Antiaircraft batteries of men who had yet to leave their own shores set up emplacements in town squares. Verse written by a gunner tells of anti-aircraft guns "searching among the stars," while "searchlights pry/Into thin clouds."[9] Undoubtedly the most poignant of verse by civilians are Dylan Thomas's elegiac lines inspired by a fire bombing and entitled, "A Refusal to Mourn the Death, By Fire, Of a Child in London," its pathos matched only by poetry of the Holocaust.

Unlike the First World War's early poetry, from the outset there were few expressions of noble sentiment this time. A taunt in verse was aimed at the soldier, who "put to shame earthquake and plague," to "maim the crazy and the lame." The warrior usurps the divine by becoming "the God whom frenzy pleases."[10] In the rhetoric of a recruiting drive, a sailor poet heard "the butcher bird sing,"[11] and a schoolmaster poet described "The New Learning" of hatred, through which "The human mind does silly things."[12] A soldier-poet's lines telling of the aloneness and vulnerability of a young man "Pried from the circle where his family ends," and "no hero of old tales,"[13] could be a late eighteenth-century plaint for the peasant torn from his land for military service. Another poet picked up the World War I soldier-poets' theme to see beneath "the medals and the glory" that corpses are not "magnificent or stately;" nor are bones "elegant that blast has shattered."[14]

Although the scales had fallen from everyone's eyes when they were faced with another bloody war, there was nearly universal agreement from beginning to end that this one had to be fought. An elegy for a fallen guardsman extolls his risking "against his will" the "dreadful danger," that "all had shared."[15] Here is no ecstatic self-sacrifice, but a grim facing of fear despite the urge to live. Yet as the poet's *persona* gazes at the dead soldier, unable to comprehend death's finality, he imagines him awakening "at break of dawn somewhere, fed up, courageous, vain," and swearing, starting in once more. No rosy dawn of resurrection, this; simply a mortal struggle lived over and over again by gritty men who did what they had to. There was far less written of the soldier's hardships in this poetry than there was in World War I. The soldier-poet knew this time that he did not hold a monopoly on suffering—especially when liberating troops began discovering the horrors that inspired Stephen Spender's "Memento," about the Nazi death camps where eyes "sunk jellied in their holes," look out from faces of "clenched despair," and hands are "like rakes with fingernails of rust."

The World War II soldier had inherited what the Great War veteran had learned, but he knew also that he did not stand alone as victim of an establishment. There was little cause for disillusionment and sense of betrayal. Peer or laborer, soldier or civilian, all were vulnerable. The soldier was no longer set apart, by either his gallantry or his sacrifice.

In the Second World War the character of military culture became more ambivalent because when everyone was a combatant, the old distinctions lost meaning. Similarly, because neither military nor social elites had much public stock, old ideas of military chivalry lost ground. Unconventional methods fostered in special units such as the Royal Marine Commando and Special Air Service, and the deceptions carried on by Intelligence and espionage agencies bore little resemblance to traditional ideas of military honor. Few were troubled by these innovations, and those who suffered from overly nice scruples were dismissed as obsolete. Yet, there remained as always the nagging problems of moral constancy, ethical responsibility, and their transmission as irreducible demands.

That is why Evelyn Waugh's *Sword of Honour* trilogy—*Men at Arms* (1952), *Officers and Gentlemen* (1955), and *Unconditional Surrender* (1961)—is probably the most important novel fiction about the Second World War. In it Waugh perpetuates the memory of a tradition of chivalry which he believed had reached its last stages of decline in the Great War and had finally become alien in British society. Himself a wartime officer in the Royal Marines and later the Royal Horse Guards, Waugh recounts the fortunes of his vaguely autobiographical hero, the over-aged Guy Crouchback, an officer in the fictitious Corps of Halberdiers.[16] Crouchback and the other characters are symbolic of stages in martial England's declining moral fortunes.

Throughout the wry, detached, and blackly comic satire runs a theme of decay, symbolized in "the Decline of the House of Crouchback." The questing hero's inward journey is from the amateur soldier's early idealism to despair at the futility of war. For Waugh the Second World War manifested a moral descent which had begun at the close of the Middle Ages. British military culture had fallen shamefully during the Imperial age, and the rare truly honorable soldier was seen by his comrades in arms as a dupe, easily outstripped by opportunists in a race for promotion and advantage, and persecuted by unimaginative fools and zealots.

The first of the trilogy, *Men at Arms*, serves to define Waugh's military ideal and its antithesis. Waugh locates the war in a historical twilight. Guy Crouchback's father Gervase has "been born in full sunlight and lived to see night fall." The flagging aristocracy is distinguished from the modern age's bourgeois warmongers, profiteers, and appeasers: "On one side stood the Crouchbacks and certain inconspicuous, anciently allied families; on the other stood the rest of mankind." Guy is destined to be the last of the male line. His eldest brother Gervase has been killed in France, and another, Ivo, has committed suicide in a fit of depression. His sister Angela has married the entrepreneur Box-Bender, and Guy himself has been divorced by his wife Virginia.

Crouchback, his name (Cross-back) associating him with the Crusaders, has a spiritual affinity with his ancestor Roger de Waybrooke (Way-broke), of the Second Crusade. Apparently Waybrooke was shipwrecked at St. Dulcina in Italy, and fell gallantly helping a petty prince in a local power struggle, "a great journey still all before him and a great vow unfulfilled." Castello Crouchback rose on the ruins of St. Dulcina, and here the Crouchback generations have dwelt in self-imposed exile, an outpost of civilization and culture surrounded by superstitious peasants, fascists, and petit bourgeoises.

At first, Guy is rejected for enlistment because of age, while everyone else is "feverishly occupied in disencumbering himself of responsibilities." Discussing his enlistment attempts with his brother-in-law, Crouchback appears to Box-Bender merely "smug" in his dedication. Box-Bender is incredulous that Guy actually wants to *serve* when everyone else is cynically maneuvering for advantage.

His effort to enlist finally rewarded, Guy's ideas about war seem anachronistic. When he expresses indignation at Russia's invasion of Poland, no one sympathizes. The pragmatic Box-Bender sneers, " 'You'd have a general strike and the whole country in collapse if you set up to be just.' " Crouchback's suspicions build when the Finns' defeat proves that optimistic news reports have been lies, and that courage and justice have no bearing on the outcome.

Yet, while Guy does not admit his own love of war even to himself, it serves an emotional need for military romance. Poland's dismemberment is his opportunity for righteous exultation at "a just cause." Similarly, Germany's invasion of Denmark and Norway hold for Guy the promise of sporting action, "very nice for the Halberdiers." With the frightening simplicity of the inspired amateur, Guy learns to adore his regiment and its routines, much as an old Regular might have taken pleasure in discipline and mess tradition as rites of purification which "would work their magic." But Guy's genteel introduction to military life, derived from the peacetime military aesthetic, is deceptive. He has yet to discover that the soldiery best suited for modern war is the kind that takes readily to the brand of inhumanity it has to destroy.

His unit's move to a former boys' boarding school, Kut-al-Imara, named for a humiliating episode of British arms in the East during the Great War, prompts Guy to contemplate moral decline. In his naiveté he looks on military life and the war itself as a moral antisepsis, like the carbolic the battalion uses on its new quarters. Ironically, obsessive rituals of cleanliness and order mask the filth and chaos of war and war lovers.

The novel introduces the one-eyed Brigadier Ritchie-Hooke, a tribal atavism not blind to war's realities, yet with no vision of war's ethical ends. For him war-as-game—"biffing," he calls it—is a quest for adventure and personal glory. The assembled officers, "silent as in a monastery refectory" as they await Ritchie-Hooke's address, present an illusion of withdrawal from worldly cares, as if they have retrogressed to the condition of "scared schoolboys." The appearance is sinister in its deceptiveness, for institutionalizing of irresponsibility disguises too easily the responsibility of military command. For Ritchie-Hooke command is an exhilarating release from moral restraint.

Although Guy is not long in learning that he and his comrades in arms are not soldiers in the best tradition of arms, he is content for a time to play the game. Affecting a military moustache and monocle, he reflects that "After all, . . . his whole uniform [is] a disguise, his whole new calling a masquerade." Becoming a bemused participant in a war he cannot comprehend, Crouchback at first is like a schoolboy romantic, his imaginings of war childishly sanitary. He recalls that, while awaiting his first command, "Troy, Agincourt and Zululand were more real . . . in those days than the world of mud and wire and gas where Gervase fell." Classical, medieval, and Imperial epic battle grip his imagination, while the most recent and ghastly of conflicts escapes his thought.

Crouchback's closest acquaintance Apthorpe personifies another sort of romantic military game-playing. With his Anglican high church aunt he stands for Imperial England, imbued with the romance of dominion, material possession, and power. Apthorpe is inordinately proud of his mounds of esoteric baggage, meant to give the impression that he has been the archetypal ruling Briton on the exotic fringes of Empire. Like the romance of Empire itself, these material acquisitions are a sham of their owner's true worth; self-interested conquest only apes the true quest.

The theme of quest, true and false, is dominant; allegorical representations of the grail are by turns serious and comic, sacred and profane. When a priest speaks to Crouchback of " 'this terrible time of doubt, danger and suffering,' " Guy bridles and replies that for him it is " 'A time of glory and dedication.' " He seems to see as his destiny a completion of Roger de Waybrooke's abbreviated crusade. Guy's grail is the fulfillment of military service, its symbol present at a mass evidently to be associated with the miraculous vision in Arthurian legend:

Presently a sacristan came in and drew the black curtains from the east windows; brilliant sunlight blinded their eyes, momentarily, to candles and chalice.

Guy's increasingly paranoic companion Apthorpe seeks a hilariously improbable grail in the shape of his precious portable field toilet. Its function speaks for its owner's aspirations as questing warrior! The covetous Ritchie-Hooke appropriates it, and Apthorpe's quest to get it back is consummated when the booby-trap the brigadier has installed explodes.[17] The thunder box's fate, and the benumbed Apthorpe's ending up in the grass on all fours like an animal, signal the beginning of his descent into madness. Apthorpe's wasting body is an apt symbol for the deterioration of Britain's Imperial impulse. Similarly, his suicide seems to stand for the Second World War, born of self-destructive policies and ending the British Empire. By 1945 independence for most British possessions was all but accomplished fact.

Despite Guy's mystical fervor and high intentions, his first assay proves as misdirected and abortive as Roger de Waybrooke's. Guy's battalion is diverted to Dakar, a French African colony under Vichy rule. Following Ritchie-Hooke's orders, he engages in an unauthorized patrol ashore, and along with his mischievous commander, he suffers official censure and disgrace. Ritchie-Hooke's quest, whether in barracks or in battle, is an exhilarating game, affording him all the irresponsible devilry of youth. A lovable old child left over from World War I, he delights in the practical joke, the contest, the need to be one-up, on his subordinate Apthorpe, on his own force commander, and on his enemy, no matter what the cost. His martial instincts are the source both of his military successes and his self-injury. " 'There are no Sundays in the firing line,' " he declares; nor is there any inhibiting code of arms.

Ritchie-Hooke goes ashore at Dakar to play his version of the legendary beheading game. He keeps Guy in the dark. Guy has no idea that his own mission to carry out reconaissance ashore and to bring back a coconut as proof is merely a diversion for Ritchie-Hooke's private escapade. Ritchie-Hooke returns, mischievously triumphant, with a human head. Guy, whose crusading ancestor's escutcheon bore "turks' heads," wins only a coconut and disgrace. The would-be serious warrior has been made to play only a mock game, so that the gamesman might play in earnest. For Ritchie-Hooke men are pawns in a game of chance. Guy has been used, and like his spiritual forebear, he has been diverted from his rightful path by events he cannot control.

The Second World War was no more a time for epic heroes to wage war for private sport and fame than it was for Imperial jingoists or high-minded romantics. Ritchie-Hooke is relieved of command by prosaic authorities, and retires into decent obscurity. Guy is held wholly responsible for his own part in the antic operation because, while few want to accept much responsibility themselves, they are quick to assign blame. *Men at Arms* shows an end of legitimate pride and chivalric sentiment. Waugh saw in their place a military spirit that had become opportunist, authoritarian, and bureaucratic.

This tragic inevitability is shown in Apthorpe's plummet from bombastic vigor to paranoia and suicide. The titles of *Men at Arms'* three books reflect successively stages in Imperial England's self-destructive moral course: "Apthorpe *Gloriosus*" (reminiscent of the Plautine soldier-braggart-clown and his dramatic successors); "... *Furibundus*" (like Seneca's mad Hercules *Furens*); and "... *Immolatus*" (suggestive of the fate of Hector's Troy). All of Waugh's characters are a bit self-destructively mad in their obsessive quests. Apthorpe has held an ideal image of himself as English *b'wana*, and Ritchie-Hooke has pursued the Great War's early heroic ideal. Guy himself has cherished a romantic delusion that the facade of officership he has found in his first Halberdiers' mess embodies the spirit of chivalry.

Although Apthorpe and Ritchie-Hooke let Guy down, they too are after more than mere material advantage. Like Guy, they have no proper place in a society grown secular and acquisitive. After the ill-fated raid, a couple of officers chat offhandedly: " 'Both Uncles gone the same day.' 'Funny, I was thinking the same.' I rather preferred Crouchback on the whole." The romance of Empire, the spirit of chivalry; yet it is the spirit of chivalry in its personification as Crouchback which has survived, no matter how tarnished. That both Guy and Apthorpe have been lame, and that Ritchie-Hooke receives a leg wound seem to have symbolic importance as part of a long literary tradition of warriors whose leg wounds have been evidence of imperfection, vulnerability, and fallibility.[18] They err but not from bad intentions.

Everyone else has more in common with Trimmer, Virginia's lover who has a larger part in *Officers and Gentlemen* than in *Men at Arms*. They are upstarts who trim sail with the wind if they can get something. Even the Irish priest at the little English church where Guy takes mass is interested in the number of Halberdiers attending because his parish is paid a "capitation" fee. Like Ritchie-Hooke, he uses soldiers to collect heads for his own purposes. The veil of banality that has fallen over England's spirit of chivalry is apparent in Guy's incapacity for artistic endeavor after Virginia leaves him. The poetry has gone out of soldiering, and mere prose is left.

The concept of the "Man at Arms" reflected in Waugh's novel is synonymous with a moral tradition of service and sacrifice for ethical ends. "Soldier" ceases to mean either a Regular or Reservist. It is an *idea*, grounded in centuries of cultural growth, and held as belief by loyal and chivalrous spirits. Whoever is charged by the state to aid in its defense, whoever holds to the *idea* of "soldier," and whoever lives by it is a true "Man at Arms" in

Waugh's novels. Paradoxically, his fiction and the Allied man at arms' conduct throughout the Second World War are themselves the best arguments against a theory of moral decline. Military culture never was more noble in its means and ends. What the *Sword of Honour* trilogy reveals about men's baseness is true, but the essence of Waugh's military ideal was upheld by the many servicemen and -women in that war.

FROM WORLD WAR II TO THE FALKLANDS WAR

> If wars were limited in ages past, the reasons why they were so have little relevance for us today.[19]

With the war over, a system of compulsory national service in the Territorial Army was instituted and remained in place until 1957. The new pattern of alliances and enmities in Europe, together with the new technology of weapons and delivery systems, nullified the strategic protection afforded by the English Channel, which formerly had been a major factor determining the character of British arms. England joined the community of continental Western Europe in the shadow of the Eastern bloc's Warsaw Pact nations, and became a major partner in the North Atlantic Treaty Organization (NATO). For the first time the army's peacetime character became like that of Fortress Europe's traditional armies: a mass of temporary soldiers, commanded and trained by cadres of professional officers and NCOs who were their squadrons' and battalions' real spine. Peacetime national service at home, in Germany with the British Army Of the Rhine (BAOR) and elsewhere in a dwindling collection of Commonwealth possessions, was much despised by England's temporary soldiers. It violated a sensibility born of centuries-old tradition. Although compulsory national service enticed some men to sign on as Regulars when their stint was done, few conscripts became enthusiastic amateurs.

The idea of a mass British Army of temporary soldiers could be justified only as long as it appeared that nuclear warfare could be assimilated into the land battle's tactically traditional conventions, as artillery had been some four centuries earlier. The illusion survived as a basis for NATO tactical doctrine almost to the mid–1960s, and was accepted enthusiastically by regular officers and NCOs, many of whom had been in the Second World War or had served in the British Commonwealth Division with the United Nations in Korea. They carried forward their amateur élan into a training environment with bleak realities beyond their experience or imagination, and practiced the new "nuclear tactics" with their old panache.

The idea was this: Facing each other on a battlefield they viewed like a big chessboard, opposing commanders tried to maneuver each other's forces into areas of ever-decreasing size by feinting, attacking, and blocking all but predetermined lines of approach and withdrawal. The tactical doctrine of dispersal replaced the old emphasis on "concentration of force," and junior officers had to achieve skills of independent command and initiative earlier associated with the temperament of the inspired amateur. Once an enemy was contained within a sufficiently small perimeter, the nuclear "knockout punch" would be delivered. NATO exercises seemed a reasonable sport, predicated on the certainty that fear would dictate the game rules. Neither side would exceed prudence by using a nuclear device larger in destructive power than the one-kiloton so-called nominal bomb, adequate only to vaporize a battalion.

That was in the early 1960s, when the brinkmanship game was being played by statesmen, in the conviction that the superiority of Western technology made diplomatic power gambles fairly safe. Since then, however, little serious consideration has been given to the idea of levels of escalation. Now the talk is of preemptive or retaliatory strike on a hemispheric scale, as the likely alternative to conventional war. The relatively lighthearted strategic and tactical fictions of the 1960s have dissipated, and Britain's NATO troops have returned to doctrines based in the main on the tactics of highly mobile conventional war, while with a sense of futility perhaps, they train also for protective measures against nuclear, biological, and chemical warfare.

Whatever the eventuality, there would be little or no mobilization time, so that the value of a trained reserve has diminished. Reflecting the new reality, the British Army was retailored during the 1960s as a force-in-being, with highly trained regulars still positioned on the Continent. The Territorials suffered massive reductions in 1960 and again in 1965. Both among Territorial and regular regiments there were amalgamations to streamline the army. Regiments were redesignated with new titles, and their men paraded to consecrate new colors. The experience was wrenching for men whose regiments were their families; but the regimental spirit forged in the eighteenth century somehow adapted and prevailed as the traditions and battle honors of old regiments were perpetuated lovingly in the new.

It was not only the advance of technology and the nature of the strategic threat in Europe which altered the army's character. While America's emergence as the West's major superpower had broadened its strategic concerns to hemispheric proportions, England at the end of its Imperial phase in the late 1940s was divesting itself as gracefully as possible of its possessions before they tore loose anyway. One by one, Palestine, Malaya, and territories in the West Indies and southern Africa became self-governing. The most significant of these events for the army was India's Independence. In August of 1947, Britain's Imperial Army in India became the armies of India and Pakistan, and the last of its British officers and home battalions withdrew.

A generation of British regulars in India had given their lives to the idea of Empire, as if it would never end. The wrenching force of Independence is revealed poignantly in Paul Scott's vignette of modern India, *Staying On* (1978). When the army departs, an elderly British military couple remain to live out their days in a former hill station. The novel, a tragic tale of gradual isolation, alienation, and death, is a microcosm of the decay and death of the British Raj. The age that had molded Kipling's Tommy and had made the British regular the model of military professionalism had ended.

Ironically, the new technology which had brought about mass armies had by the 1960s offered a prospect of war so total that protracted combat between mass armies in Europe seemed impossible. Similarly, the new realities which expanded Britain's strategic concerns to include Europe and the whole Western Hemisphere accompanied a contraction of its immediate interests. The commercial impetus which in the eighteenth century had sent Britain's Volunteers and regulars abroad had come to an end. For these reasons, through the 1970s the British Army began to resemble in numbers and role the late Restoration army more than it had at any time since the seventeenth century. British regulars even still patrolled the streets of Belfast as once King Charles II's Embodied Militia might have patrolled English towns in search of Commonwealth men.

The British regular of the 1970s and 1980s has combined ideally the qualities of the eighteenth century's Volunteer with those of the nineteenth century's Regular. The evidence for that assertion is the superb band of professionals who fought their splendid little war in the Falkland Islands, a feat both magnificent and peculiar. Unlike the United States, which has labored to maintain strategic integrity in its hemisphere ever since the enunciation of the Monroe Doctrine, Britain has not expected any longer to have to protect territorial interests outside Britain, especially in the Americas. It was mere aberrational politics which made the Argentine descendants of Spanish conquistadors forget the lesson England's sailor-soldier Sir Francis Drake had taught the Armada three centuries earlier in the Renaissance's dawn of British military professionalism.

Argentina's junta did not count on either the British political will or military skill when their forlorn conscripts, commanded by arrogant and inept officers, occupied the "Malvinas." British national pride rode on this remote remnant of Britain's possessions. Only three days after Argentina's invasion of the Falklands on April 2, 1982, and only two days after the United Nations Security Council's resolution calling on Argentina to withdraw, the first elements of the British task force were on their way to begin "Operation Corporate." With all negotiation exhausted, the task force's land elements went ashore on 21 May. Only three weeks later on 14 June, after a rapid advance and some brisk engagements, a mere seven battalions forced the unconditional surrender of a dug-in defensive force of 12,000.

The oddity of the Falklands War is instructive in underscoring the passing of Britain's age of military amateurism. The war was an anachronism, perhaps reminiscent of a time when small forces of tough, drilled, and disciplined Regulars kept the map red by taking on Zulus, Boers, and Sudanese Dervishes. But there were differences. Along with professional competence and

determination, there were verve, flexibility of mind and action, and belief in
the moral necessity of the enterprise, which at the start of the Great War
had separated the old regular from the temporary soldier. The Falklands
War was never in danger of turning out like the battle for Majuba Hill, a
shocking defeat by Boer farmers in 1881, made possible because of the British
regulars' arrogance and rigidity of mind. Indeed, the Falklands War reflected
the British regular soldier's historical legacy of a tradition of professionalism,
but tempered with the best qualities of spirited amateurism.

This unique combination of qualities derived from a tradition of three
centuries was manifested in the makeup of the task force's land formations.[20]
The Royal Marines of 3 Commando Brigade were the spiritual heirs of
Kipling's "kind of giddy harumfrodite—soldier and sailor too," the soldier
of Her Majesty's ships, who in the heyday of Empire was "landin' 'isself
with a Gatlin' gun to talk to them 'eathen kings." Although the Royal Marines
belong, strictly speaking, to the Admiralty, their traditions and history are
inseparable from the army's, and therefore have their place in this history
as well as in the army's ceremonial order of regimental precedence. Regiments of the army served the Admiralty in British men-of-war both before
and after the first regiment of Marines was raised in 1664. To this day the
colors of several line regiments bear the naval crown. The nineteenth-century
Marine regular's unconventional role was typical of an age which, since late
in the previous century, had seen the growth of Light Infantry and Rifle
regiments to wage the skirmishing kinds of imperial wars thought so lacking
in propriety by the traditionalist officers of Guards and line regiments.

Aside from their operations as shore defense and protection for naval and
coastal gunners, Marine battalions served at the Somme and in other major
engagements of the Great War. However, the unorthodoxy associated with
the Royal Marines' historical tradition properly came into its own only with
the flourishing amateur spirit of the Commandos early in the Second World
War. In 1940 the originally separate units of army commandos and Royal
Marine commandos were conceived because of history's lessons taught by
ill-armed but fanatical and desperate irregulars: the Spanish guerrillas of the
Peninsular War, the Boer commandos, and Palestinian freedom fighters of
the 1930s.[21] This idea that small groups of enthusiastic amateurs with a cause
would prevail over larger and conventionally trained forces was a return to
the thinking of Charles II's early architect of the Restoration's administration,
Edward Hyde, Earl of Clarendon,[22] in his treatise inveighing against a standing army of professional soldiers. The difference, however, was that the
Second World War expert in irregular warfare was seen as a kind of soldier
with positive virtues of his own, rather than simply as an untrained citizen
whose enthusiasm and moral superiority supposedly would guarantee success.

The Commandos attracted adventurous men, ready for excitement and
careless of their own lives. They were amateurs in spirit, and both in terms

of conventional skills and untried concepts of operations, they were amateurs by any measure of military competence, too. Indeed, a raid on Guernsey when the force was just over a month old was reported by one of the Commando officers himself as "a very amateurish affair."[23]

There was a lot of opposition to the Commandos among Regular Army officers. Sir Winston Churchill remembered:

The idea that large bands of favoured "irregulars" with their unconventional attire and free-and-easy bearing should throw an implied slur on the efficiency and courage of the regular battalions was odious to men who had given all their lives to the organized discipline of permanent units. The colonels of many of our finest regiments were aggrieved. "What is there they can do that my battalion cannot? This plan robs the whole Army of its prestige and of its finest men. We never had it in 1918. Why now."[24]

The events which since those early days have made the Commandos a legend of military professionalism need no retelling here. By the time of the Falklands War, the Royal Marine Commandos had become exemplars of the traditional British military spirit of amateurism, incorporated into the regular's professional ethos.

The 5th Infantry Brigade, which included the 2nd Battalion of The Parachute Regiment, fought in the Falklands War side by side with 3 Commando Brigade. The "Paras" ' link with the Commandos dates from 1941, when 2 Commando became 11 Special Air Service Battalion, and later, The Parachute Regiment.[25] No account of the regiment's exploits is needed, beyond mention of the 2nd Battalion's outstanding performance as a unit of 5 Brigade in the Falklands.

The Special Air Service (SAS) was in the Falklands, its history consummately reflecting the British professional's spirit of amateurism. It was the spirit of amateur dash and initiative, fostered by the Second World War's least conventional demands, which had brought the SAS into being. Its original recruiting source in 1941 was the eccentric Long Range Desert Group (LRDG), or "Popski's Private Army," a remarkable collection of impressarios, whose unorthodox methods were reflected even in their flamboyant and unmilitary dress. The LRDG was roundly despised even by fellow wartime soldiers who had embraced the norms of the regular, but they were also admired for their exploits and envied for their freedom from traditional military constraints. From the LRDG grew the Special Air Service Brigade, soon to become the SAS Regiment. There could be no more professionally "correct" background for its first moving spirit, Lieutenant David Stirling of the Scots Guards, and no more professionally disreputable background for its first fifty or so volunteers than "Popski's Private Army." Stirling had already departed from the professional norm, however, because at the time he was serving in the Commandos.

After extraordinary exploits in the Second World War, the SAS was disbanded briefly, until its special skills were required for the British effort in Malaya. Reconstituted as the Malaya Air Scouts, the regiment soon got back its old name. Furthermore, in 1947 a Territorial Army regiment, the Artists Rifles, was redesignated the 21st SAS Regiment (Artists) T.A., and began supplying volunteers to the Regular Army component. The Artists Rifles, formed in 1859 by Lord Leighton, the eminent British classical painter and sculptor, was from its inception the very paradigm of military dilettantism and social consciousness. Those characteristics have brought a tradition of color and flair to the modern SAS, appropriate to the regimental motto, "Who dares wins." The SAS has become the model of professionalism in irregular warfare. What had happened, really, was the professionalizing, institutionalizing, and regularizing of unorthodoxy, so that the SAS men's unassuming manner both conceals and manifests an enormous capacity for orderly and efficient violence.[26]

Other units in the Falklands perpetuated the British Army's tradition of loyalty and duty associated with the professional soldier, dating from its beginnings in Charles II's retinue of Royal troops. A Medium Reconnaissance Squadron of the Blues and Royals was a reminder of the first regiments of cavalry created by Charles II. The "Blues," originally the Royal Regiment of Horse and later The Royal Horse Guards, date from 1660, and the 1st or Royal Dragoons, later known simply as the Royals, were formed in 1661. The regiments amalgamated in 1969 as the Blues and Royals (Royal Horse Guards and First Dragoons). Equally regarded originally as the Monarch's troops were two battalions of Foot Guards. The Scots Guards whose 2nd Battalion saw action in the Falklands were formed by Charles II in 1660. The Welsh Guards, the most junior of the regiments of Guards, were formed only in 1915, perpetuating and renewing in modern war the Regular Army's early tradition of service to the Monarch. The regiment's 1st Battalion served in the Falklands.

This revealing composite portrait of a force of amateur-professionals in which Guards regiments served with Royal Marines, The Parachute Regiment, and SAS men was completed by the presence of the 1st Battalion, 7th Gurkha Rifles. Following an honored tradition of mercenary service to the British Monarch, the Gurkhas are a living memory of the days of the Raj. With their British officers, the NCOs and men of the army's Gurkha battalions still are volunteers from the Kingdom of Nepal. They have been so since the Gurkha War of 1815, when British Regulars learned to respect the Gurkhas' fighting qualities and welcomed them as comrades in arms.

With India's Independence in 1947, Britain retained four Gurkha battalions (later increased to six), perhaps in no small part as an expression of good faith, gratitude, and affection. The Gurkhas repaid British trust with the same loyalty and professionalism which had made them a feared legend. The intense family feeling is captured in *Bugles and a Tiger*, whose author,

John Masters, had lived for years as an officer in a prewar Gurkha battalion. The unique bond between the Gurkhas and their British officers has shown the strains of the modern age, in which benign paternalism has become anachronistic.

The presence of the Gurkhas in the Falklands evokes nostalgia about a passing time. That may have been their last battle under the British flag. Today, they are relegated mainly to border patrol duties on Hong Kong's frontier with the People's Republic of China. While the British government pledges to continue their service in purposeful roles when Hong Kong becomes a possession of the People's Republic, their future in the twenty-first century seems in doubt. These riflemen *ne plus ultra*, with military virtues once so valuable on the frontiers of Empire, may not have a place much longer.

The Gurkhas' uncertain position casts in relief a challenge facing the British Army as a whole. The Falklands War was probably a welcome diversion for the army's Gamesmen, the officers and men who held values and traditions derived from the Great War's army. Through those earlier ranks had passed both Regular and temporary soldiers, their inspired amateurism hardening into resolve for some and dissipating in disillusionment for others. The same spirit was in the dedication and competence of the next generation of amateurs who fought another world war, and who in turn transmitted their ethic of service to the soldiers who have served since. However, the Falklands War was an anomaly in British military history. Without an Empire to defend, and with the age of the Nuclear Endgame already arrived, the British Army's present ethos is as threatened as the Gurkhas' future.

NOTES

1. Edmund Blunden, *Poems 1930–1940* (London: Macmillan & Co., 1940), pp. 210–14.

2. R. Money Barnes, *A History of the Regiments & Uniforms of the British Army* (London: Seeley Service & Co. Ltd., 1957), p. 266.

3. Evelyn Waugh, *Men at Arms* (Harmondsworth: Penguin, 1952). Subsequent citations are to this edition.

4. George Herbert Clarke, *The New Treasury of War Poetry* (Boston: Houghton Mifflin Co., 1943), p. xxxi.

5. Brian Gardner, intro., *The Terrible Rain* (London: Methuen, 1966), p. xviii. The poetry quoted in this chapter is from this collection.

6. A. S. J. Tessimond, "England."

7. Denton Welch, "Rural Raid."

8. Charles Hamblet (RAF), "Bombs on My Town."

9. H. B. Mallalieu, "Readiness Standby."

10. J. Brownowski, "Man, Take Your Gun."

11. Charles Causley (RN), "Recruiting Drive."

12. Ian Serrailler, "The New Learning."

13. John Manifold, "The Recruit."

14. Ruthven Todd, "These Are The Fruits."

15. G. A. Wagner, "Guardsman."

16. Waugh is mentioned in Hilary St. George Saunders's *The Green Beret: The Story of the Commandos 1940–45* (London: Michael Joseph, 1949), pp. 65, 68, 213. For parallels between Waugh's personal experiences and his novels, see Jeffrey Heath, *The Picturesque Prison: Evelyn Waugh and His Writing* (Montreal: McGill-Queen's University Press, 1982).

17. The "thunderbox" episode bears associations with the long literary tradition relating to the magus Roger Bacon's brass talking head, which is reputed to have shattered thunderously. By inference, Apthorpe as symbol of British imperialism is a false magician, infatuated with power at the cost of national virtue.

18. Waugh's art is very allusive. As with the "beheading game," leg and foot woundings have a lengthy history of myth and symbol relating to flawed warriors; for example, Achilles, Bran (*Mabinogian*), Peleus, the Fisher King (Sir James Frazer, *The Golden Bough*), Maurice (Emile Zola, *La Débâcle*), Bourne (*The Middle Parts of Fortune*), John Ball (*In Parenthesis*), and the puzzling scarred boot worn by Alaine Robbe-Grillet's soldier in *In the Labyrinth* (1959, trans. 1967).

19. Bernard Brodie, *Strategy in the Missile Age* (Princeton, N.J.: Princeton University Press, 1959), p. 311.

20. For a table of land forces (excluding SAS Regiment personnel), see William Fowler, *Battle for the Falklands* (London: Osprey, 1982), p. 12.

21. Saunders, *Green Beret*, p. 21.

22. See Chapter 1.

23. Saunders, *Green Beret*, p. 30.

24. Sir Winston Churchill, *The Second World War*, Vol. 2 (Cambridge: Riverside Press, 1951), p. 371.

25. Hilary St. George Saunders, *The Red Beret: The Story of the Parachute Regiment at War 1940–45* (London: Michael Joseph, 1950).

26. *The Winter War*, an account of the Falklands War by two journalists who accompanied the troops, is particularly poignant in capturing the flavor of hard professionalism spiced with amateur verve, the more so because the young correspondents' glimpse at these traditional soldiers from the outside. Neither has had military service. See Patrick Bishop and John Witherow, *The Winter War* (London: Quarter Books, 1982).

CONCLUSION

A HISTORICAL OVERVIEW OF BRITISH MILITARY AMATEURISM

NEC Aspera Terrent[1]

The hundred years from the midseventeenth to the mideighteenth century saw the growth to maturity of British Constitutional monarchy and, with it, the emergence of Britain's army as a truly national institution. The upper class's obsession with maintaining the status quo was a fearful reaction to changes occurring subtly and irresistibly. As military culture developed through the eighteenth century, the army became conservative and tradition-bound, its evolution reflecting the national temper.

The commercial spirit of the age made for a time of contracts. In Britian, the consequence of an astute ministerial eye to commercial profit was a policy of Crown recognition of private, yet quasi-Imperial, agencies in the New World, the most important of which were the Honourable East India Company, founded in 1600, and the Hudson's Bay Company, founded in 1668. Even religion placed great emphasis on the Covenant as a divine business arrangement, and the Puritan-impelled Parliamentary soldier had chosen what he believed was his covenant with God over his covenant with his King. A contracted professional soldiery was of several kinds. Some followed the wars as individuals, finding employment where they could. Also, nations with a shortage of other kinds of export goods contracted out complete military units, while sometimes maintaining limited control to ensure that they would not be employed against the national interest. Still other units fought as auxiliaries with another nation's army, though as national contingents wholly under home control.

In effect, statesmen regarded soldiers as commodities in a mercantile structure which established relationships between nations. Thus, national commercial enterprise as military adventure would eventually bring about a merging of Regular soldiers' mercenary motives and patriotic sentiments, expressed later as Britain's nineteenth-century romance of Empire. This professional mercenary ethos accounts, however, for only part of the military culture that had emerged in the seventeenth century. England's Civil War had produced a citizen-soldiery which was perpetuated in the Commonwealth's standing army, and later in the Militia of the Restoration and eighteenth century. This "Constitutional" force, as distinct from the "mercenary" army of Regulars,[2] was the result of a strong new ideological element in the hitherto largely pragmatic profession of arms. Opposing views during England's Civil War had been a complex web of political, social, and religious issues. Theoretically, loyalties had been to ideals of faith and government, rather than to individual leaders. The Cavalier army had fought not only for Charles I, but also for the principle of monarchy. Similarly, the Parliamentary army had fought in defense of a particular theological position.

From the end of the Commonwealth period, the mercenary perception of military service as a profession had to be reconciled with the newer perception of an ideologically motivated soldier. Thus, two traditions would merge, each imparting an essential element to the developing military culture:

There was the old, honourable soldierly pride of the mercenary, and there was the newer, but well-established tradition of the disciplined armies which fought for religion and national constitutional freedom.[3]

From the Commonwealth period onward, Crown authority by itself was no longer adequate moral license to practice the profession of arms. The English Parliament had seen to that, and with the Restoration, kept a sharp eye to ensure that the army did not become wholly the sovereign's personal retinue. If the army was not to be feared and wooed, it had to be controlled and limited.

Yet the army still was acknowledged by statesmen as a necessity for civil order, national defense, and prosecution of the nation's economic aims abroad. Control of both the army and government was a major Constitutional problem during the Restoration, because of a general principle governing the relationship between an army and the state it serves:

[S]ocieties are orderly and peaceable only in so far as they have solved this double problem, of the subordination of military force to the political government, and of the control of a government in possession of such force by legal restraint and the popular will.[4]

The corollary dilemma for the military profession was the soldier's need to reconcile his loyalty to his sovereign with his loyalty to the state as embodied in Parliament. For most of the period, this difficulty was manifested in the emergence of two virtually distinct military bodies: on the one hand the Regular Army, essentially mercenary and loyal to the monarch; the Militia, a Constitutional force more given to parochial loyalties and initially conceived as a counterbalance to the army. The difference in political orientation between the two forces diminished steadily as England's successive monarchs and ministers established the precedents and ordinances which produced a true Constitutional monarchy after the so-called Glorious Revolution of 1688. In the meantime, a large and unruly Embodied Militia tyrannized the countryside, and earned the fear and hatred once reserved for mercenary Regulars.

Through the eighteenth century, the army and militia imparted their ethos to each other and became more similar in composition and custom as England's military interests abroad drew more men into active service. The Restoration and most of the eighteenth century had brought relief from internecine strife and major foreign wars, although there were the "Irish Problem" and many little campaigns elsewhere. This was a period of profound distrust of armies and loathing of military men. Exploration and exploitation of the New World brought new wealth, and complacency set in among the middle and upper classes. War-weariness became self-satisfaction, and disillusionment with war and hatred of the soldiery became disregard and contempt.

Yet a parallel tradition, more Gallic than Anglo-Saxon, persisted. English infatuation with French philosophical idealism, manners, and fashions was a feature of the Restoration. While English officers and common soldiers alike professed contempt for the fighting abilities of the "froggies," they also were thoroughly receptive to French notions of military *gloire* and *honneur*. The incompetent dandies who officered Britian's army, and the rank and file who were abused by their superiors and despised by their society, grew to hold a deep conviction about the romance and honor of "soldiering." The militia, far more important politically than effective militarily, was useful for aspiring members of the squirearchy who thought to earn prestige and influence by prancing in uniform on horseback. Meanwhile, the professional military created an insular subculture of its own as a source of fierce pride and loyalty.

An oath of loyalty to sovereign and state, regular pay, a strong sense of military honor derived from the special nature of soldiering, and an emergent love of country during a period of fierce international competition—all were causes for the soldier's sense of superior otherness. As England's prosperity continued, views toward the soldiery mellowed from active hatred to good-humored indulgence and condescension tinged at times with irritation. Regular soldiers and militiamen alike were targets for the comic satire of novelists, artists, poets, and pamphleteers, the more so as military culture became discrete and eccentric.

Society's contempt was somewhat justified. Many officers fell woefully short of the ideal, especially in the early eighteenth century. Military specialization had brought a need for commanders with knowledge, skill, and imagination, qualities few officers possessed. While the rank and file were the scum of society, they had to be desensitized further to become capable of maneuvering with machine-like precision and to endure point-blank fire without flinching. Discipline ceased to be merely a means of troops being kept from crime, desertion, fighting among themselves, and abusing civilians. Now brutality and rum became basic tactical expedients. Firepower at close range won battles, so that concentration of fire, and steadiness in withstanding preparatory cannonading became paramount military virtues. Commanders reposed their faith in their officers' loyalty and their men's steadfastness, and while lipservice was given to professional knowledge, intelligence was generally distrusted among officers and men alike.

Military thinking corresponded to the mechanistic thought of the age. A military force was a well-ordered mechanism, in which all the parts—infantry, cavalry, artillery, and various support services—functioned as part of a coordinated whole, in theory, anyway. Infantry formations were rigidly geometric, the squares, columns, and lines answering the compulsively rationalistic will to order that characterized the age. The rank and file who made up those squares, columns, and lines were not so reasonable that they were impervious to fear and fatigue. Unless "reason" were imposed through rigorous punishment and repetitious drill, the common soldier was in danger of disturbing the perfect symmetry of the whole. Thus, soldiers who had little cause to love their calling anyway were subjected by their officers and sergeants to a kind of discipline that made fear of punishment worse than fear of death.

The discipline needed for this machine-like precision was conducive to the professional soldier's toughness of spirit which later would give the nineteenth-century Regular Army its special character. During the eighteenth century, however, when British soldiers were responding to brutal treatment by achieving extraordinary feats of arms, countercurrents in society were advancing the cause of the dignity of the individual, which found expression in the French Revolution and the American War of Independence. Meanwhile, successive levies for service abroad had swelled the ranks of the Embodied Militia with unwilling citizens. In Marlborough's time warfare had been limited, and the Regular Army had been only slightly larger than at the Restoration. Even as late as 1793 the Regular Army numbered only about 15,000 in England and about twice that abroad.

In the closing years of the eighteenth century, there was a constant need for troops in America and wherever European powers competed for territory. The ranks were filled through every base ploy: "crimps" got men drunk and delivered them to recruiting sergeants for bounty, and press gangs abducted unfortunates from the streets. The victims were amateurs beyond doubt, although many filled the ranks of regular regiments. Before the century ended, society's view of the soldier was changing. Loathing and contempt gave way finally to pity, reflected especially in poetry, as a prelude to the romanticizing tendencies of the early nineteenth century. However, attitudes toward the soldier as a collective abstraction bore little relationship to reactions in individual encounters, and changes in public sentiment did little to alleviate the misery and neglect that were the common soldier's lot.

Although cynicism and materialism after the Restoration had not been fertile soil for the growth of military ideals, an aristocratic military code nevertheless soon flourished. In the past the professional captain of war had honored the old codes of chivalry (perhaps rather hollowly) as his own. With the establishment of a truly national army, small though it was, the military profession had perpetuated and elaborated upon chivalric codes of conduct for everyone who bore arms. While the code had class connotations for officers, it was also universal, as regimental honor began to assume first importance. As the penchant for private dueling might suggest, officers embraced a convention of jealousy for their personal honor, and did not share much concern for the honor of the profession's corporate institutions. An officer's loyalty was primarily to his class, rather than to his regiment or the officer corps.

In the eighteenth century, the regiment became an institution with nearly mystical significance, and was the focus of the soldier's life, sentiment, and *esprit de corps*. It was the evolution of the regiment as an institution as well as a tactical organization which determined the nature of military culture in Britain's armies. Because officers did not find permanent attachment to one regiment to be in their interests, it may be fair to say that professional noncommissioned officers were the main repositories of the regimental spirit and the military ethos it sustained through the eighteenth and nineteenth centuries.

Officers of both the army and militia sought purchase of commissions in higher ranks wherever vacancies appeared, and remained the profession's gypsies until the practice was abolished late in the nineteenth century. Many officers, both regular and militia, identified themselves permanently with a single regiment, but that identification was not unalloyed with social pretension, economic advantage, and political ambition. Nevertheless, although the evolution of the regimental ethos would not be complete for another century, the regiment became fertile soil in which a true military culture took root.

While nurturing a spirit of professional dedication, the regimental ethos also was characterized by parochialism and ignorance. A regiment was a little world, with its own uniform, customs, and routines, and it demanded absolute fidelity. Perhaps much of the reason for the growth of a distinct culture was the rejection and isolation of the military by a society at first fearful and resentful during the Restoration, and afterwards complacent and contemptuous. The soldier thus was thrown back on his own kind for self-respect and a sense of belonging. For Regulars on foreign garrison duty in Africa, India, America, and the West Indies, their nearly permanent exile drew them together as military families and outposts of British society.

Although soldiers had been despised or ignored from the Restoration on, the military ethos penetrated the culture of civilian society, largely as a result of the squirearchy's vested interest in the militia as a source of political power and social prestige. Moreover, the military profession promised a reasonable career for the squirearchy's leftover sons when land inheritances and church livings either were not available or did not provide prospects suitable to the temperament of a profligate or adventurous young man.[5]

In time the relationship between military and civilian cultures became reciprocal, ensuring a continuation of amateur spirit from outside the profession. Although the English never bred a military caste equivalent, say, to the Prussian Junkers, there were "military families," for whom it was traditional that one or more of each generation's sons would become Regular Army officers. Thus, family pride often coincided with the demands of the code of arms in requiring an officer to practice *noblesse*. *Noblesse* had long ceased to be limited merely to aristocratic behavior; it perpetuated the feudal notion of mutual obligation which bound leader and led. The sentiment between the landed gentry and yeoman tenantry had retained a strongly feudal quality, which carried over into relationships in the Militia.

The Regular Army also exercised a benevolent if cruel sort of feudalism, because its officers were of the same gentry that provided Militia officers. As warfare became logistically more complex, and military organizations became more specialized and self-contained, it was in the Army's interest for officers, noncommissioned officers, and rank and file to care for each other's welfare. An officer's duty therefore came to include responsibility for discipline, rations, quarters, and the physical well-being of his soldiers. Of course, actual practice fell woefully short of the ideal. In fact, officership in the early eighteenth century probably was worse than at any time before or since. However, an ideal of the officer's paternalistic responsibility for his men was universally accepted in theory; and at least in some instances, most notably during Marlborough's command, responsibility actually was practiced.

Unlike the eighteenth century with its reverence for the past and its love of order and stability, the nineteenth century was a time of sweeping change throughout Europe. Vigor, motion, progress, and free expression of feeling were the new gods. "*Activité, activité, vitesse*," Napoleon's dictum for his generals before launching his armies into Austria, exemplified the spirit of the age. It was a time of revolution on all fronts: political, social, technological, scientific, and artistic. Military culture was exposed to new realities as soldiers experienced modern war for the first time. But while the physical and psychological impact on Continental armies was profound, the British Army was as tradition-bound as the social system it mirrored. It was in the interests of the upper classes from whom were drawn the army's senior officers to maintain the status quo; and they resisted change imposed by civilian progressives in government.

The need for change was not urgent, because the Royal Navy kept the-hearth safe. However, before Nelson's destruction of the French fleet at Trafalgar in 1805, the Napoleonic threat had brought about frenzied activity. From 1803 to 1805, in every English hamlet and village companies of local Militia called "Fencibles," "Yeomanry," and "Volunteer Cavalry" were raised for defense, and they drilled enthusiastically in glorious uniforms. In 1804 the Militia numbered almost 500,000. In 1805 compulsory training for home defense began, and the militia was used to reinforce the Regular Army. By 1808 the total force had expanded to 650,000, and at Waterloo most of the 36,000 British troops were in fact untried militiamen.[6] Performing with the steadiness of regulars, they took, 15,000 casualties, a number equal to the strength of the entire home army only a decade earlier. Waterloo was the British militia's nova, however; and it languished for the rest of the century.

If the Romantic Age brought effusions of sympathy for soldiers, the politics of power united with a romantic national ideology to glorify war. In the face of a new kind and scope of warfare, soldiers of all ranks, regular and militia alike, remained steadfastly backward. In the spirit of British racism and jingoism, the soldier began to believe it his God-given mission to impose his law on the Empire. With the stabilizing of the Empire's boundaries, there was an end to calls for large levies on short notice, and the frontiers of Empire were left to the Regular Army, its regiments jealously guarding their honor. While Reactionism on the Continent after the Congress of Vienna had resulted in large conscripted armies in Austria, Prussia, and France for repression of liberal-minded citizens, there was no comparable threat in England. With the Regular Army able to look after the Empire, the militia soon withered into obscurity. A connection between Regulars and Militia hardly existed for most of the nineteenth century, and even the confused double-ranking system of "brevet" and "army" ranks for Militia officers on active service was abolished in 1858.

Wellington's campaigns against Napoleon, and later the Crimean debacle, gave the lie to the old military myth that war was glorious. Europe's citizen-soldiers and whole societies touched by war experienced disillusionment born of suffering. Many began to see chivalry and military honor as bestiality in disguise, and the military would-be hero and martyr as just a poor victim. Britain's military romantics who had not felt war's torments remained un-moved, however. Even the famous ride of the Six Hundred was made a glamorous event, although the sordid reality behind the Light Brigade's charge should have made it a monument to the incompetent and professional apathy of the British Army's regular officers.

On the Continent industrial technology, mass production, the advent of the railway and telegraph, and the supplanting of the musket with the rifle changed warfare. Military science had grown to include national policy, mobilization planning, and the logistics of mass deployment. The officer corps of Europe embraced a "cult of professionalism"[7] and became true students of their calling. The rank and file who were conscripted in large batches did not have even the satisfaction of being led straight into battle. Rather, their generals marched them to and fro *en masse* to outmaneuver an enemy they rarely saw face to face. Courage, individual skill at arms, and even group discipline and esprit no longer meant much, so that the idea of military honor remained more personal than institutional. There was the-honor of the officer corps and of the nation, but nothing comparable to the British love of regiment.

Unlike Prussia's war against Austria in 1866 and against France in 1870, Britain's wars in the same period were less destructive. Because battles consisted of colonial skirmishes between Regulars and primitively armed natives, British officers could afford to remain courageously ignorant, and the troops could keep their fierce pride. Under these unique conditions, the British Army kept its special idea of military honor. French "*honneur*," for example, seemed quite unlike British "honour"—the one aristocratic, individual and romantic, and the other rather middle class with aristocratic pretensions, institutional and prosaic. For the nineteenth-century British ranker, the idea of "military honor" was centered in his regiment, and cut across demands of honor imposed by class, rank, or individual conscience.

Because war in the nineteenth century had become more national and political than dynastic or commercial, the Regular began to look on himself as defender of his nation's institutions and faith. He was less likely to regard himself as a mercenary and more likely to express his duty as a patriotic obligation. His attitude reflected a shift in national sentiment, for the Romantic concept of "nation" extended to a new sense of ethnic identity. This racial militancy prodded Britons to subdue and proselytize among "lesser breeds without the Law," and gave an amateur dimension of cultural messianism to the Regular's sentiment.

Racism acted as self-fulfilling prophecy. The British Tommy, imbued with unshakeable belief in his superiority, performed prodigious feats against the most improbable odds in India and Africa. Yet that same conviction led to complacency and to the Indian Mutiny (1857), defeat at Kabul (1838), near disaster in the Crimea (1855), and humiliation at Majuba Hill (1881). The invincible dominion of Britishness and the British Army had become an article of faith, and Kipling's warning knell, "Recessional" (1897), went largely unheeded:

> Far-called, our navies melt away;
> On dune and headland sinks the fire:
> Lo, all our pomp of yesterday
> Is one with Nineveh and Tyre!
> Judge of the Nations, spare us yet,
> Lest we forget—lest we forget!

Few Britons faced up to their insular idyll's inevitable end. Britain's armies went away to fight; no civilian at home had ever endured unpleasantness from any soldiers but his own, whose roistering was an occasional nuisance usually confined to garrison towns. Whereas continental Europe's armies after Napoleon were part of the fabric of civil life to quell internal unrest, Britain's small Regular Army at home was not much more than a minor ceremonial institution, and the rest of the Regular Army was Britain's absentee housekeeper of the Empire. The Militia was a source of social prestige for the squirearchy and not much more. Officers at home were valuable as fashion plates and as marital prospects for the daughters of the upper middle class, and the other ranks, when thought of at all, were lauded by the literate classes merely as admirable abstractions.

As a wave of liberal reform for Britain's working classes early in the nineteenth century was overborne by national prosperity and upper-class conservatism, the kind of compassion Goldsmith, Wordsworth, and Cowper had expressed for the common soldier faded. Conscription had ceased with an end to military involvement in continental squabbles, and the wholly volunteer Regular Army comfortably helped to alleviate a pressing overpopulation problem in industrial areas. No longer were there hordes of discharged citizen-soldiers who had been dragooned into service to return as derelicts. The Regular Army's rank and file were usually out of sight and out of mind.

Predictably we cannot find in the literature of Britain's nineteenth century a war novelist in the European sense—no Stendhal, Tolstoy, or Zola. One finds only some fanciful and amusing fiction about the previous century's English mercenaries, a few novels of manners in which officers are only incidentally military men, and a body of jingoistic poetry and prose which romanticizes the Regular soldier and his lot, imparting an aura of glory to military mediocrity and even defeat. Most nineteenth-century British literature about the soldier is parochial in tone, and does little to evoke feeling about war and military life. Few Britons were interested in what seemed hardly to concern them in the halcyon days of Empire, and Kipling's effusions did little to dispel the euphoria.

Rare are the events that change radically and permanently the way men think about themselves and their world. The Crucifixion, the Haj of Mohammed, and the French Revolution shattered old faiths and built new ones. The Great War was another such event. It marked a renewal in human affairs, and in Britain's military history it was an end of innocence. Earlier wars had not done much to shape British military culture and institutions. Rather, political, social, and economic conditions had determined the soldier's ethos. Wars before the nineteenth century might seem to have taken a long time (e.g., the Hundred Years' War and the Thirty Years' War); but in reality the state of war had been a statesman's conception, while individual sieges had lasted weeks, and open battle had lasted a few hours. Even modern wars in nineteenth-century Europe had been brief, because victory went quickly to the side which had best mastered the principles of concentrated firepower, rapid communication, and mass manpower. Warfare, even the first so-called total war waged by Napoleon, had remained limited for the British. Only in America had the four years of civil war meant nearly continuous field maneuver by mass armies over a protracted period. Yet even in that conflict, its level of sustained intensity did not approach that of the Great War.[8] The Great War was incalculably more "total" than anything the British soldier had experienced. It was long enough and was of such intensity that it would radically alter his conception of who he was, what his purposes were and should be, what he believed in and should believe in.

With the Great War the military calling had to reconcile a conception of the soldier as a regular in the traditional sense with that of the temporary citizen-soldier. The aim of the old regular had been to "soldier" well; that is, he had found satisfaction in the routines of military life. By contrast, the wartime soldier's aim in war was to gain an end result; soldiering was not an end in itself. For him, soldiering and war were a brief interlude in an otherwise unmilitary life. In 1881 the army had undergone an organizational reform, so that the Militia and Yoemanry were affiliated with Regular Army regiments. Being few in number, the officers and men of these units trained only a few days each year. The Cardwell System, so called after the initiator of a decade of military reforms, also had assigned "military districts" to regular regiments for recruiting purposes. Thus, by the Great War the Regular Army resembled the militia because of the regional identity of regiments.

There the resemblance ended. With reforms instituted in 1908 by the War Secretary Richard (later Viscount) Haldane, the Territorial Force had come into being. Incorporating the Militia and the more socially elite regiments of Volunteers and Yeomanry, the Territorials preserved the true amateur's enthusiasm for arms and a jingoistic fervor of Empire. The Territorial Force was virtually ineffective, however, until mobilized for the Great War, when the distinction between professional and amateur would be obliterated. It was their glory and tragedy that, although formally established only for home defense according to Englishmen's ancient rights, whole units volunteered for overseas duty when war was declared in August 1914.

By the war's end, twenty-one divisions of Territorials had seen overseas service. The technology of mass war had given new life to the British Army's ethos of amateurism. Britain's first true citizen army imparted its character to each generation of soldiers that came after, until the present. The British soldier's achievement in the Falklands War was only the latest, and perhaps the last and finest, expression of the amateur spirit in the British profession of arms.

GAMESMEN AND ENDGAMESMEN

Some lately recalled reservists—and even long-service regulars—found this sudden exposure to gigantic stress more than they could bear. Occasionally, under the swift contagion of fear, NATO units simply broke and melted away—but not often.

. . . .

Within a fraction of a second the...fireball, with temperatures approaching those of the sun, was over 2,000 meters in diameter and reached down towards the centre Birmingham.

General Sir John Hackett[9]

It is a paradox of history that technology, which brought the amateur spirit into its own with mass war, ultimately will assure its disappearance. The amateur spirit has always brought to war and soldiering the exhilaration of the game and a belief in great ends to be won. The reality of the Nuclear Age will negate both those characteristics of amateurism which for a time have given the military profession its romantic coloring.

The synthesis of the spirit of amateurism and the spirit of professionalism has been consummated only in time for a new distinction to appear. The two kinds of warrior for the nuclear age are the traditional "Gamesman" soldier, and the new "Endgamesman." For the first time in history there is a kind of warrior who finds his fulfillment in not going to war. The nuclear warrior's idea of military honor lies wholly in his identity as *potential* combatant only. His role is deterrence, and if he becomes an *actual* combatant, he considers his honor lost. His credo is, "If we have to go to war, we've already lost." This new kind of warrior is not found in the traditional units and formations of the army, because his business is intercontinental nuclear ballistics. He is committed to the inaction of continual preparedness, in the recognition that if he must go to war he already has incurred the guilt of weakness and the shame of defeat in the game of international posturing.

Faced head on, that idea cannot be dressed up in red coat and burnished helmet, to march to the drum amid waving flags. The martial stir of blood and the racing heart which the traditional soldier has felt in the presence of military ceremonial are evidence of a destructive impulse societies no longer can afford to indulge. What has been emotionally seductive to amateur and professional soldier alike now is seen by the new nuclear warrior and much of British society as intellectually repulsive, because it speaks of self-annihilating instincts. By this measure, the soldier's traditional function, the waging of war, becomes a badge of his inadequacy in playing a game he dares neither win nor lose too absolutely. Thus, the modern military ethos is fast becoming one of readiness and restraint, without fulfillment. The war ecstasy may be indulged with relative safety only in war games or in conventional war-as-game; that is, in limited campaigns of which the Falklands War was typical.

Until recently, the British army has needed soldiers cast in the traditional mold, to fight conventional wars with limited means and ends. These have been the men who have fought former campaigns, which by nuclear standards have been less than "total." They have sweated and died as they always have, bloodily and earnestly. They have played the ultimate game, because their wars have still had rules of sorts, even if, as was often the case in Malaya, the only rule has been that there is some chance of survival through will and skill.

Traditionally, the military profession has been regarded as essentially monolithic. That is, the common denominator has been that every general and every cook have in some way been engaged in the orderly application of force. Within the context of that broad function, British soldiers have been seen, and have seen themselves, as professionals and amateurs, Regulars and Reserves, and various combinations of each. The Great War diminished that distinction, until the single difference among Britain's fighting men was an intangible line between those who had been in the trenches and those who had not. Today, that separation made by battle experience is losing its significance in many quarters of the military world, because the idea of war in the nuclear age has become associated with loss of everything, including military honor, which formerly has been associated with fighting well.

Customs and codes of conduct have hitherto been built by military professional amateurs, amateur professionals, and reluctant temporary soldiers alike, on the idea of battle as the soldier's consummation. Now a new distinction has emerged: the traditional soldier who trains for limited conventional wars and fights them, and the nuclear warrior who mans a console and trains to trigger Apocalypse. The military Gamesman and Endgamesman each has his own distinctive characteristics and ideas of military professionalism which he finds difficult to reconcile with the other's. The Gamesman is essentially conservative in holding to a traditional conception of the profession of arms, while the Endgamesman has a new and pragmatic ethic. Indeed, their purposes are as mutually antagonistic as their temperaments.

Officers of the traditional combat arms are still imbued with the regimental mystique. Cast in Morris Janowitz's classic idea of the "heroic image," they are comfortable either in camouflage smock or girt with ceremonial sword.[10] While avoiding overt reference to valor, gallantry, glory, and patriotism, they are fundamentally tribal and romantic. They speak of responsibility in terms of "command," and of "their" soldiers with affection. They pride themselves on decisiveness in crisis and imaginativeness of conception, while perpetuating a misleading myth of endearing incompetence and languor. They are poetic, somewhat eccentric, and given to youthful enthusiasms. Their troops are as aggressive as, but tougher and more resilient than, Kipling's Tommies, and far more able to exercise initiative.[11]

The other warriors, prosaic Endgamesmen, the majority of whom are not of the army, began to appear in the mid–1960s, with the death of an idea that nuclear war could be limited and contained. In the language of military sociology they are cast in the "competitive" image.[12] Their technical knowledge and skills are more complex than those required of the Gamesmen.

The officers prefer to administer and maintain resources and material rather than to command men, and the men and women themselves are technically skilled workers rather than fighters in the traditional sense. Like their staff officer progenitors, Endgamesmen are prudent in acting and speaking only with higher sanction. Temperamentally conformist, obedient, and highly competent, they are trained to respond immediately and predictably to commands and situations. The Endgamesman type is thoroughly reliable, and will never act on his own initiative where there is doubt. He is most comfortable in neat and unostentatious uniforms of civilian cut, which, together with his briefcase, fit him for his operations room environment. He cooperates readily with both military and civilian co-Endgamesmen, but unlike the Gamesman he does not make a fetish of personal loyalties or regimental romance. Professional attachments are to "systems," and he gauges virtue by organizational effectiveness.[13]

Whereas the Endgamesman finds the Gamesman a dangerous, if somewhat comic, anachronism, the Gamesman finds the Endgamesman bleakly functional, civilian, and unwarlike. Ironically, each mistakes the other, because the Endgamesman's potential destructiveness is infinitely greater than that of his more traditional comrade in arms. A further irony is that the daring and somewhat erratic Gamesman who professes love for mud and blood, and is ready to take a chance in limited war, is committed to a notion of war-as-game, with rules and some modicum of order. It is this attitude, characteristic of the youth of Siegfried Sassoon's generation, which is captured in Evelyn Waugh's portrayal of the boyish old brigadier, Ritchie Hook, in *Officers and Gentlemen*. Ritchie Hook's "games" psychology of war, born of the Imperial army and his early soldiering days in the Great War, had been transmitted intact to the soldiers who fought in the Falklands. Meanwhile, the thoroughly rational and unromantic Endgamesmen manned their consoles in their antiseptic subterranean fastnesses in the unlikely event that the Falklands War should precipitate the nuclear Endgame.

With the advent of nuclear technology, conventional war has returned to a state Daniel Defoe's mercenary Captain Carleton might approve. Once more the traditional profession of arms has become the preserve of officers capable not only of waging limited war, but also of ensuring that it *remains limited*. Military virtue is seen to lie neither in victory nor in a just war waged for just ends. Rather, the conventional warrior must wage war with the aim of avoiding finality, either in victory or in defeat. The difference, though, is that his purpose in prolonging and limiting the contest is not profit— merely humanity's survival through avoidance of a nuclear alternative.

After coming into full flower in the British Army by the summer of 1916, the age of military amateurism has waned. Although literature after World War I showed a withering of amateur verve, the seeds of its spirit burgeoned for a time with the Second World War. The citizen-soldiers of that adventure probably saw the last of true military amateurism in the British Army. In the postwar years, irregular warfare brought about an institutionalizing of the amateur's ethos among regulars, much as it had in the nineteenth century, when for a time the militia virtually disappeared. This professional amateurism showed up brilliantly in what was probably the last of Britain's small wars.

The Falklands War, an anachronism even in Britain's postwar and post-Imperial period, was an occasion for the British Army to engage in conflict similar in scope to an eighteenth-century "Cabinet" war or a campaign on India's Northwest Frontier. Perhaps with that moment of glory, the time has passed for the kind of soldier who at home could evoke the amused exasperation of the *Spectator*'s satires and, in battle abroad, could stir the world's admiration for his discipline, daring, and courage. While the Falklands War was an appealing anomaly in British military history, the advent of the nuclear warrior will surely end the army's spirit of amateurism.

THE LANGUAGE OF THE NUCLEAR AGE AND THE FUTURE OF MILITARY LITERATURE

> The depersonalization of the destructive process may yet render the principle of humanity as archaic as the principle of chivalry may already have become.[14]

In years to come, a backward glance may show that the literature of our time is the closing chapter in the history of military amateurism. Traditionally unmilitaristic, English culture has not produced literature in the language of martial splendor since the ages of Anglo-Saxon epic and chivalric romance. From the Restoration until World War I, military language was a jargon confined to the military community, and a literary metaphor for sexual war, used archly by fashionable writers. After brief disrepute between World Wars, military language has emerged in the Nuclear Age as a common possession of all classes, warrior and civilian alike. Reflecting the militarized state's loss of moral distinctions, it tailors attitude. The bleakly functional siege argot of nuclear strategy is a universal idiom, as General Sir John Hackett's prose scenario, *World War Three*, shows.

O'Brien's premise in George Orwell's *Nineteen Eighty-Four* that "war is peace" is fundamental to the Nuclear Endgamesman's ethos which allows for no distinction between peacetime "soldiering" and the continual war of deterrence. Similarly, the civilian, presuming an ambient state of hostilities, both accepts and uses militaristic language. The ephithets and rhetoric are technological or pseudotechnological, abstract, superficially value free, and ostensibly objective and rational. The new militarism differs from its classic description before the Second World War. The distinction which Alfred Vagts drew in 1937 between the "military way," the reluctant use of force for just ends, and "militarism," an infatuation with warlike pursuits celebrated with ceremonial pomp, is as valid now as then. However, the new bellicosity is prompted more by dread of annihilation than by military romanticism, and the ceremonies of warlike sentiment are more subtle in appearing to be their opposite. Nuclear language is less overt than Edwardian patriotic excesses, more insidious, and more pervasive, as Britain with its allies has adopted a siege mentality. The language of strategic diplomacy is an idiom of aggrieved innocence and pacific optimism. "SALT," "START," and "SDI," euphemistic acronyms whose meanings are universally understood, obscure underlying hostile design.

Since the seventeenth century, British society has come full circle from the early technical jargon of limited war, through three centuries of military idiom as the soldier's role-defining symbol and as literary metaphor, back to a language of siege. In the Restoration when Daniel Defoe's probably apocryphal Captain Carleton is supposed to have soldiered, an elite brotherhood of initiates were familiar with the encyclopedic mysteries of fortification: "quinque-angle," "counterscarps," "rampires," "cavalieros," "argins," "curtains."[15] Rather in the same way, the modern civilian speaks familiarly of "fail-safe" and "ICBM," but without necessarily any direct experience of arms and only a vague notion of the characteristics, destructive power, and even appearance, of nuclear missile systems. By contrast, the language of the Restoration's mercenary and regular was as limited as war itself. Warfare had its own pedantry, and as weaponry became more effective, it developed its own rules and conventions which set limits on destructiveness and drew clear distinctions between soldier and civilian, war and peace. Mercenary officers subscribed to a pseudochivalric ceremoniousness which, like speech and uniform, set the soldier apart from civilian society.

Although technology continued to change warfare, the eighteenth century's dynastic and colonizing wars were limited and not very dangerous, compared even to nineteenth-century wars. Distant and not very threatening, warfare had a chance to develop its own aesthetic. Ornate cannon castings, fine wood stocks inlaid with mother-of-pearl, and uniforms to shame peacocks manifested a common attitude toward the military profession as appealingly exotic. Fashion was as important as functionality. The technical language of war thrived on the Continent, where the British army acquired its battle skills. Understandably, French was fashionable among the army's linguistic Beau Brummels. Society regarded the British officer as remotely amusing, and this voguish vernacular was looked on as exasperating affectation. In 1711 a young lady complained to the *Spectator* that British officers on the Continent were killing and dying indecorously, in French.[16] Railing schoolmarmishly about officers giving "accounts of their performances in a jargon of phrases which they learn among their conquered enemies," she offers an officer's letter: *"reconnoitre," "pontoon," "fascine," "hauteur," "defile," "mar-aud," "corps de reserve," "gasconade," "cartel," "carte blanche," "commandant," "chamade."*[17]

When civilian society could regard war as a not very serious pastime, its idiom could serve as a comic literary metaphor for the war of the sexes. Alexander Pope's mock Horatian epic poem, "The Rape of the Lock" (1712), is an extended metaphor for sexual siege, its heroine Belinda's outworks negligently defended by her nymph "militia of the lower sky." The contemporary reader would have understood the slighting reference to the militia. Notoriously ill-trained and ill disciplined, they were as important to defend Britain against a possible French invasion as their mythic counterparts are in guarding Belinda's feminine honour.

John Clelland's *Fanny Hill* (1749) is replete with siege, sally, dueling, discharges of shot, battery, engines, mining, and equestrianship. The young Cornet always treats his companion decorously, according to the rules of erotic combat.[18] Fanny reports, "[T]hough all modesty and reserve were banished from the transaction of those pleasures, good manners and politeness were inviolably observed." A popular book among English sporting gentlemen was Pierre Laclos's *Les Liaisons Dangereuses* (1781). Its military title does not disappoint:

I . . . carried her towards the . . . field of glory: . . . she had already yielded to her happy conqueror; . . . I adopted a purity of method; . . . I departed in no respect from the true principles of this war, which we have so often remarked is like the other. Judge me then as you would Frederic of Turenne. I forced the enemy to fight when she wished only to refuse battle; by clever manoeuvres I obtained the choice of battlefield and dispositions.[19]

All this sexual *double entendre* in the military idiom did not imply that British society was militaristic. Indeed, the case was quite the opposite, because the common literary device continued only so long as war was remote and soldiers were merely comic and pernicious. "A soldier," explains Lemuel Gulliver reasonably to a Houyhnhnm in the eighteenth century's most famous satire, "is a yahoo hired to kill in cold blood as many of his own species, who have never offended him, as possibly he can."[20] In Laurence Sterne's *Tristram Shandy* (1760–1767), Uncle Toby and Corporal Trim's war gaming may be seen as a metaphor, with absurdly erotic undertones, for life's bathos.

The isolation of British military culture continued into the nineteenth century, and the military metaphor survived for a while. For instance, Charles Lamb asked rhetorically who would "beat the drums of . . . retreat" for the "march of science," and he complained about excessive legislation "placing guards at the very outposts of possibility."[21] Lamb's correspondence spans the time of Napoleon's campaigns, yet contains hardly a hint of English involvement. For most of the British public this first "total war" was still confined and distant, and England looked on, when it looked at all, like *Vanity Fair*'s picnicking spectators at Brussels. At midnineteenth century, the public who were reading news about the Crimea and the battle for the Redan would have known all about the red cavalry overalls of the gorgeous 11th Hussars, nicknamed the "Cherrypickers," and their scandalous "clothes Colonel" Lord Cardigan. But they probably had little idea of what a *redan* was.[22]

The glamour the British public saw in the miserably mismanaged feats of British arms in the Crimean War was matched only two years later by patriotic indignation at atrocities by rebellious Indian troops at Lucknow. After the Sepoy Mutiny of 1857, Queen Victoria's government frankly acknowledged India's importance to the national economy by converting "John Company's" (the Honourable East India Company) army into troops of the Crown. From then on, the commercial impetus which had long been a basis for mercenary recruitment also became the regular's love of duty and Empire.

Much of the grievance leading to the Mutiny had been a failure of British military leadership of Indian troops. To address the problem, Academy-trained subalterns of the public school sort were sent to replace the old "Company" officers in Indian regiments. At an appropriate moment in their professional lives, they married Englishwomen of "good" family, raised their families in the army's cantonments, and sent their sons back to English public schools.

Because of these practices, and the climate of Imperial pride, the so-called great game of Empire gave the British army new legitimacy in the public's eyes. Meanwhile, British commercialism abroad was taking on an aspect of Imperial glory and military romance. Officer's affectations of speech and the rank and file's Hindustani slang reinforced a heroic self-image reflecting the nation's romantic jingoism. The "message English" of C. S. Forester's Curzon (*The General*), who serves in the Boer War and World War I, and the fashionable "cavalwy lithp" were like linguistic uniforms for the British officer in *"mufti"* having his *"chota peg."*[23]

The British Indian Army was a proud and brutal subculture of long-service men subsisting on the margins of English civilization. The soldiers who looked to their regiments and their comrades as their only objects of faith had their word stock as a bond. For acceptance the recruit had to "get his knees brown" linguistically by using "hobson jobson": *"banduk,""bhisti,"* *"jildi," "pani lao."*[24] At home the mythology of the Army's exploits on Indian's Northwest Frontier imparted a spirit of romance even to the Tommy's cockney slang, echoed in Kipling's epic-ballad style.

While the Tommy's subculture remained separate in Britain, the jargon of universal militarism had been growing on the Continent from the beginning of nineteenth-century modern military professionalism. The mobilization and movement of mass citizen armies and resources meant that military education and planning had to go beyond battlefield tactics to embrace

national strategy, so that generals and statesmen understood the same pragmatic jargon of political militarism. The apparently scientific "principles of
war" reduced men to bloodily bloodless embodiments of the physical laws
of mass, expressed as various international equations of the "balance of
power."

With World War I the British language of militarism expressing jingoism,
optimism, and righteous hatred became the metaphor of the gentry's blood
sports and the public school boys' games. The linguistic reversal reveals a
shift in attitudes. Whereas sexual combat had been represented through a
metaphor of war when limited war was not a threat, the Great War's sporting
metaphor described war when it had become too vast for comprehension.
Ironically, the sportsman's euphemism expressing the amateur's love of the
hunt and the game became most popular when war was least a game and
civilian attitudes least sporting. Journalistic accounts are full of the Boche
being "knocked for a six" and Huns being "run to earth." Meanwhile, the
most dehumanizing and destructive word in military science was "attrition,"
a substitution of linguistic ingenuity for tactical imagination.

Until World War I, the argot of national strategy had been confined to
power elites, and Britain's frankly military romanticism was innocently, if
suicidally, endearing. With Britain's initiation as a nation-in-arms, the British
Army became somewhat civilized, while civilian society became militarized. Early in the war patriotic young officers educated in the classics unquestioningly accepted Horace's famous line, *Dulce et decorum est pro patria
mori*. But Wilfred Owen's tragically sardonic war poem "Dulce et decorum
est" was a new idiom discrediting the old militarism. Better to live for justice,
than to die in squalor for a lie. The literary tradition of siege metaphor having
lost its appeal, the title of Frederic Manning's *The Middle Parts of Fortune*
reversed the tradition. At first suppressed under its original title as *The Middle
Parts . . .* , the novel appeared as *Her Privates We*.[25] By either name, the novel
used a sexual metaphor for a peep beneath the skirts of martial glory.

The tactics of mass ended the British regular as a cultural type. As Robert
Graves (*Goodbye to All That*) records, civilian soldiers at first tried taking
Hindustani tucks in their linguistic tunics. However, by war's end the prewar
Regular's spirit and speech were in tatters. The unsoldierly citizen warrior's
argot was unmilitarily prosaic. "Blighty" came to mean the longed-for wound
just serious enough for evacuation home.[26] French military jargon still pep-
pered the technical language of trench warfare: "*parapet*," "*parados*," "*trav-
erse*." But the new gallicisms, expressive of weary frontline fatalism, were
"*sanfaryan*" ("*ce ne fait rien*") and "*napoo*" ("*moi non plus*"). The Great War
and Britain's first citizen army ended the old army as a discrete culture with
its own linguistic signifiers, and between wars military jargon, metaphor,
and literature were in disfavor.

Universal literacy and democratization had placed the state's jargon of
militarism within popular reach. The language of technology gained impetus

from World War I onwards; and what has seemed scientific, value-free, and inventive has seemed good. Especially since World War II military technology and combat tactics have become progressively interdependent. Cast in the pragmatic image of technology, industry, and commerce, many military men have begun to find status in the prestige jargon of science, and only members of the traditional combat arms cast themselves in military tribalism's "heroic image."[27] The ethos of the technician and logistician is becoming dominant in some parts of the military community, and the prestige idiom is civilian and entrepreneurial: "human relations," "input," "feedback," "dissatisfiers," "offsets," "cost effectiveness," and the new-minted "survivability." Even the disreputable "attrition" has returned as a bureaucratic verb for personnel reduction: "to attrit."

With universal militarizing, military argot as role signifier has virtually disappeared. The difference between the early civilian language of militarism until World War I, and the language of the Nuclear Age, is its universal uniformity. That has been the effect of (1) reduced class stratification since World War I, (2) universal literacy, (3) electronic news media, (4) and hemispheric confrontation, which has erased the margins of the potential battlefield.

No longer the language of strategic science, the new mode is an international language of science militarized. "Exocet" and "SAM" are common linguistic currency, and "silo" has ceased to evoke arcadian nostalgia. The result of this familiarity with linguistic form without direct knowledge is semantic confusion. "Preemptive strike" and "deterrence," for instance, both are and are not like "attack" and "aggression."

This loss of distinction between military action and mere reaction is implicit in the Nuclear Endgamesman's complex roles as soldier and citizen, military commander and technician. As a result, accepted definitions of classic professionalism (expertise, responsibility, corporateness) do not seem to apply much to the Nuclear Endgamesman. His competence and knowledge are consummate, but they are confined primarily to technology rather than to military science as such. Neither the decisions of grand strategy nor those of minor tactics are as much his business as is the technical expertise to evolve scenarios and contingency responses and to act on them, if necessary, without reflection.

The spirit of amateurism has always presupposed a gaming element; that is, respect for the adversary's fighting qualities, observance of rules of combat, and love of the game. How those elements may apply to the Nuclear Warrior is hard to see, as he prepares for a single act of total annihilation. The Endgamesman may be as devoted to his duty as the old regular, and he may have an amateur's affection for the strategic and technological mechanisms of deterrence. As well, he may have the military ideologue's dedication to a cause, but he is denied the amateur's love of chivalry, campaigning, and rituals of military life. What that signifies for ideas about the military virtues and for the future of military literature which presumes a moral norm is uncertain. Whether even language soon will be able to sustain military literature to show the truth of a new kind of warrior is not known. The literature of military amateurism may cease to be written with the passing of the British Army's traditional soldiership, the Gentlemen of the Blade.

NOTES

1. "No difficulty frightens us"—the motto of a dozen British Fusilier regiments and regiments of the line.

2. For "mercenary" and "Constitutional" see J. R. Western, *The English Militia in the Eighteenth Century: The Study of a Political Issue 1660–1802* (London: Routledge & Kegan Paul, 1965).

3. George Clark, *War and Society in the Seventeenth Century* (Cambridge: Cambridge University Press, 1958), p. 100.

4. Michael Howard, ed., *Soldiers and Governments* (London: Eyre & Spottiswoode, 1957).

5. Clark, *War and Society*, p. 98.

6. R. Money Barnes, *A History of the Regiments & Uniforms of the British Army* (London: Seeley Service, 1957), p. 107.

7. John Gooch, *Armies in Europe* (London: Routledge & Kegan Paul, 1980), pp. 39–44.

8. For comparative tables of national casualty totals, see John Terraine's *The Smoke and the Fire: Myths and Anti-Myths of War 1861–1945* (London: Sidgwick & Jackson, 1980).

9. General Sir John Hackett, *The Third World War* (London: Sidgwick & Jackson Ltd., 1978), pp. 18, 372.

10. Morris Janowitz, *The Professional Soldier* (Glencoe, Ill.: Free Press, 1960).

11. John Laffin, *Tommy Atkins: The Story of the English Soldier* (London: Cassell, 1966), pp. 194ff.

12. Maury D. Feld, "Military Self-Image in a Technological Environment," in *The New Military*, ed. Morris Janowitz (New York: Russell Sage, 1964).

13. The paradigms of "Gamesman" and "Endgamesman" were coined by this author, in his address, "Just Games," contained in "Report of a Leadership Symposium Held at RRMC June 1981," ed. D. Lang (Victoria, Canada: Royal Roads Military College).

14. Guenter Lewy, "Superior Orders, Nuclear Warfare, and the Dictates of Conscience," in *War and Morality*, ed. Richard A. Wasserstrom (Belmont, Calif.: Wadsworth Publishing Co., 1970), p. 130.

15. quinque-angle: pentagonal design for fort's perimeter.

counterscarps: outer slope or wall of ditch or moat.

rampires (arch.): ramparts; earth embankment surrounded by parapet encircling a fort.

cavalieros (arch.): elevated entrenchments within a bastion.

argins: earthworks.

curtains: the part of the rampart and parapet between two bastions or gates.

16. *Spectator*, Miss Leonora Shepheard, No. 165, 8 September 1711.

17. *fascine*: bundle of faggots; fascines were laid across soft or marshy ground for passage of horses, wagons, artillery.

hauteur: high ground, often the ground of tactical importance.

gasconade: a feint or sally in force, to give a deceptive impression of strength.

cartel: a written agreement between nations at war, especially as to exchange of prisoners (usually involving their word, or "parole," not to engage in further combat). (Also, a written challenge, especially a duel.)

carte blanche: literally a blank sheet of paper, signed by a commander ready to acknowledge defeat, upon which the victor may name the conditions.

chamade: a parley for surrender conditions, exchange of prisoners, payment for release of prisoners on their parole.

18. Cornet (or "Cornet of Horse"): The cavalry equivalent of ensign of Guards, or second lieutenant of line infantry. Originally, the fifth and junior commissioned officer of a cavalry troop, who carried the standard. His sexual significance is obvious.

19. Pierre-Ambroise-François de Laclos, *Les Liaisons Dangereuses* (1781), (London ed., 1796); numerous editions and translations into several languages. Richard Aldington's trans., *Dangerous Acquaintances*, New York (undated) is quoted here, pp. 278–79.

Frederic Turenne: Frederic Wilhelm, "the Great Elector" (1620–88); Henri Turenne, Vicomte de La Tour d'Auvergne (1611–75), both consummate commanders and innovative tacticians of the Thirty Years' War, when field maneuver was replacing siege.

20. Jonathan Swift, *Gulliver's Travels* (1726), ed. Louis A. Landa (Boston: Houghton Mifflin Co., 1960), p. 199.

21. Charles Lamb, . . . *Letters* (New York: Random House, 1936), pp. 305, 997.

22. *redan*: fortification consisting of two walls or parapets set at an angle pointed toward the enemy, and open at the back.

23. *mufti*: civilian clothes (a word forbidden in fashionable "home" regiments).

chota peg: lit: small drink; a scotch and soda, gin and tonic, etc.

24. bondook: (Hindi: *banduk*): rifle.

bhisti: water bearer. (Kipling's Gunga Din, of course; but for "Gunga," see also "gungy.")

jildi: Hurry up!

pani lao: Hindi: *pani*: water; *lao*: bring). Tommy's standard command to a *bhisti*.

gungy: Hindi/Urdu: *gunga*, *gunda*: unclean (in the religious sense) or dirty.

25. *Middle Parts* . . . was first published by Peter Davies in limited edition, 1929. The expurgated version, *"Her Privates We,"* with sanitized language, was published in 1930. Republished, London, Granada Publishing, Ltd., 1977.

26. Blighty: (from Hindi *Bilyati*: country, homeland). For an Indian Army soldier, the word meant simply "England," but for the Great War's citizen-soldier it meant a wound serious enough for evacuation to England, but hopefully not permanently damaging.

27. Feld, "Military Self-Image."

BIBLIOGRAPHY

HISTORIES, COMMENTARIES, AND CRITICISM

Barnes, R. Money. *A History of the Regiments & Uniforms of the British Army*. London: Seeley Service & Co., Ltd., 1957.

Baugh, Albert C., ed. *A Literary History of England*. New York: Appleton-Century-Crofts, 1967.

Bergonzi, Bernard. *Heroes' Twilight*. New York: Coward McCann, 1965.

Bishop, Patrick and Witherow, John. *The Winter War*. London: Quarter Books, 1982.

Bond, Brian. *The Victorian Army and the Staff College, 1854–1914*. London: Eyre & Metheun, 1972.

Brodie, Bernard. *Strategy in the Missile Age*. Princeton, N.J.: Princeton University Press, 1959.

Bunting, Josiah, III. "The Military Novel." *Naval War College Review* 26, No. 3, Sequence No. 246 (November-December 1973).

Child, John. *The Army of Charles II*. London: Routledge & Kegan Paul, 1976.

Churchill, Sir Winston. *The Second World War*. Vol. 2. Cambridge: Riverside Press, 1951.

Clark, Alan. *The Donkeys*. New York: Universal Publishing and Distributing Corp., 1961.

Clark, George. *War and Society in the Seventeenth Century*. Cambridge: Cambridge University Press, 1958.

Corvisier, Andre. *Armies and Societies in Europe, 1494–1789*. Bloomington: Indiana University Press, 1979.

Edwards, T. J. *Regimental Badges*. Aldershot: Gale & Polden, 1953.

Farwell, Byron. *Mr. Kipling's Army*. London: W. W. Norton, 1981.

Feld, Maury D. "Military Self-Image in a Technological Environment." In *The New Military*, ed. Morris Janowitz. New York: Russell Sage, 1964.

Fortescue, J. W. *A History of the British Army*. Vol. 1. London: Macmillan & Co., 1918.

Fowler, William. *Battle for the Falklands*. London: Osprey, 1982.

Fussell, Paul. *The Great War and Modern Memory*. London: Oxford University Press, 1975.

Gardner, Brian. *The Big Push*. London: Cassell, 1961.

———. Intro., *The Terrible Rain*. London: Methuen, 1966.

George, D. Lloyd. *War Memoirs of David Lloyd George*. London: Odhams Press, 1939.

Girouard, Mark. *The Return to Camelot*. New Haven, Conn.: Yale University Press, 1981.

Gooch, John. *Armies in Europe*. London: Routledge & Kegan Paul, 1980.

Graham, Dominick. "England." In *Fighting Armies of the World*, ed. R. A. Gabriel. Westport, Conn.: Greenwood Press, 1983.

Hackett, John. *The Profession of Arms*. London: Times Publishing Co., 1962.

Hargevik, Steig. *The Disputed Assignment of Memoirs of an English Officer to Daniel Defoe*. Stockholm: Almquist & Wiksell, 1974.

Harries-Jenkins, Gwyn. *The Army in Victorian Society*. London: Routledge & Kegan Paul, 1977.

Heath, Jeffrey. *The Picturesque Prison: Evelyn Waugh and His Writing*. Montreal: McGill-Queen's University Press, 1982.

Howard, Michael, ed. *Soldiers and Governments*. London: Eyre & Spottiswoode, 1957.

Huntington, Samuel P. *The Soldier and the State*. Cambridge, Mass.: Harvard University Press, 1957.

Janowitz, Morris. *The Professional Soldier*. Glencoe, Ill.: Free Press, 1960.

Keegan, John. *The Face of Battle*. New York: Viking Press, 1976.

———. "Regimental Ideology." Sandhurst: Royal Military College, 1982.

Knightley, Philip. *The First Casualty*. New York: Harcourt Brace Jovanovich, 1975.

Laffin, John. *Tommy Atkins: The Story of the English Soldier*. London: Cassell, 1966.

Lewy, Guenter. "Superior Orders, Nuclear Warfare, and the Dictates of Conscience." In *War and Morality*, ed. Richard A. Wasserstrom. Belmont, Calif.: Wadsworth Publishing Co., 1970.

Mason, Philip. *A Matter of Honour*. Harmondsworth: Penguin, 1974.

Perlmutter, Amos. *The Military and Politics in Modern Times*. New Haven, Conn.: Yale University Press, 1977.

Ropp, Theodore. "The Military Officer and His Education in the Next Quarter Century." *Signum* (June 1976).

Saunders, Hilary St. George. *The Green Beret: The Story of the Commandos 1940–45*. London: Michael Joseph, 1949.

———. *The Red Beret: The Story of the Parachute Regiment at War 1940–45*. London: Michael Joseph, 1950.

Skelley, Alan Ramsay. *The Victorian Army at Home*. Montreal: McGill-Queen's University Press, 1977.

Terraine, John. *The Smoke and the Fire: Myths and Anti-Myths of War 1861–1945*. London: Sidgwick & Jackson, 1980.

"Tradition." Vol. 65. London: Belmont-Maitland Publishers, 1972.

Vagts, Alfred. *A History of Militarism: Romance and Realities of a Profession*. New York: W. W. Norton, 1937.

Western, J. R. *The English Militia in the Eighteenth Century: The Study of a Political Issue 1660–1802*. London: Routledge & Kegan Paul, 1965.

SOURCES FOR CONTEMPORARY ACCOUNTS, ESSAYS, AND LETTERS

Addison, Joseph, Steele, Richard, et al. *Spectator* (1710–14). Cincinnati: Applegate & Co., 1857.

Aitken, James, ed. *English Letters of the XVIII Century*. Harmondsworth: Pelican Books, Ltd., 1946.

Bairnsfather, Bruce. *Bullets and Billets*. Letchworth: Garden City Press, 1916.

Bonham-Carter, Victor. *In a Liberal Tradition: A Social Biography 1710–1950*. London: Constable, 1960.

Boswell, James. *Life of Johnson* (1740). Ed. R. W. Chapman. London: Oxford University Press, 1953.

Dawson, A. J., intro. A *"Temporary Gentleman" in France: Home Letters from an Officer in the New Army*. London: Cassell, 1916.

Defoe, Daniel. "An argument shewing that a standing Army, with Consent of Parliament, is not inconsistent with a free Government, & c...." London: Printed for E. Whitlock, 1698.

———. "A brief Reply to the History of standing Armies in England. With some Account of the Authors." London: 1698.

Guibert, Hippolyte de. *Essai General de Tactique* (1781); quoted and summarized in Cyril Falls, *The Art of War*. London: Oxford University Press, 1961, pp. 25–28.

Housman, Laurence, ed. *War Letters of Fallen Englishmen*. London: Victor Gollancz, 1930.

Hyde, Edward. "Of War." In *A Book of English Essays 1600–1900*, eds. Stanley V. Makower and Basil H. Blackwell. London: Oxford University Press, 1912, pp. 24–32.

McGuffie, T. H., ed. *The Common Soldier at Peace and War 1642–1914*. London: Hutchinson, 1964.

"Platoon Commander" [anon.]. *Hospital Days*. London: T. Fisher Unwin, Ltd., 1916.

Richards, Frank. *Old Soldiers Never Die*. London: Faber & Faber, 1933.

Strachey, J. St. Loe, ed. and intro. Donald Hankey. *A Student In Arms*. Toronto: McClelland, Goodchild & Stewart, 1917.

Tiddy, R. J. E., intro. *The Mummers' Play*. Oxford: Clarendon, 1923.

Tiplady, Thomas. *The Soul of the Soldier; Sketches from the Western Battle Front*. New York: Fleming H. Revell Co., 1918.

Treves, Sir Frederick, ed. *Made in the Trenches*. London: George Allen Unwin, Ltd., 1916.

Woodhouse, A. S. P., ed. *Puritanism and Liberty: Being Army Debates (1647–49) from the Clarke Manuscripts....* London: Dent & Sons, 1938.

Wragg, H., ed. *Letters Written in Wartime (XV-XIX Centuries)*. London: Oxford University Press, 1915.

NOVEL FICTION, POETRY, AND COLLECTIONS OF PROSE AND VERSE

Aldington, Richard. *Death of a Hero*. London: Chatto & Windus, 1929.

Austen, Jane. *Pride and Prejudice* (1797). New York: Signet, 1961.

Blunden, Edmund, *Poems 1930–1940*. London: Macmillan & Co., 1940.

———. *Undertones of War* (1928). Rev. ed. London: Cobden-Sanderson, 1930.

Clark, George. *War and Society in the Seventeenth Century*. Cambridge: Cambridge University Press, 1958.

Clarke, George Herbert. *The New Treasury of War Poetry*. Boston: Houghton Mifflin Co., 1943.

Cowper, William. "The Task" (1782). *Poems by William Cowper, Esq.* Vol. 2 (1785). Reprinted in facsimile. London: Scolar Press, 1973.

Defoe, Daniel. "The Military Memoirs of Capt. George Carleton from the Dutch War, 1672. . . . " (1728). *Memoirs of an English Officer*. Ed. Martin Seymour Smith. London: Victor Gollancz, 1970.

———. "Of Captain Misson." *The History of the Pirates*. Vol. 2 (1728). Reprinted in *The Augustan Reprint Society Publications*, no. 87, ed. Maximillian E. Novak. Los Angeles: Wm. Andrew Clark Memorial Library, University of California, 1961.

Dryden, John. "Cymon and Iphigenia" (1700). *The Poetical Works of John Dryden*. Ed. George R. Noyes. Cambridge, Mass.: Riverside Press, pp. 890–98.

Eliot, George. *Adam Bede* (1859). Rev. ed. New York: Airmont Publishing Co., 1966.

Fielding, Henry. *Tom Jones*. New York: Signet, 1963.

Ford, Ford Madox. *The Good Soldier* (1927). New York: Vintage Books, 1955.

———. *It Was the Nightingale* (1933). Philadelphia: J. B. Lippincott Co., 1933.

———. *Parade's End* (1924–28) [Tetralogy]. Intro. Robie MacCauley. New York: Vintage Books, 1979.

Fussell, Paul, intro. *Siegfried Sassoon's Long Journey: Selections from the Sherston Memoirs*. New York: Oxford University Press, 1983.

Gardner, Brian, ed. *Up the Line to Death: The War Poets 1914–18*. London: Eyre & Methuen, 1964.

Goldsmith, Oliver. *The Citizen of the World* (1762). Ed. W. A. Brockington. London: Blackie & Son, undated.

———. *The Vicar of Wakefield* (1762). Toronto: Macmillan, 1942.

Graves, Robert. *Goodbye to All That* (1929). Harmondsworth: Penguin, 1960.

Hackett, General Sir John. *The Third World War*. London: Sidgwick & Jackson Ltd., 1978.

Jones, David. *In Parenthesis*. London: Faber & Faber, 1937.

Jones, Harry, ed. *War Letters of a Public School Boy*. London: Cassell, 1918.

Kersh, Gerald. *They Die with Their Boots Clean*. London: William Heinemann, Ltd., 1941.

Kipling, Rudyard. Rudyard Kipling's Verse: *Definitive Edition*. [Ed. not cited.] London: Hodder & Stoughton, 1940.

———. "A Madonna of the Trenches." *Debits and Credits*. New York: Doubleday, Page & Co., 1926.

Laclos, Pierre-Ambroise-François de. *Les Liaisons Dangereuses* (1781). (London ed., 1796); numerous editions and translations into several languages; Richard Aldington's trans., *Dangerous Acquaintances*, New York (undated).

Lonsdale, Roger, ed. *The New Oxford Book of Eighteenth Century Verse*. Anon., "Sir Dilberry Diddle, Captain of Militia . . . " (1766). Oxford: Oxford University Press, 1984.

Manning, Frederic. *The Middle Parts of Fortune* (1929). Intro. Michael Howard. London: Granada Publishing Co., 1977.

Raymond, Ernest. *Tell England* (1922). London: Corgi, 1973.

Sassoon, Siegfried. *Memoirs of an Infantry Officer*. London: Faber & Faber, 1930.

Service, Robert. "Rhymes of a Red Cross Man" from Foreward and *Envoi* of Service's collected war poetry. Toronto: Ryerson Press, 1931.

Sherriff, Robert C. *Journey's End*. New York: Brentano Press, 1929.

Smith, Nicol, ed. *The Oxford Book of Eighteenth Century Verse*. Oxford: Clarendon, 1926.

Swift, Jonathan. *Gulliver's Travels*. Boston: Houghton Mifflin, 1960.

Thackeray, William Makepeace. *Vanity Fair* (1847–48). Ed. F. E. L. Priestley. Toronto: Macmillan, 1911.

Waugh, Evelyn. *Men At Arms*. Harmondsworth: Penguin, 1952.

Wells, H. G. *The World of William Clissold*. 2 Vols. New York: George H. Doran, 1926.

Williamson, Henry. *The Patriot's Progress*. London: Sphere Books, 1930.

Wordsworth, William. "Guilt and Sorrow" (1842). *The Poetical Works of William Wordsworth*. Ed. E. de Selincourt. Oxford: Clarendon, 1940, pp. 94–127.

Index

About the Author

G. W. STEPHEN BRODSKY is a retired Canadian Forces infantry officer, with service in conventional and airborne units. His tours of duty have included West Germany (NATO), Cyprus (UN), Kashmir (UN), and the United States where he was a Distinguished Honor Graduate of the US Army Ranger School. His degrees in Literature are from Queen's University and the University of Victoria. He has instructed at the Canadian Forces Officer Candidate School, Staff School, and Royal Roads Military College where as Special Lecturer he specialized in Literature of War and military ethics. He has contributed to such publications as *Fighting Armies of the World* (Greenwood Press, 1983), *Signum*, and *Seventeenth Century News*.

Recent Titles in
Contributions in Military Studies
Series Advisor: Colin Gray